Gottinger · Elements of Statistical Analysis

Hans W. Gottinger

Elements of Statistical Analysis

Walter de Gruyter Berlin · New York 1980

Library of Congress Cataloging in Publication Data

Gottinger, Hans-Werner.
Elements of statistical analysis.

Bibliography: p.
Includes index.
1. Mathematical statistics. 2. Probabilities.
I. Title.
QA 276. G 645   519.5   80–10104
ISBN 3-11-007169-X

CIP-Kurztitelaufnahme der Deutschen Bibliothek

Gottinger, Hans-Werner:
Elements of statistical analysis / Hans W. Gottinger. – Berlin, New York : de Gruyter, 1980.
ISBN 3-11-007169-X

Satz: Tutte, Druckerei GmbH, Salzweg/Passau.
Druck: Karl Gerike, Berlin.
Bindearbeiten: Lüderitz & Bauer Buchgewerbe GmbH, Berlin.

Preface

This book has been designed as an introductory textbook on an elementary level with emphasis on application in the behavioral sciences, yet, it is of sufficiently methodological orientation to being used as a one-semester course for undergraduate studies that requires only a limited background in high school algebra, except for the more technical, starred chapters.
Furthermore, it can be used as a supplementary text in connection with broad coverage textbooks in statistical analysis, or even as a self-instruction manual, for beginning graduate students in comprehensive programs of economics, sociology, psychology, education, system and industrial engineering, or related fields. Equipped with this material the student should be able to work out simple problems for himself arising in his specific field of study. For this purpose a number of problem sets are given for self-instruction.
The present book emerged from a half-year lecture course, repeatedly taught at the University of Bielefeld, the University of California, Santa Barbara and at the Technical University Munich – in different departments, to students of different backgrounds.
Formally the book is organized in 10 chapters, for some chapters, e.g. 3*, 4* and 9*, technical supplements and survey-type material have been added to enhance better understanding of key concepts.
It attempts to be well balanced given its limited scope between methodology, statistical analysis and techniques. For the uninitiated among the readers it appeals more to intuition and common-sense reasoning, yet the material is presented in a reasonably rigorous fashion. Various options are left to the reader regarding further study on more advanced technical aspects, for this purpose a bibliography is added. Finally, this is to express my great appreciation to de Gruyter, Berlin for its cooperation in designing the book and for making possible last-minute changes in the text.

Bielefeld, März 1980 *Hans W. Gottinger*

Contents

Part I.
Foundations of probability and utility

1. Methodology of Statistical Analysis

1.1 Conception of Statistics

All conceptions of statistics agree that statistics is concerned with the collection and interpretation of data. The data may be pertinent to an immediate practical action or decision, for instance, which best course of action – if available – to pursue under a situation of uncertainty or complete ignorance. But data may enhance knowledge without being immediately pertinent to a practical action, as in measurements of outcomes of natural laws or physical processes.

In application, the distinction between practical action and enhancement of knowledge is rarely clear-cut. Often, in real-life situations, it turns out that provision of knowledge is a *sine qua non* condition for choosing reasonable actions.

An essential ingredient of problems called „statistical" is that the relevant data are imperfect; we must always deal with uncertainty.

It is natural to ask why there should be a separate discipline of statistics. Certainly data are often collected and interpreted by people with little or no knowledge of statistics. The justification for statistics as a separate discipline lies in the hope that there will be general principles common to diverse applications. Some statistical principles consist of little more than common sense, and while statistics must ultimately be consistent with common sense, the implications of common sense in complicated problems are far from obvious. Much statistical reasoning can be conveyed by informal discussion of examples that illustrate simple uses and misuses of statistics, but for a deeper grasp of the subject, a more systematic and formal development is needed. Broadly speaking, the modern approach to statistics can be characterized by the words *inference* and *decision*, which refer to the processes of drawing conclusions and making decisions in the light of available data, or determining what additional data should be obtained before concluding and deciding. 'Conclusion' is used here in a technical sense, defined by J.W. Tukey (1960), as 'a statement which is to be accepted as applicable to the conditions of an experiment or observation unless and until unusually strong evidence to the contrary arises'.

1.2 History of Bayesian Statistics

A systematic treatment of utility and subjective probability according to Ramsey, de Finetti and Savage has stimulated the discussion on the foundations of mathematical statistics and its relationship to statistical inference. The core of this discussion is based on the 'behavioristic' interpretation of a statement (rather than of a 'theorem') implicitly derived by the English Clergyman Thomas Bayes (1763)*.

The proponents of this behavioristic interpretation of Bayes' statement are called Bayesians and their arguments have led to the Bayesian analysis in statistics. There are different kinds of Bayesians, but they all agree at least on the following point: It is possible to draw statistical conclusions from the conditional probability $P(H|E)$, that is the probability of a hypothesis H (to be true) given that the event E has been observed (to be true). The so-called 'Bayes Theorem' then is a trivial consequence of the product axiom of probability theory. However, it is more than a belief in this 'theorem' that distinguishes someone to be a Bayesian, it is the general acceptance of the idea to use a concept of intuitive probability in statistical theory and practice, to motivate this concept on a decision-theoretic basis and beyond that to find many applications in the experimental sciences.

There are two essential characteristics of Bayesian statistics and they can be listed in a simplified manner as follows.

(1) Probability evaluation is based on experience, intuition, and personal assessment combined with a number of consistency criteria relating to a rational person.
(2) Treatment of statistical data is continuously revised on the basis of new information, or evidence that is available to the decision maker (statistician).

Modern Bayesian statistics, in general, rests on three main construction blocks, consisting of:

(1) the game-theoretic studies of von Neumann and Morgenstern.
(2) the statistical works of J. Neyman and A. Wald.
(3) the subjective probability interpretations of F. P. Ramsey, B. de Finetti, B. O. Koopman, L. J. Savage et al.

Some of these elements have been developed within the classical statistical theory. A combination of all of these elements, however, forms the foundations of Bayesian analysis. Furthermore, there are two external factors that support this view, e.g. the philosophical attitude that most or all

---

* Th. Bayes, 'An Essay towards solving a problem in the Doctrine of Chances,' Philosophical Transactions of the Royal Society 53, 370–418 (Reprinted in: Biometrika 45, 1958, 293–315).
In crude form Bayes derived the statement that the probability of a 'certain cause' will be subject to change given that certain events will occur. In this statement the probability concept is used inductively for the first time by inferring from a small sample to the whole population.

scientific inferences result from 'inductive' rather than 'deductive' reasoning and the psychological viewpoint that 'statistics is a theory of the uncertain environment in which man must make inferences'. (Petersen and Beach, 1967), e.g. that human information processing is just an 'inconsistent' case of optimal information processing of data as required by statistical inference. Much of what Bayesian statistics has received as inputs in terms of new ideas is based on results obtained in experimental areas (such as psychology); to some extent, therefore, one could speak of a behavioral approach to statistical methodology. Although this process started from Bayes' fundamental work and reached the time of de Laplace, it has been cut off after de Laplace and only quite recently has been rediscovered by the 'Bayesians'. It is therefore illuminating to give a brief account of the main events in the development of statistical methodology. In the nineteenth century there was an increasing awareness among statisticians that a connection between probability theory and various methods of using data in a consistent fashion should result in a construction of a theory of statistical inference. Such a theory would permit predictions on the basis of a wise use of data and with tools provided by probability theory.

There were studies in this direction by Quetelet, W. Lexis, F.Y. Edgeworth, K. Pearson, culminating in the work of R.A. Fisher's *Statistical Methods for Research Workers* (1925). J. Neyman developed Fisher's ideas further and around 1940, say, statistical theory was firmly based on this standpoint – 'Fisher as seen through Neyman's eyes' (F.J. Anscombe, 1961) – which still prevails among eminent contemporary statisticians, although their number is slightly decreasing over the past decade. Since 1940 the theory of statistical decisions emerged paralleling the more orthodox theory of the Neyman-Pearson school.

In the more recent theory you structure any statistical problem as a decision problem where the statistician is engaged in a game against nature, and the only way of gaining information is by doing experiments. Again here two phases can be distinguished. The first phase was introduced by A. Wald's *Theory of Statistical Decision Functions* (1950). This theory still adopts a frequentistic interpretation of probability. The second phase is truly 'Bayesian', it emphasizes the point that the structure of a decision problem consequently requires a behavioristic interpretation of probability, that is a non-frequentistic concept of personal probability.

Now, what is it that makes the Bayesian method so attractive for many experimental situations that are not restricted to social or behavioral sciences but also extend to certain problems in the natural sciences (see I.J. Good, (1969)).

What are the specific prerequisites for the application of the Bayesian method, what specific kinds of information do we need?

• First of all, we need a statistical specification in an observational model in which observations are assumed to be realizations of random variables represented by a set of conditional probability distributions, conditional by a set of parameter values (states of nature). Let us assume, we have a finite number of states of nature, say m, and denote them by $\theta_1, \ldots \theta_m$, and furthermore let us have a finite number of outcomes, denoted by $t_1, t_2, \ldots t_n$. Then we can calculate for all $m \cdot n$ combinations of states and outcomes the direct probability of an outcome, given a state, denoted by $P(t|\theta)$.

• Second one needs a utility or loss function indicating the relative desirability of available decision acts for a given set of parameter values.

• Third, one needs a marginal probability distribution over the parameter space, i.e. an a priori (subjective) probability distribution.

Now the first condition has been universally accepted by all relevant schools of statistics, e.g. by the Bayesians as well as by the classical school – there is no disagreement about that. The second condition has been introduced by A. Wald, but only the third requirement is typical for the Bayesian method. It is this requirement which is most controversial for classical statisticians, and, as we shall see, centers around the validity and interpretation of Bayes' theorem.

Let us first deal with the third requirement (in natural conjunction with the first one), which, in general, leads to the inference rather than the decision problem, and then see how and why Bayes' theorem is essential for its formulation.

In the frequentistic interpretation of probability in terms of the limit of long-run frequencies it is impossible for the statistician to measure uncertain events (which are not repeatable) by probabilities.

In the frequentist's view an uncertain event on which no past history exists, is either considered to be not measurable by a probability or the probability of zero or one (and one does not know which) is assigned.

'If we ask the probability that the 479th digit in the decimal expansion of π is a 2 or a 3, most people would say 2/10, but the frequentist, if he answers the question at all, must say 0 or 1, but that he does not know which'. (J. Cornfield, 1967, p. 44). The frequency concept in connection with the construction of significance levels, errors of type I or II, confidence intervals etc. only answers the question as to how certain we feel on the basis of the given data (a posteriori distribution) but does not answer the question as to how certain we feel in advance when we still don't know the data (a priori distribution).

We could characterize an individual's state of uncertainty with respect to a proposition by the betting odds he would offer with respect to it. Consider an event (proposition) A and let P(A) be the probability of this event, for which you would receive \$1 in case the proposition A is true, otherwise you receive nothing. Let A be the proposition 'it will rain tomorrow' and somehow you arrive at a probability (estimate) of $P(A) = 1/3 = p$. Then, in other words, you would be willing to pay 33 cents in exchange for receiving \$1 provided the event A occurs or the proposition A is true. This is equivalent in ordinary language to saying that you bet on an amount \$1 at odds p to $1 - p$ on the occurrence of A. In some way p could be considered as your entrance fee to enter a betting contract. Of course, if p is greater than unity, you are certain to lose whether or not A is true. You wouldn't consider such a bet 'fair' and most likely refuse to accept such a bet. On the other hand, suppose you want to bet on 'rain' and pay $p = 20$ cents, and also bet on 'no rain' and pay $q = 30$ cents, in this case your betting partner wouldn't consider such a bet as fair, since whatever proposition turns out to be true he would have to pay \$1 and only receives 50 cents in return. Such a probability assignment could be termed 'incoherent'; to have a coherent assignment you have to select probabilities which sum up to one. Hence, fair betting implies coherent assignments of probabilities and this can be shown to satisfy Kolmogorov's finite additivity axioms of probability theory (see Chapter 2. .1). [Also, the notion of conditional bets can be introduced by considering events which are not mutually exclusive, i.e. if an individual smokes he will develop lung cancer, if he doesn't then there is no bet.] The construction of personal probabilities via a betting contract is obviously related to the concept of conditional probability and this again will quite naturally lead to the formulation of 'Bayes' theorem'. This will be shown next. In the following exposition we draw heavily on Cornfield's review.

Let there be two classes of proposition, A and B, every class contains mutually exclusive propositions. For simplicity, let us first assume that class A contains two propositions: an individual has or has not developed lung cancer during some definite time interval. The class B may contain two propositions, either the individual is found to be a smoker or a non-smoker. Extension to more than two possibilities in each class presents no difficulty. Now the proposition space would consist of four points

$$A_1 B_1, \; A_1 B_2, \; A_2 B_1, \; A_2 B_2,$$

all A's and B's are not mutually exclusive. $A_1 B_1$ would mean 'the individual has developed lung cancer and is a smoker'. $P(A_1)$, $P(B_1)$ would be the unconditional probabilities, but one could also define the conditional probability $P(A_1 | B_1)$, i.e. the probability of developing lung cancer given that one is a smoker. It could be defined by

$$P(A_1 | B_1) = P(A_1 B_1)/P(B_1). \tag{1}$$

Now on the basis of Kolmogorov's axioms of finite-additive probability together with (1) we could derive Bayes' theorem in a straight-forward fashion. By symmetry, and dropping the subscripts we have

(2) $$P(B|A) = P(BA)/P(A) = P(AB)/P(A),$$
$$\text{so that } P(AB) = P(B|A).\ P(A).$$

As can easily be seen, B is the union of the mutually exclusive events $A_1 B$, $A_2 B, \ldots$ so that $P(B) = P(A_1 B \text{ or } A_2 B \text{ or} \ldots)$, and by the additivity axiom

$$P(A_1 B \text{ or } A_2 B \text{ or} \ldots) = P(A_1 B) + P(A_2 B) + \ldots,$$

hence (3) $P(B) = \sum P(A_i B)$.
Now (2) can be changed to

(4) $$P(A_i B) = P(A_i) P(B|A_i).$$

If we start from (1), reformulate the numerator according to (2), and the denominator according to (3) and (4) we get

(5) $$P(A|B) = \frac{P(B|A) P(A)}{\sum_i P(B|A_i) P(A_i)}$$

This is 'Bayes' Theorem'.
Making a notational change by identifying the propositions $A_1, A_2, \ldots$ with states of nature $\theta_1, \theta_2, \ldots$, and the propositions $B_1, B_2, \ldots$ with the outcomes $t_1, t_2, \ldots$, we have 'Bayes' Theorem' in the form.

(6) $$P(\theta|t) = \frac{P(t|\theta) P(\theta)}{\sum P(t|\theta_i) P(\theta_i)}, \quad \text{where}$$

$P(\theta|t)$ is referred to as the a posteriori probability (posterior probability), $P(\theta)$ as the a priori probability (prior probability), and $P(t|\theta)$ as the likelihood.
(6) expresses the fundamental fact of 'learning by experience' in terms of the relation of prior and posterior probability.
It is the interpretation of this result which has triggered most of the controversy rather than the mathematical deduction, which is, without doubt, a correct one.
Let us first observe some properties of this relation.
(1) If $P(t|\theta) = 1$ and yet $\bar{t}$ (not t) has been observed (to be true), then $P(\theta|t)$, the posterior probability, is zero, i.e., an initially plausible hypothesis is rejected by the test.
(2) If $P(t|\theta_i)$ is the same for all i, then the posterior probability is equal to the prior probability, i.e., any additional information would not change the posterior probability.
(3) If $P(\theta) = 0$ then also $P(\theta|t) = 0$. If a proposition is initially false, then no information whatsoever will change the initial probability assessment.

I. In the philosophy of science an influential school of thought stressed the view that scientific conclusions based on past observations are not deductive. The theory of inductive inference originating with the work of David Hume in the last century has been elaborated and virtually extended to a philosophical school of thought by Rudolf Carnap.

Carnap's *LogicalFoundations of Probability* (1950) is just a straight-forward extension of his general principles of induction in scientific inference. Harold Jeffreys in his *Theory of Probability* (1961) devised five 'essential' rules of inductive inference under which 'Bayes' Theorem' could be subsumed as representing one important case of probabilistic inference.

II. Bayes' theorem has been accepted and used by Laplace, but some decades after Laplace the first critical voices have been heard. They centered around the construction of prior probabilities, in particular, how could one justify any assignment of probabilities to various states of nature. There were objections by Boole and Cournot, but much later – in the development of the theory of statistical inference under K. Pearson and R.A. Fisher –Bayes' theorem was not used at all and outrightly rejected by R.A. Fisher (1941). 'The theory of inverse probability [i.e. Bayes' theorem] is founded upon an error and must be wholly rejected. Inferences regarding populations from which known samples have been drawn, cannot by this method be expressed in terms of probability'. This questions the possibility of assigning prior probabilities to various states of nature. Frequentists, in particular, are troubled by the concept of prior probability. H. Cramér (1946) points out: '... the foremost weakness of this argument is that the prior frequency function $\pi(m)$ is in general completely unknown... Also irrespective of this, the argument suffers from the fundamental error that the true value of m is in most cases not the result of a random trial and may therefore never be regarded as a stochastic variable. Usually m is simply to be regarded as a fixed though unknown constant ... and on the whole under such circumstances no prior frequency function exists. Bayes' theorem is therefore practically useless for the theory of error and its use in this field should be replaced by the method of confidence limits.'

This and similar criticisms will probably in many cases be based on special interpretations of the probability concept. These points of view imply, roughly, that one only accepts the probability of something if this something can be registered in experiments which can be repeated. The probability can then be approximated by the relative frequency of this something in a long series of trials. On the other hand, if the numerical value of a probability is interpreted as representing the degree of belief a prior probability statement (on some parameter or state of nature) should be fully legitimate.

Yet, it should be mentioned that while an advocate of subjective probability will find no 'ideological' barrier to apply Bayes' theorem in statistical inferences, the theorem can be used when making these inferences by a non-Bayesian. One cannot criticize Bayes' theorem on grounds that it is used by Bayesians, as come critics do, since provided non-Bayesians agree that statistical inferences should be based on an revision of data in the light of new information there is no effective alternative open to them other than Bayes' theorem. However, the trouble is, that they have to find a frequency interpretation for the prior probabilities, whereas the Bayesian is much more flexible in view of his probability concept. Let us see where the real source of difficulty is located.

If θ is a random variable with a well-defined frequency distribution, which is known then the frequency distribution is the prior probability function and there should be no controversial point between Bayesians and non-Bayesians in this case. Controversies will arise if θ is an unknown constant (not a random variable) and has no past history. Then according to the frequentist the probability is not defined, the Bayesian, however, would apply his subjective probability concept. It is obvious that the effect of the prior probability on the posterior probability will be diminishing to the extent that more and more information will become available through the likelihood which would modify the initial prior probability. As a consequence of this, two scientists (or statisticians) having initially quite different priors will eventually arrive at the same posterior probabilities when faced with a sufficiently large body of data – provided the priors are all non-zero. This fact has been rigorously proved in a paper by D. Blackwell and L. E. Dubins (1962).

As regards the nature of prior probability assignments the Bayesian would certainly utilize any information contained in samples of past data to construct his prior, in this case it is said that his prior is 'data-based' (A. Zellner, 1971, 2.3). This does not necessarily mean that all conditions will be satisfied that permit the specifications of a frequency distribution, e.g., if we deal with small samples of data, for instance. In other cases prior information may be obtained on the basis of introspection, casual observation or even from plausibility arguments, this could be referred to as a 'non-data-based' prior. It is clear that differences of opinion between statisticians are most likely to occur by the use of non-data based priors. To arrive at a prior probability judgment it is often convenient, and in the spirit of the Bayesian approach, to separate information (as represented by data or other sources) from probability analytically and to consider the process under which different degrees of subjective information will induce corresponding probability evaluations. One can then argue that the probability assessments represented by the prior have a sound information-theoretic basis. Work in this direction has been done by Gottinger (1973, 1974).

A particular problem which could arise is the case of complete ignorance or 'knowing a little'. In this case it has been suggested by H. Jeffreys (1961) that if the unknown parameter θ lies in some finite range its probability distribution should be taken as uniformly distributed. This proposal corresponds to the Laplacean principle of 'insufficient reason' where equal probabilities are assigned to completely unknown states.

As R.L. Plackett (1966) observed, when the number of observations is sufficiently large the likelihood will have a sharp peak at the maximum likelihood estimate of θ, so in forming the posterior distribution only a small interval of the prior distribution is relevant. Therefore it is sufficient to introduce a 'locally uniform' or 'gentle' prior distribution for an unknown parameter centering around the maximum likelihood estimate, but taking any form outside the range since these values get multiplied with only negligibly small likelihoods so that the posterior distribution is barely affected by this.

III. The concept of a loss function – as introduced by A. Wald – is essentially a counterpart of von Neumann-Morgenstern's utility function (1947) which came up around the same time. It is another basic element of Bayesian analysis, however, here the emphasis lies on 'decision' rather than 'inference'. A. Wald and some of his followers were inclined to think of any statistical inference problem in terms of a statistical decision problem. This view seems plausible for certain activities of the statistician (such as hypothesis testing which could be looked upon as preferring certain decision rules over others), but would not pertain to problems where the statistician only wants to observe and then draw conclusions on the basis of observations – such as choosing between rival cosmological theories, or in a medical diagnosis problem where conclusions may result in decisions (regarding the medical treatment of the person concerned) but they may also be valuable for themselves. In a statistical decision problem we consider m possible states of nature $\theta_1, \theta_2, \ldots, \theta_m$, and n possible outcomes $t_1, t_2, \ldots, t_n$. We assume that the statistician (decision-maker) can choose among a set of possible decision acts, denoted by $a_1, a_2, \ldots, a_r$. Now define a decision function as a real-valued function with the characteristic property

$$d(a_k, t_i) = \begin{cases} = 1, & \text{if } t_i \text{ results in } a_k \\ = 0, & \text{otherwise.} \end{cases}$$

Hence a decision function is a rule which assigns for a given state of nature an act a to the outcome t.

Consider a finite number, say p, of possible decision functions $d_1(a_k, t_i)$, $d_2(a_k, t_i), \ldots, d_p(a_k, t_i)$, among which you have to find the 'best' decision function. In order to establish a selection criterion A. Wald introduced the concept of a loss function $l(a, \theta)$ that could have a positive, negative or

zero value. By choosing among decision rules you would prefer rules which result in the smallest losses. By definition, $l(a, \theta)$ is a random variable. The loss function, as a real-valued function, is in fact the negative counterpart of von Neumann-Morgenstern's utility function. Therefore, all their utility axioms that are required to prove the existence of such a function apply equally to Wald's loss function. One particular result of von Neumann-Morgenstern that matters here is the continuity property for gambles. This property is a direct consequence of the archimedean type axiom of utility theory. Roughly, the property implies that as long as there do not exist infinitely large positive or negative utilities (losses) it only matters that utilities (losses) are ordered according to their expected values.
Suppose you have three losses l_1^*, l_2^*, l_3^* with $l_1^* < l_2^* < l_3^*$. According to the continuity property we claim that $l_2^* = (p^* l_1^*, \bar{p}^* l_3^*)$ where $(\ldots, \ldots)$ is a gamble with $p^* \in (0, 1)$, $\bar{p}^* = 1 - p^*$.
Furthermore we would have

$$l_2^* < (p l_1^*, \bar{p} l_3^*) \qquad \text{for } p > p^*,$$
$$l_2^* > (p l_1^*, \bar{p} l_3^*) \qquad \text{for } p^* > p.$$

On the right-hand side we observe the expected loss (gamble), the problem then is to minimize the expected loss:

$$E[l(d, \theta_j)] = \sum_i [\sum_k l(a_k, \theta_j) d(a_k, t_i)] p(t_i | \theta_j) = R(d, \theta_j),$$

the risk function.
Having defined the expected loss we would like to choose those decision rules that improve the risk function stepwise. We say a decision rule d_1 is at least as good as d_2 if and only if $E[l(d_1, \theta_j)] \leqq E[l(d_2, \theta_j)]$ for $j = 1, 2, \ldots, m$. If the strict inequality holds for at least one j then we say d_1 *dominates* d_2. A decision function is *admissible* if it is not dominated by any other decision function.
To compute the expected value of $l(a, \theta)$ over all possible states of nature, we set $E(l(a, \theta)] = \sum_j l(a, \theta_j) P(\theta_j | t)$ for every possible a. To choose an a which would minimize $E[l(a, \theta)]$ is called Bayes' decision rule, given the chosen prior probabilities. Thus there is a family of Bayes decision rules, corresponding to the possible prior distributions for the states of nature.
It can be proved that Bayes' decision rule is both necessary and sufficient for admissibility. This would put everyone – arguing for admissibility but denying the existence of prior probabilities – in an almost untenable position since every decision rule which is admissible is also a Bayes' decision rule relative to a particular set of prior probabilities. Finally, a few words should be said about the relationship of the decision and inference in Bayesian statistics.

In business and industry, actions must be and are taken in the face of uncertainty about nature. In such a framework the application of decision theory seems most natural and profitable, although technical problems such as assigning prior probabilities and specifying utilities will arise. The scientist, on the other hand, seeks to broaden and deepen his understanding of the laws governing his science. He performs experiment after experiment, and essentially revises his findings in the light of new information provided by additional experiments. Decisions are involved but often they are coupled with problems of inferences.

When the aim of a statistical analysis is that of describing or making inferences about nature, whether this will be the population of a country or the laws governing a physical or social process, in these cases the highly structured theory of decision making may not be so appropriate. One view of the Bayesian approach to statistics, motivated by such considerations as these, is that it provides a vehicle for the reduction of data, transforming problems into 'no-data' problems, the data being used to generate a posterior distribution. Summarizing, the Bayesian approach to statistical inference is based on an argument of the following form:

(i) It is the business of the scientific experimenter to revise his opinions in an orderly way with due regard to internal consistency and the data, and so

(ii) one has to develop techniques for the orderly expression of opinion with due regard to internal consistency and the data, but

(iii) the only orderly expression of opinion with due regard to internal consistency is the Bayesian one, and

(iv) the only orderly revision of those opinions with due regard for the data is through Bayes' theorem, therefore

(v) the Bayesian approach to statistical inference is the most 'natural' one.

1.3 A Quality Control Example

More than by any philosophical discourse on Bayesian analysis it is illuminating to introduce the key Bayesian ideas by a simple example, modified from one originally given by Schlaifer (1969). The purpose is only to give you some concrete feeling for the important ideas. Technical terms will be defined mostly in the context, and details will be developed later.

An automatic machine has just been adjusted by an operator, and we are uncertain as to how good an adjustment has been made. In principle it is possible to make an exhaustive and mutually exclusive list of *events* or *states of the world* that are relevant to the problem: one of these events surely obtains but we are uncertain as to *which one*. The word "event" can be interpreted informally as "something that might happen" or "something that might be true." But an event may refer to something that has occurred already but is unknown to us, and this is the situation in the example we are now presenting. The events of the example can be described by the probability p that the machine will turn out a defective part. For simplicity it is assumed that there are only four events (representing adjustments of the machine) and they can be described by values of p: p = .01, .05, .15, .25.

You can think of p in terms of betting odds (see Sec. 2.3). Whichever p is of the four possibilities – .01, .05, .15, .25 – we assume that it will remain constant during the production run now being contemplated, which consists of 500 parts.

If we knew that p = .01, which represents the best possible adjustment, we would be satisfied with the operator's adjustment. If, on the other hand, we knew that p = .25, we might be tempted to change the adjustment in the hopes of improvement. Suppose that there is a mechanic who can, without fail, put the machine in the best possible adjustment. We are told that the time needed by the mechanic to make the necessary adjustment should be valued at $ 10. The problem is to decide whether or not to incur this $ 10 cost.

We shall for the moment assume that just two *acts* or *decisions* might be taken: (1) *acceptance* of the adjustment, that is, do not check it; (2) *rejection* of the adjustment, that is, have it checked by the master mechanic.

For each possible combination of event and act, we assess the *expected net cash flow* that will ensue if that act is taken and that event obtains. To explain this, we shall assume first that $.40 is the *incremental* cost needed to rework a defective part, regardless of how many defective parts are produced. The incremental cost of a non-defective part is, of course, $0. Now if the probability p of a defective part is .01, the probability of a non-defective part is 1 – p = .99. To calculate the expected cost of a defective part for a production run of one, given the best adjustment, we *weight* $.40 and 0 by the respective probabilities, .01 and .99, as follows:

$$(.01)\,\$.40 + (.99)\,\$0 = \$.004.$$

If we equate the probability with long-run relative frequency, this equation can be interpreted as follows. In the long-run, .01 of the parts are defective and an incremental cost of $.40 is incurred, .99 are non-defective and the incremental cost is 0. *On the average in the long run*, then, the cost of defectives per part produced, the expected cost per part, is $.004. Since a decision is to be made about a production run of 500 parts, we then multiply $.004 by 500 to get $2.00, the expected cost of defectives per 500 parts produced, that is, per production run. The use of long-run frequencies is introduced to help to visualize the concept of expectation. Expectation and probability

also have meaning even if there is a single unique choice, never to be repeated; then the idea is that of betting odds, not long-run relative frequencies.
Similar calculations for $p = .05$, $p = .15$, and $p = .25$ give expected costs for the act of acceptance as $10, $30, and $50.
For the act of rejection, the computation is even simpler. Regardless of the event that obtains, the mechanic achieves the best adjustment $p = .01$,, so that the expected cost of defective product is

$$500[(.01)\$.40 + (.99)\$0] = \$2.00.$$

In addition to this we must count the $10 for the mechanic's time, which also is the same regardless of the machine's actual adjustment. Hence the expected incremental cost for rejection is $2.00 + $10 = $12.00

All this information can be summarized in a *payoff table.* This is a two-way table in which the row headings are possible events, column headings are possible acts, and the entries are expected incremental profits or costs, as the case may be, for each event-act combination. Table 1–1 is the payoff table for the present problem.

Table 1–1: Payoff Table

Event	*Act*	
p	Acceptance	Rejection
.01	$ 2*	$ 12
.05	10*	12
.15	30	12*
.25	50	12*

With this information alone it is frustrating to decide whether to accept or reject. Acceptance is clearly the better act if $p = .01$ or .05, but rejection is better otherwise, as is indicated by the asterisks in Table 1. If the event is known, the best decision is obvious, but the problem is a problem of uncertainty as to which event obtains. Your decision depends on your assessment of the probabilities to be attached to the four possible events. How do you arrive at the needed probabilities? Suppose that there is extensive evidence on the history of the fraction of defective parts in 1000 previous long production runs under similar conditions in the past, and that this history is summarized in Table 1–2. The needed probabilities are assessed by the relative frequencies.
The basic criterion for decision can now be applied: choose that act for which expected cost is lowest (or, for which expected net revenue is highest).

Table 1–2: History of Fraction Defectives

Fraction Defective	Relative Frequency
.01	.70
.05	.10
.15	.10
.25	.10
	1.00
(Number)	(1000)

For each act, we take costs from Table 1–1 and probabilities from Table 1–2, and weight the costs by the probabilities. The expected cost for acceptance is

$$(.70)\,\$2 + (.10)\,\$10 + (.10)\,\$30 + (.10)\,\$50 = \$10.40\,.$$

Similarly, the expected cost for rejection is

$$(.70)\,\$12 + (.10)\,\$12 + (.10)\,\$12 + (.10)\,\$12 = \$12.00.$$

According to the decision criterion, the better act is to accept. (We assume that a decision must be made without getting more evidence.)

Suppose next that we ask for some measure of how willing we would be to make a terminal decision now, rather than to seek additional evidence. Alternatively, how much doubt is there that the decision that looks best is really best? One approach is to contemplate action in the light of perfect information. By this we mean the following. As we now consider the decision problem we do not know what adjustment obtains; but before a terminal action is taken, we will somehow find out the actual adjustment, then refer to Table 1–3 and be assured of making the better decision. Expected costs would therefore be

Table 1–3: Costs of Action in the Light of Perfect Information

p	Cost
.01	\$ 2
.05	10
.15	12
.25	12

The expected cost of action in the light of perfect information is

$$\begin{aligned}&(.70)\,\$2 + (.10)\,\$10 + (.10)\,\$12 + (.10)\,\$12 =\\ &= \$1.40 + \$1.00 + \$1.20 + \$1.20 = \$4.80\end{aligned}$$

In the long run, if the adjustment is $p = .01$ in a fraction .70 of all the setups, etc., and *if we always take the better action for the adjustment that obtains,* the average cost per run is $4.80. In the absence of perfect information the best action was acceptance, and its expected cost, $10.40. The difference between $10.40 and $4.80 or $5.60 represents the *expected value of perfect information.* That is, if perfect information could be bought, we would be willing to pay up to $5.60 for it, but no more.

Still using a long-run interpretation, we can interpret $5.60 in another way. In the absence of perfect information, we always accept. Hence .10 of the time we accept when p = .15 and incur a cost $30 − $12 = $18 greater than the cost with perfect information. In another .10 of the time, when p = .25, acceptance entails a cost $50 − $12 = $38 above the cost with perfect information. In the remaining .80 of the time (p = .01 or .05) acceptance is best. The expected saving from perfect information is therefore

$$(.10)(\$18) + (.10)(\$38) + (.80)(\$0) = \$5.60,$$

and this is again the expected value of perfect information.

This last interpretation has used the idea of *opportunity loss*, or simply, *loss*, which often substantially clarifies decision problems. Loss does *not* mean negative income; rather it is the absolute difference between the payoff for a *given act and event* and the payoff for the *best act for that event.* Table 1–4 gives the payoff table and the corresponding loss table in the example.

Table 1–4:

Payoff Table

Event p	*Act* Accept	Reject
.01	$ 2*	$12
.05	10*	12
.15	30	12*
.25	50	12*

Loss Table

Event p	*Act* Accept	Reject
.01	$ 0	$10
.05	0	2
.15	18	0
.25	38	0

It is clear that the expected *loss* of acceptance is equal to the expected value of perfect information:

$$(.70)(\$0) + (.10)(\$0) + (.10)(\$18) + (.10)(\$38) = \$5.60.$$

The expected loss of rejection is

$$(.70)(\$10) + (.10)(\$2) + (.10)(\$0) + (.10)(\$0) = \$7.20.$$

The difference between expected loss of the two actions, $7.20 − $5.60 = $1.60, is necessarily the same as the difference between expected costs, $12.00 − $10.40 = $1.60.

Now consider another new action: obtain more, but not perfect, information and then make the choice between acceptance and rejection in the light of this information. For illustration assume that this information consists of a sample of size $n = 1$, that is, a single part is made by the machine and inspected. Suppose that the part turns out to be defective. (We defer the question of whether it was wise to take a sample of size 1). Prior to this sample we assessed probabilities for the four adjustments as equal to the relative frequencies of Table 2, namely, .70, .10, .10, and .10. Simply because they are prior with respect to the sample, we call these *prior probabilities.* Since the part is defective, we presumably now put less probability on the better adjustments, more on the poorer ones; the extent of revision is not obvious.

The revision of probabilities is accomplished by *Bayes' theorem,* as we now show.

(1) Determine the probability of the observed sample given each possible adjustment of the machine.

(A) If $p = .01$, the probability of a single defective in one trial is .01.

(B) If $p = .05$, the probability of a defective is .05.

(C) If $p = .15$, the probability of a defective is .15.

(D) If $p = .25$, the probability of a defective is .25.

Each of these probabilities for the sample result given p is called a *likelihood.*

(2) Calculate the *joint* probability of the sample result in conjunction with each of the four adjustments: for each adjustment, multiply the prior probability for the adjustment by the likelihood of the sample for that adjustment.

(A) The probability that the sample comes from the best adjustment is the prior probability .70 times the likelihood .01, or $(.70)(.01) = .007$.

(B) The probability that the sample comes from the second best adjustment is $(.10)(.05) = .005$.

(C) The probability that the sample comes from the third best adjustment ist $(.10)(.15) = .015$.

(D) The probability that the sample comes from the worst adjustment is $(.10)(.25) = .025$.

If we add the four numbers .007, .005, .015, and .025, to obtain .052, we may interpret .052 as the prior probability of the observed sample. That is, each of the four numbers is the probability that the sample comes from one of the four adjustments. Since the four adjustments are assumed to be only possible ones, the sum .052 represents the probability of a defective part in the light of the prior distribution for the adjustment of the machine. In the long run, .052 of samples of $n = 1$ following new setups are defective. It follows that $1 - .052 = .948$ of samples of $n = 1$ following new setups would be non-defective, so the prior probability of a good part is .948.

(3) Compute the probabilities assigned to each of the four adjustments after

the sample, the *posterior* probabilities. In long-run terms it is easy to see how to do this. An observed defective happens .052 of the time. An observed defective from the best setup happens .007 of the time. Hence *on all occasions in which a defective part occurs,* it comes from the best adjustment $.007/.052 = .1346$ of the time. Similarly, we get posterior probabilities $.005/.052 = .0962$, $.015/.052 = .2885$, and $.025/.052 = .4808$ for the other adjustments. Table 1–5 summarizes the process just described.

Table 1–5: Revision of Prior Probabilities by Bayes' Theorem

Adjustment	Prior Probability	Likelihood	Joint Probability	Posterior Probability
.01	.70	.01	.007	.1346
.05	.10	.05	.005	.0962
.15	.10	.15	.015	.2885
.25	.10	.25	.025	.4808
Total	1.00	–	.052	1.000

The revision of probabilities in the light of sample evidence can be thought of as a blending of the information in the sample to be analyzed with all other information, the other information being expressed quantitatively by the prior probabilities. From the Bayesian view, this process is the essence of statistical inference. The posterior distribution expresses the inference independently of the decision problem at hand, or of whether or not there is an immediate decision problem.

Finally, consider the problem of whether or not it looked wise, before sampling, to examine one part before making a terminal decision between acceptance and rejection. (We do not examine the possibility of taking still larger samples but the same principles apply and indeed point the way to determination of the *best* sample size). Before sampling the expected cost of acceptance, the better act, was \$10.40. In contemplating in advance a sample of size one, we know from the reasoning above (which could have been carried out before the sample was actually taken) that the probability of a defective is .052; a non-defective therefore has probability $1 - .052 = .948$. We know also that if a defective occurs, rejection will be the best act and that its expected cost will be \$12.00.

Similarly, it can be shown that if a non-defective occurs, acceptance is the best act and its expected cost is \$9.11. Hence the expected cost of taking a sample of size one then making the best terminal decision is

$$(.948)\,\$9.11 + (.052)\,\$12.00 = \$8.64 + 0.62 = \$9.26$$

The difference between \$10.40 and \$9.26, or \$1.14, is the *expected value of sample information.* As between an immediate decision to reject or accept and a deferral of that decision until a sample of one is taken, we prefer the sample so long as its cost was less than \$1.14.

1.4 Conclusion

The machine-setup problem, simplified as it is, illustrates most of the important ideas that we shall be dealing with. Similar examples in everyday life problems can be discussed along these lines, even if the payoffs are not given in monetary terms (see D.W. North, 1968). It shows the logical elements of any problem of decision under uncertainty, and demonstrates how statistical inference could fit into the analysis of a decision problem. Whether or not it is worthwhile to break down a decision into these elements is a matter of judgment. For many problems of business or everyday life, we prefer a purely informal analysis. But even when we may not care to push through an analysis in detail, the kind of reasoning described here is often helpful. It reminds us that an essential step is simply to think hard about the actions that are open to us. (The listing of possible actions is an informal, intuitive, creative task that does not lie within the scope of statistics as such.) It reminds us that any proposed action must be evaluated against not one but all the relevant states of the world. Assessments of the probabilities of alternative states of the world are a part of the decision process. Finally, it reminds us that the probabilities of something happening and its consequences must be assessed separately. We should not exaggerate the probability of nuclear war, for example, simply because the consequences would be so terrible.

Frequently we find ourselves in situations in which we must digest evidence even though no immediate decision is called for. In this way we build up knowledge that can be drawn upon when specific decisions do arise. The process by which we do this is called statistical inference, as opposed to statistical decision theory, although decision theory is fruitful in suggesting how inference should be approached. From the Bayesian point of view, the objective of inference is to attach probabilities to uncertain events, to revise these probabilities in the light of new evidence, and sometimes to condense a listing of probabilities by one or more numerical measures.

The machine-setup example of this chapter has introduced the key steps of a Bayesian decision-theoretic analysis. The distinctive features of the approach are the assignment of probabilities to events and payoffs to consequences, the decision rule of maximizing expected payoffs, and the revision of probability assignments in the light of new evidence.

Suggested Readings

Anscombe, F. J.: Bayesian Statistics, American Statistician 15, 1961, 21–24.

Blackwell, D., and L. E. Dubins: The Merging of Opinion with Increasing Information, Ann. Math. Statist. 33, 1962, 882–893.

Box, G. E. P. and G. C. Tiao, Bayesian Inference in Statistical Analysis, Reading (Mass.), 1973

Cornfield, J.: Bayes Theorem, Review of the International Statistical Institute 35, 1, 1967, 34–49.

Cramer, H.: Mathematical Methods of Statistics, Princeton, 1946.

Fisher, R.A.: Statistical Methods for Research Workers, 8th Ed., Edinburgh, 1941.

Good, I. J.: A Subjective Evaluation of Bode's Law and an Objective Test for Approximate Numerical Rationality, Journal of American Statist. Association, 64, 1969, 23–66 (with discussion).

Gottinger, H. W.: Subjective Qualitative Information Structures based on Orderings, Theory and Decision 5, 1974, 1–29.

Gottinger, H. W.: Qualitative Information and Comparative Informativeness, Kybernetik 13, 1973, 81–94.

Gottinger, H. W.: Grundlagen der Entscheidungstheorie (Foundations of Decision Theory), Stuttgart, 1974.

Jeffreys, H.: Theory of Probability, 3rd ed., Oxford, 1961.

v. Neumann, and O. Morgenstern: Theory of Games and Economic Behavior, 2nd ed., Princeton, 1947 (Appendix).

North, D. W.: A Tutorial Introduction to Decision Theory, IEEE Trans. System Science and Cybernetics, Vol. SSC-4, 3, 1968, 200–210.

Petersen, C. R., and L. R. Beach, Man as an Intuitive Statistician, Psychological Bulletin 68, 1, 1967, 29–46.

Plackett, R. L.: Current Trends in Statistical Inference, J. Roy. Statist. Society, Ser. A, 1966, 249–267.

Schlaifer, R.: Analysis of Decisions under Uncertainty, New York, 1969.

Schlaifer, R.: Probability and Statistics for Business Decisions, New York, 1959.

Tukey, J. W.: Conclusions us Decisions, Technometrics 2, 1960, 423–433

Wald, A.: Statistical Decision Functions, New York, 1950.

Zellner, A.: An Introduction to Bayesian Inference in Econometrics, New York, 1971.

2. Finite Probability

2.1 Definition and Interpretations of Probability

A *probability measure* assigns to every *event* under consideration a number, called a *probability* such that

(1) The probability of any event is non-negative.

(2) The probability of an event consisting of two mutually exclusive events is the sum of the probabilities of the two individual events.

(3) The probability of the event consisting of all the events under consideration is 1.

In the axiomatic approach to probability, probability is a primitive or undefined concept, just as a point is a primitive concept of geometry. When people talk of defining probability, they have in mind the interpretation of probabilities in practical applications of the theory. The question is one of usefulness for applied work.

Consider a physical object, such as a ball. (Certain technical complications of this example are here ignored.) As a convention the total volume of the ball can be taken to be unity, corresponding to axiom (3) of probability theory. Any part of the ball can be defined as an "event", for which the "probability" is the ratio of its volume to the volume of the ball. Hence the "probability" of an event is always non-negative (axiom 1). Consider any two mutually-exclusive parts of the ball. The "probability" of the two parts together is the sum of the "probabilities" of the two parts separately (axiom 2). This does not say that probability *is* volume, but rather that the formal theory of probability can be applied to volumes.

Another interpretation is closer to our interest. Consider a group of 100 people who have been asked a series of questions, each of which can be answered by "yes" or „no," abbreviated Y or N. Looking at question 1, suppose we find 54 Y's and 46 N's. The relative frequency of Y is $54/100 = .54$ and of N is $46/100 = .46$. These relative frequencies are non-negative and they add to 1, the relative frequency of Y *or* N. The example can be extended by looking at the answers to the first two questions. Any response can be represented as YY, YN, NY, or NN. The *relative frequencies* of these four response categories are again non-negative numbers that add to 1.

In the Bayesian approach, long-run relative frequencies are rather metaphysical, though often enlightening intuitively for visualizing probabilities, as we did in Chap. 1. The Bayesian interpretation of probability need not appeal to long-run relative frequency; its intuitive content can be expressed in terms of betting odds. This interpretation is called the *subjective pro-*

bability interpretation. Subjective probability is discussed at length in the next sections and Chap. 3*.

2.2 Subjective Probability and Betting

Along the lines of Savage (1954, 1971), we can give a simple economic interpretation of probabilities in terms of betting and show how this ties up to a consistent construction of probability in terms of Kolmogorov's axioms.
Let us assume a probabilistic experiment with events A, B, C, ... is to be performed (or has been performed and the result is still unknown to the experimenter.) Subjective probability reflects an individual's degree of belief that some prediction will be verified. This is the meaning of sentences 'horse A will probably win the next race', 'President F will probably not be reelected' (given the present amount of evidence). A straight-forward way to measure an individual's subjective probability is to propose a bet. This requires the notion of a betting contract: to place a bet on the event A a person must find a second individual (bank) who is willing to bet on A (not A), and they must agree on the terms of the bet. A bet on the event A is then a contract which contains the risk (for the individual concerned) to lose p dollars if A occurs in order to win s dollars if A occurs. The bet will appear *fair* to the person if it preserves a certain kind of symmetry, i.e. if he is indifferent between the alternative (i) risking p dollars if A occurs to win s dollars if A occurs, and (ii) risking s dollars if A occurs to win p dollars if $\bar{A}$ (not A) occurs.
Therefore, if the bet appears fair the person's odds are p : s and his subjective probability for A would be $P(A) = p/(p+s)$. Obviously, we have $P(A) \geqq 0$ and $P(A) + P(\bar{A}) = 1$. Regarding the probability of the universal event (which is always true), we see that a person should risk an arbitrarily large bet on S, and bet nothing on $\bar{S} = \emptyset$ (the impossible event). [Note that 'impossible' and 'certain' could be used in a relative, subjective sense which, in general, is weaker than 'logically impossible' or 'logically certain'.]
Hence $P(S) = 1$ and $P(\emptyset) = 0$.
Now let us show how the concept of conditional probability fits into the construction of betting behavior. We set $P'(H) = P(H|B)$ for every event H in S. Here is an elementary intuitive argument that these subjective conditional probabilities should satisfy the product rule of probability theory. The universal event for the conditional probability experiment has been reduced from S to a subset B, but otherwise no further information is available, e.g. about subsets of B. Now a bet involving two horses, for example,

* This is equivalent to otherwise used notations $P(A \cap B)$ or $P(AB)$.

should be independent of the other horses in the race. In this way if H and K are arbitrary subsets of B then the *ratio of belief* in H to belief in K should be independent of the knowledge that B has occurred, i.e.

$$P'(H)/P'(K) = P(H)/PK) \qquad \text{or}$$
$$P(K)/P'(K) = P(H)/P'(H) = \alpha, \text{ a constant.}$$

Hence $P(H) = \alpha P'(H)$ for all subsets H of B. To determine α observe that $P(B) = \alpha P'(B) = \alpha$ and therefore, by substitution, $P(H) = P(B). P'(H)$ which is the product form of probability for the special case H in B.
Now let A be an event, not necessarily contained in B, but $A \cap B \subset B$. Hence, by analogy, we derive:

$$\begin{aligned} P(A \cap B) &= P(B) \cdot P'(A \cap B) \\ &= P(B) \cdot P(A \cap B | B) \\ &= P(B) \cdot P(A|B) \end{aligned}$$

Conditional probability is also probability in the sense of placing bets, thus the summing up condition $P(A|B) + P(\bar{A}|B) = 1$ is also valid. The additivity rule of probability $P(A \cup B) = P(A) + P(B)$, if A and B are disjoint is also easy to verify . Let $A \cup B = C$. We then have to prove $P(C) = P(A \cap C) + P(\bar{A} \cap C)$. But $P(A \cap C) = P(C) \cdot P(A|C)$ and $P(\bar{A} \cap C) = P(C) \cdot P(\bar{A}|C)$. Adding up we get

$$\begin{aligned} &P(A \cap C) + P(\bar{A} \cap C) = P(C)[P(A|C) + P(\bar{A}|C)] \\ &\quad = P(C).1 = P(C). \end{aligned}$$

Summarizing, we have

(i) $P(A) \geqq 0$ for all $A \subset S$,

(ii) $P(S) = 1$,

(iii) $P(A \cup B) = P(A) + P(B)$,

if A and B are disjoint. Therefore subjective probabilities in terms of betting behavior satisfy Kolmogorov's probability axioms (of a finite probability space).
In order to present a general economic interpretation of probability we extend the betting situation to a kind of 'mass betting' involving all agents entering the market on the basis of a betting contract. The mechanism for betting is as follows. Agent 1 places an agreed upon amount x $(0 \leqq x \leqq 1)$ in a pot and receives an A-ticket in return, agent 2 places an amount $1 - x$ in the pot and receives an $\bar{A}$-ticket in return. Hence, the entrance price of an A-ticket would be x and that of an $\bar{A}$-ticket $1 - x$. More bets could be placed by buying more tickets. An A-ticket indicates that a pot of size 1 has been set aside until the experiment has been performed (or until the transaction

in an uncertain market has taken place), and the A-ticket holder is entitled to receive the entire pot provided A has occurred.

Now let $D_A(x)$ be the effective demand for A-tickets on the market. We could treat one agent buying more than one ticket as several agents having the same personal price (consistent with his subjective probability of A). In fact, agent i may (for himself) set a personal price p_i which could be less than or equal to or greater than the bargain price x. We could then define the demand set

$$D_A(x) = \{A(x) : p_i \geqq x,\ 0 \leqq p_i \leqq 1\}, \qquad \text{and}$$
$$D_A(y) = \{\bar{A}(y) : q_i \geqq y,\ 0 \leqq q_i \leqq 1\}$$

with $y = 1 - x,\ q_i = 1 - p_i$.

As we see $D_A(x)$ and $D_{\bar{A}}(y)$ are already defined in terms of prices. Clearly, by assumption, every market demand function $d_A(x)$ defined in $D_A(x)$ would be a monotone, non-increasing step function, therefore would have the same downward slope as a demand function in conventional demand theory.

Likewise, we can define the supply sets $S_A(x)$ and $S_{\bar{A}}(y)$. In brief, $S_A(x)$ indicates the supply of all A-tickets at price x, e.g. those which would be supplied if the price were x. The corresponding supply functions would be $s_A(x)$ and $s_{\bar{A}}(y)$. Corresponding to $d_A(x)$, $s_A(x)$ would be a monotone, nondecreasing step function. One important observation has to be made which is natural in view of the duality in this two-goods market: if a person demands an A-ticket at price x then he places an $\bar{A}$ ticket on the market at price $1 - x$, hence $D_A(x) = S_A(y)$. Let us make the conventional assumption of economic theory that the market size is sufficiently great and the spacings of the personal prices are sufficiently close to justify the approximation that the curves $s_{\bar{A}}(x)$ and $d_A(x)$ intersect in exactly one point. Then we could determine the market equilibrium price of an A-ticket.

Denoting the price of an A-ticket by $P(A)$ we may summarize as follows: (i) $P(A) \geqq 0$, (ii) $P(S) = P(A) + P(\bar{A}) = 1$, and (iii) $P(A \cup B) = P(\text{A-ticket \& B-ticket}) = P(A) + P(B)$ for disjoint sets. Kolmogorov's axioms provide a suitable model for ticket prices. Therefore, in the subjective probability context, if we adopt a betting interpretation we can say that a probability $P(A)$ is equivalent to a competitive price of an uncertain commodity (event A) with value 1 or 0 depending on whether A does or does not occur.

2.3 Relation between Subjective Probability and Bayes' Theorem

In this section we will attempt to show that – although Bayes' Theorem can be used with much confidence by non-Bayesians – those Bayesians adopting a subjective view of probability will have the least difficulties to understand and apply Bayes' Theorem. The reason for this being that their subjective probability interpretation will lead most naturally to the construction of Bayes' theorem. First let us briefly summarize what we know so far about the implementation of subjective probability in real-life (uncertain) situations.

The idea of betting odds gives an intuitive feeling for subjective probability. We do not have to bet on horse races or elections in order to understand subjective probability, but we must understand that decision-making under uncertainty can be regarded as unavoidable gambling. The decision in Chapter 1 to accept or reject the operator's adjustment is an illustration: so long as there is uncertainty about the machine's adjustment, it is necessary to gamble – to choose a course of action that may turn out well or badly. The odds terminology is helpful in thinking about the unavoidable gambles that we must face, even if we would never gamble for fun.

The arithmetical relation between odds and probability is fundamental. If, say, the odds are 3 to 1 *against* a given event, then the implied probability against the event, that is, the probability that it does not obtain, is $3/(3+1) = 3/4$. The probability that the event *does* obtain is therefore $1-(3/4) = 1/4$, and the odds in favor of it are 1 to 3, that is, 1 to $4-1=3$.

The idea of subjective probability can also be expressed directly without reference to odds. Probability can be interpreted as the fraction of a contingent prize you would be willing to pay for the right to receive the prize if the contingency materialized.

Let us set up a single betting contract and see how coherent assignments of probability lead to Bayes' theorem. Suppose that there are two events A and B, and that you contemplate three kinds of bets with me. First, I can bet on A; for such a bet you assess the probability of A as P(A). Second, I can bet on A and B; you assess the probability of A and B as P(A and B).* Third, I can bet on B with the understanding that the bet will be called off if A does not obtain; you assess the probability of B given A as P(B|A), the *conditional probability* of B given A. If we let the stakes for these three bets be S_1, S_2, and S_3, my gains G can be calculated as follows. First, if A obtains but B does not, I win $(1-P(A))S_1$ from my bet on A, but lose P(A and B) S_2 from my bet on A and B and P(B|A) S_3 from my conditional bet on B given A. So

(1) $$G_1 = (1-P(A))S_1 - P(A \text{ and } B)S_2 - P(B|A)S_3.$$

Second, if A and B both obtain, I win all three bets, so

(2) $$G_2 = (1-P(A))S_1 + (1-P(A \text{ and } B))S_2 + (1-P(B|A))S_3.$$

Third, if A fails to obtain, I lose my bets on A and on A and B, while the bet on B|A is called off so

$$(3)\qquad G_3 = -P(A)S_1 - P(A \text{ and } B)S_2.$$

The determinant of the system of equations (1), (2) and (3) is

$$(4)\qquad \begin{vmatrix} 1-P(A) & -P(A \text{ and } B) & -P(B|A) \\ 1-P(A) & 1-P(A \text{ and } B) & 1-P(B|A) \\ -P(A) & -P(A \text{ and } B) & 0 \end{vmatrix} = \\ = P(A \text{ and } B) - P(A)P(B|A)$$

It is necessary and sufficient for my probability assignments to be coherent that this determinant be zero,

$$(5)\qquad P(A \text{ and } B) = P(A)P(B|A).$$

If $P(A) \neq 0$, we can solve (5) for $P(B|A)$ to obtain the definition of conditional probability used in mathematical probability, $P(B|A) = P(A \text{ and } B)/P(A)$. If we interchange A and B in the above argument, we obtain

$$(6)\qquad P(B \text{ and } A) = P(B)P(A|B).$$

The event B and A is the same as the event A and B, so

$$(7)\qquad P(B)P(A|B) = P(A)P(B|A).$$

If $P(B) \neq 0$, we obtain from (7)

$$(8)\qquad P(A|B) = \frac{P(A)P(B|A)}{P(B)},$$

which is Bayes' theorem.

2.4 Bibliographical Remarks

There are many excellent books on probability theory which cover most of the tools more thoroughly and the reader is warned not to content himself with what he has learned so far. Among the very recent books the text by M. Eisen (Introduction to Mathematical Probability Theory, Prentice Hall, Englewood Cliffs, 1969) is particular useful for a beginner, interested in rigorous probability theory, more advanced books are those by Feller (An Introduction to Probability Theory and its Applications, 2nd ed., Vol. II, J. Wiley: New York 1966), J. Neveu (Mathematical Foundations of the Calculus of Probability, Holden-Day, San Francisco 1969), and M. Loève (Probability Theory, Van Nostrand, Princeton 1961).
In the last years an entirely new brand of books has entered the market: they provide a comprehensive treatment of probability theory and statistical

techniques in connection with a dominantly Bayesian flavor, one particular noteworthy book is that of I. H. Lavalle, (An Introduction to Probability, Decision and Inference, Holt, Reinhart and Winston, New York 1970).

As has been said at the beginning it should be mentioned again that all different approaches to the concept of probability are entirely compatible with Kolmogorov's formal axiomatization of probability. However, this is more or less a coincidence. For example, the subjective approach can well be derived from qualitative assumptions of probability, in fact, the Russian mathematician S. N. Bernstein (1917) has proposed elaborate axiomatizations of qualitative probability based on order relations ($\leqq$) (not more probable than) as primitive notions. This corresponds to what de Finetti (1937), (1972) considers as axioms on inequalities among probabilities. Axiomatizations on qualitative lines can be achieved in quite different ways, one way is generating such orders ($\leqq^{\cdot}$) by betting schemes as done by de Finetti (1937) and later by L. J. Savage (1954), therefore motivating the ordering in a decision-theoretic framework. However, you could justify the order also from a different angle, arguing that an individual is only able to cope with uncertainty in a qualitative sense rather than by assigning probability measures right away.

Such an axiomatization may be based on considerations of measurement theory (Krantz et al., Foundations of Measurement, Academic Press: New York 1971) and it can be demonstrated that axiomatic systems as that of extensive measurement can be used for axiomatization of qualitative probability (see H. W. Gottinger, Subjektive Wahrscheinlichkeiten, Vandenhoeck & Ruprecht, Göttingen and Zürich 1974).

A good account of how the theory of induction is linked to subjective probability theory is given by den Finetti (1972, Chapt. 9), this idea penetrates much of philosophical studies on probability (see R. Carnap and J. Jeffreys, Studies in Inductive Logic and Probability, University of California Press: Berkeley 1970), see also the special issue of Synthese (Vol. 20, 1, June 1969).

Some proponents of the subjectivist school, de Finetti, L. J. Savage and in a different context Dubins and Savage argue that countable additivity is too much to require for a decision related theory of probability and therefore a finite additivity model would be sufficient. A different point of view is proposed throughout in probability theory and has been adopted for subjective probability theory by Gottinger (1974).

How individuals really make probability assignments (in case of prior probabilities) as compared to how they should make assignments has been subject to much recent research in psychology and statistics. Another problem is how to teach individuals to assess probabilities so that assessments conform to coherence postulates generating all properties of a probability measure. One possible avenue of research is to devise appropriate incentive systems (penalty and reward systems), such as in the case of betting, that make people comply to coherence rules. In this regard see the works of R. L. Winkler (The Quantification of Judgement. Some Methodological Suggestions, Journal American Statistical Association 62, 1967, 1105–1120), R. L. Winkler, The Assessment of Prior Distributions in Bayesian Analysis, Journal American Statistical Association 62, 776–800, B. de Finetti, Probability, Induction and Statistics, Chapt. 3 and 4, Wiley: London 1972, and L. J. Savage, Elicitation of Personal Probabilities and Expectations, Journal American Statistical Association 66, 1971, 783–801.

In fact, the entire approach of de Finetti is aimed at teaching individuals how to make probability judgements similar to teaching students how to make correct arithmetic manipulations. The difficulties most likely to be encountered are lucidly exhibited in a paper by A. Tversky and D. Kahneman, Judgement under Uncertainty: Heuristics and Biases, Science 185, 1974, 1124–1131. This paper and others by the same authors show the judgemental barries that may impair consistent probability judgments of individuals.

It should be emphasized that the split between the adherents of subjective probability and those of the frequency viewpoint does not correspond entirely to that of Bayesians and Non-Bayesians. For example, R. v. Mises, a proponent of the frequency viewpoint emphasized the validity of the Bayesian theory.

However, while it can be shown that all subjectivists are fullfledged Bayesians only a few frequentists share this view.

Suggested Readings

de Finetti, B.: La Prevision: ses lois logiques ses sources subjectives, Annales d' l' Institut Henri Poincare 7, 1937 (English translation in: Kyburg H. E., and H. E. Smokler (eds.): Studies in subjective probability, New York, 1963, 93–158).

Savage, L. J.: Elicitation of Personal Probabilities and Expectations, Jour. Amer. Stat. Assoc. 66, 1971, 783–801.

Savage, L. J.: The Foundations of Statistics, New York, 1954.

3* Interpretations of Probability

3*1 Introduction

This chapter illustrates some aspects of probability theory, and shows the various methodological difficulties associated to different probability concepts. All statistical methods are intrinsically connected with probability theory, and they depend on interpretations of the notion of probability. Various probability systems have been proposed, some more for mathematical convenience, others on the basis of new problems (for instance in decision theory) to cope with uncertainties. Many statistical methods can only be justified by the use of specific concepts of probability, in other cases it depends on the problem at hand which probability concept proves to be more appropriate. Hence, even for applied scientists, there is some basic need to become familiar with the foundations of probability because this enables you to choose statistical tools in a satisfactory way.
Even though Kolmogorov (1933) gave a satisfactory definition of probability in terms of a measure of a set, independent of any interpretations, there is no way to avoid a definite interpretation of probability, as soon as we arrive at problems of applications and measurement.

3*2 Relative Frequencies

Von Mises (1957) can be regarded as one of the founders of the frequency approach in probability theory in which we can say that the object of the theory is to provide a mathematical model suitable for the description of a certain class of observed phenomena known as random experiments. *A random experiment is an empirical phenomenon characterized by the property that its observation under a given set of circumstances does not always lead to the same outcome but rather to different outcomes in such a way that there is statistical regularity.*
This empirically established fact is sometimes called the empirical law of large numbers. In other words, in the frequency approach, one develops a mathematical theory of repetitive events. In doing so, the field of applicability of probability theory is extended enormously because all phenomena showing statistical regularity are now under consideration. Of these phenomena games of chance only form a rather insignificant particular case.
In order to understand von Mises, we should distinguish carefully between reality (the random experiment) and the mathematical model of reality he developed.

A first basic concept of his model is the notion of a *label space.*
The label space S is the set of all conceivable outcomes of a random experiment.
Many authors use the term *sample space* for this concept. In reality we deal with long (though finite) sequences of observations. The theoretical counterpart in the model of such a sequence of observations is an infinite sequence of labels x_j, $j = 1, 2, \ldots$ where each x_j is a point of the label space S. Again in reality we experience, in a long sequence of trials, that the relative frequency of occurrence of a given outcome becomes more or less constant. The counterpart of this fact is the first basic assumption that, in an infinite sequence x_j, the relative frequency of each label a_i tends to a fixed limit p_i. This limit is called the chance of a_i within the given sequence. In order to arrive at a more precise formulation of randomness, von Mises introduces the concept of *place selection.*
This concept is necessary because the notion of chance does not fully reflect all our practical experience with random experiments. Two examples illustrate this point. If we toss a coin many times, we may observe that the relative frequency of heads is approximately 0.5. If we only consider tosses with an even number, that is the second throw, the fourth throw etc., then in the new sequence the frequency of heads is again approximately 0.5. If you play roulette and if, for example, you play only red or black it is impossible to increase your chance of winning by playing according to a system. For example, it will not pay to play according to the rule: take part in the game only if red has shown up four times in a row and, in such a case put your money on black. Practical experience shows that a successful gambling system is impossible. From these examples, you might get the impression that the requirement of place selection does not impose a real restriction on the phenomenon of stabilizing stable relative frequencies.
But this is not true as the following example shows. Consider the sequence in binary form 01010101, ... The relative frequency of the occurrence of zeroes tends to the limit 0.5. In the subsequence consisting of the uneven elements of S, however, the relative frequency of the occurrence of zero is equal to 1. It is intuitively clear that this sequence does not possess a random character.
The theoretical counterpart of the insensitivity of stable relative frequencies to a change in the original sequence is the second basic assumption: the chance p_i of a distinct label a_i in a given sequence x_j be insensitive to place selections. Under this assumption chance will also be called probability, or more fully, the probability $p(a_i)$ encountering the label a_i in the sequence under consideration. We are now in a position to define explicitly the notion of a *collective*, a concept that is at the basis of probability theory as it is seen by von Mises.
Let S be a discrete label space and $K = \{x_j\}$ an infinite sequence of elements

of S. Let G be a system of denumerably many place selections. We assume that

(1) for every label a_i in S the limiting frequency p_i exists in K;

(2) $\sum_{i=1}^{\infty} p_i = 1$, the sum extended over all elements of S;

(3) Any place selection g belonging to G applied to K produces an infinite subsequence of K, in which again, for every a_i, the limiting frequency exists and is equal to p_i. Then, K is called a *collective* with respect to G and S.

Within the collective, several operations can be considered, alone or in combination. These operations lead to new collectives and new probabilities. Four elementary operations can be distinguished:

(1) Selection: a new subsequence is derived from an original sequence by means of a place selection. This operation leads to a new collective. Probabilities are not changed by it.

(2) Mixing: this is the reconstruction of the collective by taking several labels together. For instance, a sequence consisting of the numbers 1 through 6 is changed by only describing the original elements as even or odd. Probabilities change in the sense of the usual addition rules.

(3) Partition: from the original collective, a new one is formed by selecting only those elements that satisfy some specified condition. Probabilities change in the sense of conditional probabilities.

(4) Combination: from two collectives with labels a_i and b_j, we can define a new collective with the pairs (a_i, b_j) as its labels. Probabilities change corresponding to the product rule.

In this theory, probability calculus is nothing more or less than the art of going from one collective to another with the aid of the four elementary operations. A probability rule usually has the following structure: given a collective and probabilities in it, find the probabilities in another well-defined collective.

Now, what could be said about the applicability of this theory? Probability statements about single observations are excluded by von Mises' theory. This implies that it is meaningless to say that the probability of a coin falling heads in the next throw is equal to .5 or to speak of the probability of a certain individual dying next year. This fact is one of the most important consequences of his definition of probability as being a limit of a frequency in a collective. This fact causes no difficulties as long as we are interested in abstract theory. The picture changes, however, as soon as we apply the theory to large though finite sequences because then we have to say something about a single finite sequence. But any statement about some finite sequence is a statement about a single observation in a new compound collective. Notice that the rule which we have introduced explicitly is a statement about a single observation. Hence, by introducing this rule we leave the world of relative frequencies.

In the new world, statements are possible about single events given a certain amount of evidence. We can now ask what kind of rules we can expect to hold in this new world. Can the rule described above hold in general in such a world? The answer is no. Consider a number of events which, according to our rule, are thought to be impossible; then the disjunction (union) of these events is not necessarily impossible according to the same rule. This situation can be compared with a lottery: if the number of winning tickets is small in comparison with the total number of tickets (low relative frequency), it is thought to be impossible for any ticket to be a winning one. Nevertheless there must be some winning ticket. From this it appears that intuition requires some kind of additivity rule. Moreover, it becomes clear that the inference rule, as implicitly used by von Mises, is only permissible if the addition rule for 'impossible' events is not needed in the problem at hand. Actually, for mass phenomena any problem that has to do with frequencies can be transformed in such a way that the additivity rule is of no practical importance. As long as we restrict the domain in which the theory can be applied to mass phenomena where experience has taught us that rapid convergence exists (that is, the frequency limits are approached fairly rapidly), the inference rule causes no troubles and can therefore be used.

Hence we can conclude that, if we add a simple rule, von Mises reaches his goal, namely a scientific theory of probability for mass phenomena. However, we are not completely satisfied with the theory. Von Mises explicitly excludes probability statements about unique events, the outcome of one specific coin toss, for instance.

3*3 Inductive Probability

R. Carnap (1945) pointed out that the concept of probability can be given two different meanings:

(1) Probability is defined as a degree of confirmation (or belief) where it is rational to believe that a hypothesis h given the observation (or a sequence of observations) e is logically true.

(2) Probability is defined as the ratio of the number of favorable cases to the number of all possible cases, that is probability is a limit of relative frequencies of favorable outcomes over all possible outcomes in a random experiment.

Carnap called his two separate concepts probability_1 and probability_2.

The degree of confirmation or probability_1 can be defined in such a way that a hypotheses h given e is logically true if there is a real-valued function c such that $c(h, e) = r$, $0 \leqq r \leqq 1$, hence the degree of confirmation is given numerically in terms of $c(h, e)$.

Now the concept of consistency (coherence) stressing the compatibility between the qualitative relation '$\leqq$' (at most as confident as) on conditional propositions $h|e$, $h'|e'$ and the representation by confirmation functions is incorporated in the following properties:

(1) $h|e \leqq h'|e'$ if and only if $c(h, e) \leqq c(h', e')$.

(2) If $c(h, e) = r$, $r \in [0, 1]$ then $c(\bar{h}, e) = 1 - r$ where $\bar{h}$ denotes the complementary hypothesis.

(3) If $c(h, e) \leqq c(h', e')$ then $c(\bar{h}', e') \geqq c(\bar{h}, e)$.

Conditions (1)–(3) appropriately define a betting situation. Then $c(h, e)$ can be considered as a betting quotient, and it is intuitively clear that this concept is subject to a stronger restriction regarding the individual evaluation of uncertain propositions than a comparative relation between these propositions. I may bet 10:1 that there will be rain in October at some place against the proposition that there will be thermonuclear war within a year, but this is independent which numerical value the betting quotient will assume. Only a qualitative ordering of propositions really matters.

The intimate relation between betting, degree of confirmation and consistency can be seen by the following construction. Let M be the monetary payoff in case a betting contract has been established. A consistent person will only consider the following betting alternatives:

(a) In case e is logically true and h is false he will pay the amount rM and gain nothing so that the net gain amounts to $-rM$.

(b) In case both h and e are true he will pay rM and get M so that the net gain is $(1-r)M$.

(c) The bet is not valid if e is false.

It is therefore easy to see that the betting quotient is bounded in the unit interval. Otherwise, let $r > 1$ and $M > 0$ then in this case the net gain will be negative, hence a rational person would not accept such a betting contract. In case $r < 0$ and $M < 0$ an analogous argument holds.

It now turns out that the problem of accepting fair bets in equivalent to the problem of making consistent decisions in betting situations.

J.G. Kemeny (1955) has given necessary and sufficient conditions for showing compatibility between degrees of confirmation and fair betting quotients (see for some extensions also H. Richter (1972)). On the basis of certain observations people frequently bet money on uncertain propositions. If a person is willing to pay the amount rM and receives a net gain $-rM$ in case the proposition is false or he receives the amount $(1-r)M$ in case the proposition is true then this person reveals a bet $r:(1-r)$.

A bet is uniquely determined by the knowledge of h, e, r, M and by the specification of the betting contract, e.g. whether a person bets for or against a proposition.

Any such bets form a betting system. A betting system is called 'fair' if it does not contain a bet which guarantees a positive or negative net gain whatsoever. Any person accepting a bet in a fair betting system is consistent. In other words, the fairness condition is violated if the betting system guarantees a positive net gain whatever happens.

Hence the degree of confirmation is revealed by a fair betting system.

Sumarizing, if we use the notion of probability in terms of *probability*$_1$, we refer to a rational person acting consistently in uncertain situations:

(a) The probability that the next coin toss will be heads given a certain amount of data. More generally, the degree of confirmation that some hypothesis h is true given the amount of evidence.

(b) The degree of confirmation can be measured in terms of a fair betting quotient. Assume that the degree of confirmation that the next coin toss results in heads is 1/3 given e. Then a bet 1:2 is called fair.

Now Carnap (1950) uses the concept of a fair betting quotient in a special sense, independent of the personal taste of the person. Hence, with the same amount of evidence, any person reaches the same betting quotient (degree of confirmation). The concept of probability$_1$ as used by Carnap is thus independent of personal taste.

(c) Probability$_1$ can sometimes be interpreted as the estimation of a relative frequency. Carnap (1950) clarifies this with the aid of the following example. Imagine an urn filled with 60 red and 40 white balls. One ball is drawn from the urn. Assume that two players bet on the outcome of this draw. What is their fair bet? According to Carnap it is 6:4. In other words, the fair betting quotient is determined by the frequency of white (red) balls in the urn. Carnap defends this solution with the simple argument: if we use this rule for 100 simultaneous bets (one bet on each ball) the final balance is foreseeable and equal to zero. Now it is conclusive that, if we do not know the frequency of white balls in the urn, the fair betting quotient will be equal to the estimate of it.

Let us use this classification for an explanation of the difference between the classical approach and the frequency approach. The classical definition of the probability concept, originally based on games of chance closely corresponds to probability$_1$. If, in the classical sense, the probability of a coin falling heads is 1/2, this can be interpreted as a degree of confirmation that heads will occur on the next toss. It is equally possible to interpret this statement as a betting quotient – in fact the classical definition originates from such betting situations. It is not quite clear whether a betting quotient in the classical sense is independent of personal tastes. From the general context of symmetry among the possible outcomes of an experiment, one is inclined to conclude that the classical concept of probability is indeed objective, or independent of personal taste. Difficulties arise when the third criterion for probability$_1$ is considered. The classical theory does not provide the means to deal with biased coins, so an estimation of relative frequencies is impossible in the pure classical approach. This, in fact, is one of the main reasons why the classical theory had been considered unsatisfactory (see Appendix A).

Apparently, the frequency approach corresponds to the concept of probability$_2$. More carefully expressed, the concept of probability in the collective, as defined by von Mises (1957) corresponds to probability$_2$. In the application of the frequency theory, a rule of inference had to be introduced, and this rule of inference has the character of a probability$_1$ statement: Single events with a low probability are supposed to be impossible, or the degree of confirmation that such a single event occurs is equal to zero. In the sense of von Mises there is no calculus for such probability$_1$ statements. This is only justified when a sufficiently large number of observations is involved. Carnap tries to develop a calculus for probability$_1$ statements by postulating some generally agreed upon principles. His system is purely logical and hence objective although later he modified his position coming close to a subjective interpretation of probability. Let us quote him here, "that probability$_1$ is an objective concept means this: if a certain probability$_1$ value holds for a certain hypothesis with respect to a certain evidence, then this value is entirely independent of what any person may happen to think about these sentences, just as any relation of logical consequences is independent in this respect. Consequently, a definition of an explication for probability$_1$ must not refer to any person and his beliefs but only to the two sentences and their logical properties within a given language system." The hypothesis h will be sustained by experience e with a degree of confirmation c(h, e), that is a function of both h and e. In this, the expressions h and e are logical statements, void of any interpretational meaning. In deductive logic, expressions like "if e, then h" occur. In inductive logic, expressions will have the form "if e, then h with a degree of confirmation c(h, e)." The value of c(h, e) is determined by the way in which h and e are imbedded in a logical structure. Consider the example of coin tosses. Each toss can be considered as an individual. Each individual (or toss) will result in either heads or no-heads, so the outcome of any toss can be characterized by only one predicate (heads). The statements h and e express for a number of individuals (tosses) whether or not the predicate "heads" obtains. A very simple example is e = the first toss results in heads, h = the second toss results in heads and we could find for instance c(h, e) = .5. Now if we take another example, say an urn with red and non-red balls, then each draw can be called an individual. The predicate is "red",

and we are in exactly the same situation as in the example of coin tossing. Therefore, the degree of confirmation that the second drawing will result in red, if the first drawing has already resulted in red, is again .5.
Some critical remarks can be made about Carnap's theory:
First, the construction of an objective quantitative inductive logic, is not yet complete because the degree of confirmation is dependent on the weight given to experience. Different people will come to different degrees of confirmation, even if the same amount of experience is available. This suggests that the theory should move closer to a subjective theory of probability. In fact, Carnap's later work reported in (1971) supports this claim. Already at this stage Carnap's theory shares two common elements with a theory of subjective probability, as will become evident when discussing personalistic concepts of probability,
(1) the degree of confirmation is uniquely determined by a fair betting system, as it holds for the subjective concept (according to F. P. Ramsey and B. de Finetti – see also Section 3.*4),
(2) the derivation of the numerical confirmation function from a qualitative ordering of propositions (events).
The main difference between the two concepts seems to be that a 'rational person' in Carnap's theory is much less a human fellow than that proposed by proponents of subjective probability theory.
Second, the theory is much too restricted for applications outside the field of gambling games. The limitation to independent predicates excludes application to such simple problems as the throwing of a die. For this purpose Carnap and Kemeny give an extension of the theory. For the throwing of a die, the degree of confirmation that "6" will result is 1/6 if no experience is available. If some experience is available, the degree of confirmation will have a value between 1/6 and the observed relative frequency. The application of this theory leads to fundamental problems, however. Say, we are interested only in the outcome "6". Problems of this kind can be expressed in a language with the sole predicate "6". If no experience is available, then the degree of confirmation that "6" will occur in one throw is equal to 1/2. If we were to describe the problem in such a way that all outcomes "1" through "6" were considered separately and if no experience were available, then the degree of confirmation that "6" would occur is equal to 1/6. Actually, the problem is the same as for the principle of insufficient reason: given some description of a real world problem, the principle of insufficient reason will entail equally likely cases; given the logical language in which the problem is described, a logical symmetry is defined. However, a real world problem can often be described in various ways; the logical language in which the problem is expressed is often not uniquely determined. The well-known objections against the principle of insufficient reason are also valid for the choice of the

language in which Carnap's degree of confirmation is defined. The most important objection, however, is the problem of applicability. It is assumed that, in the confirmation function c(h, e), e contains all the relevant experience available. For a coin toss, this would imply all knowledge about mechanical laws, the number of times the reports about such observations can be trusted, and so on. It seems impossible to formalize all the available experience. Disagreements between famous scientists about fundamental issues with the same amount of objective experience emphasize the problem of an objective weighing of objective experience. Instead of a very large number of facts, experience will be rather in the form of a theory in accordance with those facts. Such a theory can nevertheless be wrong.

3.*4 Personal Probabilities

In this part of our review we discuss personalistic views which, starting out with a particular betting situation, attempt to define subjective probabilities in a general decision situation under uncertainty.
Evaluating situations of uncertainty which frequently occur in real life, the view that human beings assign certain numbers (probabilities) to events, appears rather strange, in many ways psychologically far-fetched. Instead, if a person talks about events being probable, less probable or more probable, he actually has in mind *qualitative probability* rather than probability measures. Therefore, it is more natural (and in applications more realistic) to establish a probability theory in qualitative terms, and then, as a second step, to ask what are necessary and sufficient conditions to ensure the existence and uniqueness of a probability measure strictly agreeing with the qualitative structure. Hence, you can argue that a qualitative theory of probability will always be more fundamental than any quantitative probability theory based on measure theory since it provides the essential link between real life or experimental evidence and an abstract mathematical theory. Traditionally, the Boolen algebra of events was a most natural structure for studying qualitative probability, but any other structure out of numerous lattice structures or even geometries might be of potential interest and usefulness, and, in fact, that structure which under the weakest conditions ensures the existence of a probability measure would be the most appropriate tool for a generalized probability theory.
If intuitive probability and personal weighing is to be used as a basic construct of this theory, then we should realize that it is by no means self-evident that quantitative personal probabilities exist. In many complex situations the intuitive weighings are often of a non-quantitative type. The idea that the weighing procedure will result in an ordering of the type 'event A is more

probable than event B' is basic. Notice that the concept of probability is introduced here as a primitive notion, based on a (qualitative) ordering relation 'not more probable than'. Thus it is supposed that a sentence 'A is more probable than B' has a qualitative meaning for the person in question. Besides such ordering relation it is necessary to formulate some properties that are generally thought relevant to the notion of subjective probability. All these properties must be laid down in an axiomatic system. Different systems are of course possible; the reader can be referred to the work of Jeffreys (1961), Koopman (1940, 1941), De Finetti (1937). Savage (1954); for a comprehensive discussion of the axiomatic foundations and some new contributions also the works of Fine (1973) and Gottinger (1974_a) could be consulted. Here we pay special attention to the work of Koopman and Savage. It is not quite clear, whether Jeffreys' probability concept is personal, it is fair to say that it goes beyond Carnap's former approach and falls short of Savage's approach. Furthermore, his axiomatic system is less transparent and intuitively appealing than that of Koopman's and Savage's. As to de Finetti many of his innovating ideas are found again in the work of Savage, also a thorough discussion of de Finetti's probability theory is given recently in his book (1972).

So we shall not treat de Finetti's theory separately.

First some remarks are in order to explain the nature of subjective probability. One of the main motivations for introducing subjective probability arose from the problem to estimate probability (distributions) in very small samples. In such a case the classical and the frequency approach didn't prove to be very helpful.

In ordinary life personal probability evaluations occur rather often, such evaluations are based on certain experiences from the past. Assume we like to know about the probability that on some day in February it will either rain or snow. Such a probability evaluation can be done on the basis of past experience (consider the number of rainy or snowy days in February since the last ten years) or on the basis of present information (e.g. the weather news from weather bureaus). Usually such evaluations are performed in a rather imprecise fashion, and some new tools of qualitative analysis have to be applied to analyze them (see Gottinger 1974_b).

A *physical probability* (also ,material probability' or 'chance') is defined as an intrinsic property of the physical world which does exist independent of particular logical rules. On the other hand, in a broader sense, a *psychological probability* is defined as the 'degree of belief' which arises in betting or similar decision situations faced by an individual. Psychological probability as such is not necessarily based on thorough considerations or consistent rules. If a person evaluates probability in a consistent fashion then we talk about subjective probabilities. Various consistency requirements have been suggested by the personalistic school, in general they are weaker (behavioristically less restrictive) than those given by the logical school of probability.

A rather general axiomatic system for intuitive probabilities (i.e. subjective or logical probabilities) has been suggested by B. O. Koopman (1940, 1941). He showed if certain assumptions on partially ordered intuitive probabilities are fulfilled then they can be represented by real numbers satisfying ordinary axioms of probability theory. We now turn toward a discussion of Koopman's system.

(a) *Intuitive Probabilities*

Koopman's work is based, on a Boolean ring of propositions a, b, c, ..., h, k, ... Without going into matters of definition we should like to use the term Boolean algebra in accordance with Halmos (1963).

(a) if propositions a and b are elements of this algebra then a *or* b (and a *and* b) belong to this algebra.

(b) if proposition b is an element of the algebra then *not* b (i.e. $\bar{b}$) is an element of the algebra (closed under complementation).

Propositions can be considered as to their probability that they will be true. For instance, b might be thought less probable than or equally as probable as c; in this case b is called infra-probable to c. It might also be that b and c cannot be compared as to their probability because we lack the required intuition for such a comparison. This kind of consideration leads to the assumption of a partial ordering defined on a set {a, b, c, ..., h, k, ...}. A partial ordering does not require that all elements be comparable; however, if elements are comparable, then the consistency requirements for an ordering are fulfilled: for any element b of the set the property of reflexivity holds ($b < b$); if a and b are comparable and if b and c are comparable and if $a < b$ and $b < c$, then a and c are comparable and $a < c$ holds (transitivity). Koopman extends the set of elements upon which the partial ordering is defined in the following way; denote the proposition "a under the presumption that h is true" by a|h; b|k can be defined in the same way. It might be possible to compare a|h and b|k as to their probability. Suppose, for example, that we have an urn with 50 red balls and 50 black balls in it. Let h and k stand for "the first ball drawn is red" and "the first ball drawn is black" respectively. Let a and b stand for "the second ball drawn is red" and "the second ball drawn is black" respectively. It is then quite reasonable to suppose that a|h and b|k are equally probable.

This example illustrates that it makes sense to define an ordering on the set of elements of the form a|h. In general, however, it is not necessarily true that we have intuition about the comparison of a|h with all propositions of the form b|k.

Therefore only a partial ordering is assumed to exist. Observe that the unrestricted proposition b in the original Boolean algebra can be written as $b|[h \text{ or } \bar{h}]$ for any h, so the partial ordering defined on the set of elements of the form $a|h$ implies a partial ordering on the elements of the original Boolean algebra.

If $a|h$ and $b|k$ are comparable and if $a|h$ is thought infra-probable to $b|k$, this is denoted by $a|h < b|k$. In Koopman's work, rules are laid down for comparison of elements of the form $a|h$ as to their probability aspect, where the set of elements of the form $a|h$ is generated from the Boolean algebra $\{a, b, c, \ldots, h, k \ldots\}$.

Some aspects of Koopman's theory are also found in Savage's work. Comments will be postponed until Savage's axiomatic construction is described. One remark should be made at this moment. The theory does not say in which cases comparability can be expected. In a subjective theory, this is a matter for the person himself. Nevertheless, comparability is crucial in the derivation of numerical probabilities, especially in connection with n-scales. For gambling problems, n-scales are inherent with our a priori ideas about probabilities. For typically subjective matters, like the probability of a strike, there are no natural n-scales. Either we have to reconcile ourselves to the absence of numerical probabilities in such cases, or we whould extend the Boolean algebra of propositions to n-scales. For instance, we could extend the class of propositions with, amongst others, the possible outcomes for 1, 2, 3, ... coin tosses. In this way, n-scales can be made available, but we still do not know whether the real life propositions are comparable with such n-scales.

If not, the theory would result in $0|u < b|h < 1|u$ for a real life proposition b under the presumption h, where 0 and 1 stand for propositions that are logically false and logically true respectively. From this, we can obtain $p_*(a, h) = 0$ and $p^*(a, h) = 1$, and this result is a trivial translation of our ignorance. If we want to apply the theory to this kind of problem, we have to assume that it is possible to compare $a|h$ with n-scales. But then, we have to introduce a comparison between real life propositions and game situations. With such a principle, we could easily define numerical probabilities without a complicated axiomatic system.

Another point to be raised in this context is the following. The whole system is built on something that could be called intuition. Is it really true that, say, the probability value for the occurrence of a strike is obtained by comparison with probability values from some gamble? It seems reasonable to assume that a comparison with gambles is only possible after you have become conscious of the probability value for a strike. This would imply that the primitive notion of probability is numerical, rather than an ordering relation.

(b) *Savage's Axiomatic System*

L. J. Savage (1954), like Koopman, derives numerical probabilities from a system of ordering relations. Savage's contribution is of special importance because of the context in which the problem is developed. Koopman introduces the "more probable than" relation as 'primitive', in a situation of uncertainty, one proposition can be considered "more probable" than another whatever this may mean. Savage, on the other hand, bases his system on a preference that we have for one act over another in an uncertain situation. It is assumed that such preferences will obey certain consistency rules. These rules are laid down in the postulates. The postulates can be interpreted in two ways. In the behavioristic approach, it is assumed that the postulates reflect more or less the actual behavior of individuals in situations of uncertainty. Whether or not people react in a consistent way is a problem belonging to the field of psychology. We are more interesed in the normative interpretation: Given some consistency rules, in what way should people react to a choice between acts in a situation of uncertainty? This is apparently a decision problem. Usually, the solution of decision problems is derived from probability theory. Savage goes the other way around. If it is possible to solve a decision problem, there must be a preference relation defined on the set of acts; if this preference obeys some consistency rules, then it can be shown under what other conditions numerical probabilities must exist. The ordering among acts implicitly defines the underlying notion of probability. Because the ordering among acts is subjective, the underlying probabilities are also subjective.

Let us consider Savage's definitions and postulates more closely. In the real world, or rather the relevant part of the real world, several possible states can be distinguished. For instance, when betting on the throw of a die, the possible states are the results "1" through "6". When confronted with a possible strike, there are (roughly) two states: the strike will or will not occur. Uncertainty can be defined as a lack of knowledge about the state of the world that obtains. Now, any act will result, depending on the state of the world that obtains, in a specific consequence. Hence, we can define an act mathematically as a mapping of the set of states into the set of consequences.

Definition 1. Any mapping of the set of states into the set of consequences is called an act.

If we make an even bet of one dollar on the outcome of a coin, there are two states of the world, the outcomes "heads" and "tails"; the two consequences are "winning a dollar" and "losing a dollar". According to the definition, there are four possible acts. Only two of these are realistic in a betting situation. If we put our dollar on "heads" state "heads" is mapped on the consequence "winning a dollar" and state "tails" is mapped on the consequence

"losing a dollar". The second realistic act is to put our dollar on "tails". Moreover, there are two hypothetical acts, viz. winning a dollar whatever outcome results and losing a dollar whatever the outcome.
The first postulate asserts the existence of a preference ordering among all acts, either realistic or hypothetical.

Postulate 1. In the case of acts, a complete ordering is defined, so if $\mathbf{f}$ and $\mathbf{g}$ are acts, then either $\mathbf{f} \leqq \mathbf{g}$, or $\mathbf{g} \leqq \mathbf{f}$, or both hold.
In Koopman's system, only a partial ordering has been assumed, thus not all propositions are a priori supposed to be comparable. Here, it is assumed that all acts are comparable, either realistically or hypothetically. In our later comments, we shall consider more closely the implications of this assumption in a normative interpretation of the postulates. At this stage, we can restrict ourselves to the remark that a preference among realistic acts at least seems to be necessary for a consistent solution to a decision problem. As to the behavioristic approach, it is rather doubtful whether the postulate would be fulfilled in complicated problems. Experiments on the measurement of utility, where even no uncertainty was involved, have shown that people are rather inconsistent in their preferences.
It is clear that the ordering among acts entails an ordering among consequences. For this purpose, identify each consequence c with the so-called constant act $\mathbf{f}_c$ that maps all states on the consequence c. The constant act $\mathbf{f}_c$ results with certainty in consequence c, and the ordering among the class of such constant acts can be identified with the ordering among consequences.
Other postulates will be needed to restrict further the class of possible orderings among acts. These postulates reflect common sense principles about preferences in a situation of uncertainty. If, for instance, the set of states S is partitioned into the subsets B and S − B and if the acts $\mathbf{f}$ and $\mathbf{g}$ are identical on the subset S − B, then the preference relation between $\mathbf{f}$ and $\mathbf{g}$ will be completely determined by the specification of $\mathbf{f}$ and $\mathbf{g}$ on the relevant part B of S. The same is true for any other pair of acts $\mathbf{f}'$ and $\mathbf{g}'$ when $\mathbf{f}'$ and $\mathbf{g}'$ are identical upon S − B. Apparently, the following postulate reflects this common sense principle.

Postulate 2. If $\mathbf{f}$ is identical with $\mathbf{g}$ on S − B; if $\mathbf{f}'$ is identical with $\mathbf{g}'$ on S − B; if $\mathbf{f}$ and $\mathbf{f}'$ are identical on B; if, moreover, $\mathbf{f} \leqq \mathbf{g}$, then $\mathbf{f}' \leqq \mathbf{g}'$ also.
This postulate makes it possible to define in a unique way an ordering relation among acts if the set S is restricted to the subset B.

Definition 2. $\mathbf{f} \leqq \mathbf{g}$ given B; if and only if $\mathbf{f}' \leqq \mathbf{g}'$, where $\mathbf{f}'$ and $\mathbf{g}'$ are modifications of $\mathbf{f}$ and $\mathbf{g}$ so that $\mathbf{f}$ and $\mathbf{f}'$ are identical on B, $\mathbf{g}$ and $\mathbf{g}'$ are identical on B, and $\mathbf{f}'$ and $\mathbf{g}'$ are identical on S − B.

From P. 2 it appears that, if the ordering given B were defined with the help of another pair of modifications, say **f**″ and **g**″, under the same rules of construction, then the same ordering given B would result as in the case where **f**′ and **g**′ are used.
It can easily be checked that $\mathbf{f} \leqq \mathbf{g}$, given B is a complete ordering. Apparently, only the specification of **f** and **g** on the subset B is relevant for the ordering relation $\mathbf{f} \leqq \mathbf{g}$ given B. It should be noted that the ordering relation $\mathbf{f} \leqq \mathbf{g}$ given B is interpreted as a (conditional) preference and not merely as a mathematical derivation.
So, if the preference ordering among acts, defined on S, is given and if the extra information that S − B does not occur is available, the conditional preference is given by $\mathbf{f} \leqq \mathbf{g}$ given B.
From probability theory, it is well-known that conditional probabilities are not defined under the condition of an event with probability measure 0. An analog for such events with probabiltity measure 0 is found in the definition of a null set:

Definition 3. The set B is null if and only if for all acts **f** and **g** holds $\mathbf{f} \leqq \mathbf{g}$ given B. Apparently, if B is null, both $\mathbf{f} \leqq \mathbf{g}$ given B and $\mathbf{g} \leqq \mathbf{f}$ given B, so all acts are equivalent given B.
We have already seen that an ordering among consequences is obtained by considering the ordering among constant acts $\mathbf{f}_c$ which map into the consequences c. Now, if by some extra information the set S is reduced to the subset B, acts that are constant on B result with certainty into the corresponding consequences. This again would imply a (new) ordering among consequences. We are not sure, however, that the original ordering among consequences is the same as the new one. This is asserted in postulate 3.

Postulate 3. If $\mathbf{f}_c$ and $\mathbf{f}_{c'}$ are constant acts; if B is not null; then $\mathbf{f}_c \leqq \mathbf{f}_{c'}$ if and only if $\mathbf{f}_c \leqq \mathbf{f}_{c'}$ given B.

The fourth postulate is trivial:

Postulate 4. There is at least one pair of consequences c_1 and c_2 so that $c_1 > c_2$. If all consequences were equivalent, no decision problem would be left; all acts would be equally attractive.
The ordering relation $A \cdot \geqq B$ for the subsets A and B of S can be interpreted as a "more probable than" relation. If there is a game that results in $ 100 earning if A obtains and $ 100 losses if S − A obtains, if there is another game that results in $ 100 earnings if B obtains and $ 100 losses if S − B obtains, and if we prefer the first game to the second, then apparently A is considered more probable than B. We may refer to the (weakly) "more probable than" relation as *qualitative probability*.
The postulates P. 1 through P. 4 do not guarantee that, if another pair of

consequences $c_3 > c_4$ is chosen, the same ordering of subsets would be found. For this reason, a fifth postulate is introduced:

Postulate 5. If the characteristic acts $\mathbf{f}_A$ and $\mathbf{f}_B$ are defined for the consequences $c_1 > c_2$, if the characteristic acts $\mathbf{g}_A$ and $\mathbf{g}_B$ are defined for the consequences $c_3 > c_4$ and if, moreover, $\mathbf{f}_A \leqq \mathbf{f}_B$, then $\mathbf{g}_A \leqq \mathbf{g}_B$.
Apparently, acts are assumed to be ordered in such a way that, if a \$100 bet on A is preferred to a bet on B, then a \$1000 bet on A must also be preferred.
The "more probable than" relation among subsets or events has the following three properties:

(i) the ordering is complete.
(ii) if $B \cap D = C \cap D = \emptyset$ (the empty set), $B \leqq \cdot C$ if and only if $B \cup D \leqq \cdot C \cup D$.
(iii) $B \cdot \geqq \emptyset$; $S \cdot > \emptyset$.

The structure of the ordering among events is determined by properties (i) through (iii). From these properties, we can derive,intuitively clear, propositions such as

(a) if $B \subset C$, then $\emptyset \leqq \cdot B \leqq \cdot C < \cdot S$
(b) if $B \leqq \cdot C$, and $C \cap D = \emptyset$, then $B \cup D \leqq \cdot C \cup D$.

From this point, we will omit the details and give a general outline of the construction of numerical probabilities. Essentially, Savage's approach is similar to Koopman's. Savage, however, introduces n-scales consisting of "almost" equally probable events, where Koopman uses n-scales consisting of equally probable events. If there are n-scales consisting of equally probable events, we could always find a combination of r of its elements such that this union is infraprobable to some given event A, and such that a union of $r+1$ elements is more probable than A. Under certain conditions, the limiting value of $\frac{r}{n}$ exists, and the numerical probability of A is defined as this limiting value. As we expected, the numerical probability of a union of r-elements of an n-scale proved to be exactly $\frac{r}{n}$. Instead of approximating P(A) by unions with the exact numerical probabilities $\frac{r}{n}$, we could just as well use unions with numerical probabilities of approximately $\frac{r}{n}$ – as long as the approximation error vanishes for a large value of n. Such approximations are used in Savage's concept of *almost uniform partitions:*

Definition 4. An n-fold almost uniform partition of B is an n-fold partition such that the union of any r elements is not more probable than the union of any $r+1$ elements.

It can be proved that the numerical probability of a union of r elements of an n-fold almost uniform partition is approximately equal to $\frac{r}{n}$. The introduction of almost uniform partitions has two advantages. First, the philosophical problem as to which cases we may expect equal probabilities is evaded. It seems difficult to define events with equal probabilities outside the field of games. Second, the weaker assumption of the existence of almost uniform partitions gives more insight into the essentials of the procedure leading to numerical probabilities. We now quote the main propositions needed for the construction of numerical probabilities. Proofs are omitted; occasionally, intuitive explanations are given. For details the reader is referred to Savage (1954).

Proposition A. If n-fold almost uniform partitions of S for arbitrarily large values of n exist, then an m-fold almost uniform partition for any positive integer m exists.

Indeed, if S can be partitioned in, say, 1000 events that are approximately equally probable, then it is possible to combine them in such a way that, say, three groups result that are equally probable up to a small approximation error (in numerical probability this error would be of the order 1/1000). These three groups certainly form a 3-fold almost uniform partition. It may be noted that a similar proposition is untrue for n-scales with equally probable events. Therefore, in Koopman's system, the existence of n-scales for all (positive) integers n is assumed.

Proposition B. If n-fold almost uniform partitions of S *for any positive integer* n *exist and if there were to be a numerical probability measure* P *such that* $A \leqq \cdot B$ *implies* $P(A) \leqq P(B)$, *then such a probability measure is unique.*

Indeed, if a probability measure exists then the combination of r elements of an n-fold almost uniform partition will have a numerical probability of about r/n. In fact, this value can be shown to be between $(r-1)/n$ and $(r+1)/n$. Now let k_n/n be the largest number of elements such that the union C_{k_n} is infra-probable to some event B. Then $C_{k_n} \leqq \cdot B < \cdot C_{k_n+1}$ and, by hypothesis, this implies $P(C_{kn}) \leqq P(B) \leqq P(C_{k_n}+1)$. Using the approximation error for C_{k_n} and C_{k_n+1} mentioned earlier, we find

$$\frac{k_n-1}{n} \leqq P(B) \leqq \frac{k_n+2}{n}, \text{ or } P(B) - \frac{2}{n} \leqq \frac{k_n}{n} \leqq P(B) + \frac{1}{n}.$$

If P(B) exists, then the limit of k_n/n exists, and P(B) is equal to this limiting value. So then P is uniquely determined.

Proposition C. If n-fold almost uniform partitions of S *for any positive integer* n *exist, then a probability measure* P *such that* $A \leqq \cdot B$ *implies* $P(A) \leqq P(B)$ *exists.*

The proof contains the following elements. Consider some specific sequence of n-fold almost uniform partitions (n = 1, 2, 3, ...). Evidently, for some subset B of S, we will expect that $P(B) = \lim_{n\to\infty} \frac{k_n}{n}$ where k_n is again defined as the largest number of elements of the n-fold partition such that its combination is not more probable than B. Thus, we have to prove that $\lim_{n\to\infty} \frac{k_n}{n}$ exists. Now consider the difference $\frac{k_m}{m} - \frac{k_n}{n}$. One can prove that this difference vanishes for large values of m and n.

Apparently, it can be proved in the same way that $\frac{k_n}{n} - \frac{k_n'}{n}$ vanishes for large values of n, and this guarantees the existence of $\lim_{n\to\infty} \frac{k_n}{n}$. The limiting value is called P(B), and this function P on the set of subsets $\mathscr{S}$ fulfills the requirements of a (finitely additive) probability measure:

(i) $P(B) \geqq 0$ for every subset B of S,
(ii) $P(S) = 1$, $S \in \mathscr{S}$
(iii) If $A \cap B = \emptyset$ then $P(A \cup B) = P(A) + P(B)$, $A, B \in \mathscr{S}$.

(i) and (ii) are evident from the definition of P. (iii) must be considered more closely. Given some n-fold almost uniform partition, we know that the combination of any $k_n(A) - 1$ of its elements is less probable than A. In the same way, any combination of $k_n(B) - 1$ of its elements is less probable than B. (Indeed, we know that there is some combination of $k_n(A)$ of its elements that is infra-probable to A, so all combinations of $k_n(A) - 1$ of its elements are less probable than A). But then any combination of $k_n(A) + k_n(B) - 2$ of (mutually disjoint) elements will be less probable than $A \cup B$. On the other hand, $A \cup B$ is less probable than any combination of $k_n(A \cup B) + 1$ of its elements. Hence

$$\frac{k_n(A) + k_n(B) - 2}{n} \leqq \frac{k_n(A \cup B) + 1}{n}$$

and, for $n \to \infty$, it appears that

$$P(A) + P(B) \leqq P(A \cup B)$$

On the other hand, we know that any combination of $k_n(A) + 1$ elements is more probable than A; any combination of $k_n(B) + 1$ elements is more probable than B. Hence, any combination of $k_n(A) + k_n(B) + 2$ (mutually disjoint) elements is more probable than $A \cup B$. Moreover, there is a combination of $k_n(A \cup B)$ elements that is infra-probable to $A \cup B$. From this, it appears that $P(A \cup B) \leqq P(A) + P(B)$. With this, (iii) has been proved. The relation between the quantitative probability measure and the qualitative probability ordering is expressed by

(iv) If $A \leqq \cdot B$, then $P(A) \leqq P(B)$.

Indeed, $C_{k_n}(A) \leqq \cdot A \leqq \cdot B < \cdot C_{k_n}(B) + 1$, so

$$\frac{k_n(A)}{n} \leqq \frac{k_n(B)+1}{n}$$

and for the limit, $P(A) \leqq P(B)$.
It can be concluded that if n-fold almost uniform partitions for arbitrarily large values of n exist, then a unique, finitely additive probability measure P can be derived. However, it is not easy to verify the existence of such n-fold almost uniform partitions. Savage aims to find a necessary and sufficient condition for the existence of such partitions. He therefore introduces the concepts „fine and tight" which we shall not discuss here. To make sure that numerical probabilities do exist Savage needs one extra postulate. He introduced the following one:

Postulate 6. If $B < \cdot C$, a partition E_i of S exists such that $B \cup E_i < \cdot C$ for all E_i. If this postulate is fulfilled, there exist n-fold almost uniform partitions of S for arbitrarily large integers n.
The postulates P. 1 through P. 6 define a unique finitely additive probability measure. Conditional probabilities could be defined in terms of this probability measure in a classical way.
At this stage, the definition of the probability concept in Savage's approach is complete. Let us reconsider the system as a whole. The first question to be answered is, as to whether the postulates should be interpreted in a normative way or in a behavioristic way. Savage admits that his postulates could be only fulfilled by an "ideal person".
In practice, the requirements of consistency are too heavy to bear for any real life person. Most acts are hypothetical, and therefore inaccessible for intuition. Moreover, acts defined on complicated subsets B of the universal event S will be void of any intuitive meaning. Savage (1954) remarks:
"The main use I would make of the postulates is normative, to police my own decisions for consistency and, where possible, to make complicated decisions depend upon simpler ones".
This implies that the postulates should not be considered as a simple reflected of intuitive preferences, but rather as a system in which the intuitive preferences are imbedded. One could say that the intuitive preferences (perhaps a bit policed for consistency reasons) must generate the more extended system as given by the postulates, see Fishburn (1964), chap. 5.
Both Koopman and Savage face the problem, in what circumstances numerical probabilities can be derived. We could attach numerical values to the events by means of intuition, but then we are not sure that these values obey

consistency requirements like for instance the addition rule. Both Koopman and Savage derive numerical probabilities that are consistent with an intuitive ordering of events as to their probability. Unlike Koopman, however, Savage relates this ordering of events to preferences among decision acts in general decision situations under uncertainty.

3.*5 Subjective Probability and Relative Frequencies

Strictly speaking, the conception of subjective probability explained in Sec. 2.2 suffices for all applications of statistics. It is possible to dispense completely with frequency probability. In this section we give a partial explanation of why this is so; the explanation will be completed later. But we must add that there is considerable gain in adoption of a dualistic position. This position admits subjective probability as fundamental, but uses frequency probability as a heuristic device – as we did repeatedly in Chap. 1 – and as a technical device for simplification of the development of statistical theory.

We now elucidate how relative frequencies, finite or long-run, can be viewed in the light of subjective probability.

(1) Consider single trials of well-constructed gambling devices and similar physical apparatus, such as roulette wheels, dice, coins, balls in an urn. It is plausible, for example, to assign a probability of 1/37 to each of the 37 possible outcomes of a single spin of a roulette wheel. By extension, the probability of any one of, say, three specific outcomes is given a probability of 3/37. The intuitive considerations of symmetry underlying such assessments suggest the "definition" of probability as the "relative frequency of favorable cases to total cases." From the viewpoint of subjective probability, the subjective judgment that the 37 outcomes are equally probable, together with the requirement of coherence, *implies* this definition. The judgment of equal probability *is* subjective, and we may not make it if, for example, we detect imperfections in the physical construction of the wheel or confront extensive sample evidence suggesting lack of symmetry.

(2) Suppose it is known that 532 voters of 1000 voted Democratic on a secret ballot. How do we assess the probability that a specified voter voted Democratic. De Finetti (1937) explains that coherence requires only that the average probability assessed for all voters must equal 532/1000. We may or may not wish to make the subjective judgment that this probability is the same for all 1000 voters. In considering an individual voter, we use .532 as a base from which we may wish to deviate in one direction or another in order to take into account any available information that differentiates this voter from the others.

(3) Notice de Finetti's discussion of the assessment of the probability of death of Mr. A in the course of a year, when it is known that the relative frequency of deaths for men of his age in his country has been about 13 in 1000 in the past. (This is essentially the situation postulated for the evaluation of prior probabilities for set-ups in Chap. 1.) If we judge it "not very probable" that this year's frequency will be very far from 13/1000, we are essentially back to the previous paragraph. We may or may not assess the probability of death for A at .013, depending on the information about A.
De Finetti points out that the choice of the group of individuals with whom we compare Mr. A is arbitrary. If we choose a large and heterogeneous group, the average probability is easily assessed by the relative frequency, but we may feel that A's probability differs substantially from the frequency. If, on the other hand, we choose a small and homogeneous group, we may feel that the probability is nearly equal for all individuals but that the average probability is more difficult to assess. These opposing advantages and disadvantages must be reconciled as well as possible.
In all circumstances the subjectivistic view leads to examination of available frequencies in assessment of probabilities. It may or may not lead to assessments equal or close to these frequencies. In those circumstances in which most people would assign a probability somewhere close to an observed frequency, however, the subjectivistic theory provides a rationalization of why such consensus exists.

3.*6 Some General Conclusions

In this chapter we have considered several axiomatic systems, all of which pretend to give an interpretation of the probability concept. As Uspensky (1937, p. 8) remarked: "Modern attempts to build up the theory of probability as an axiomatic science may be interesting in themselves as mental exercises; but from the standpoint of applications the purely axiomatic science of probability would have no more value than, for example, would the axiomatic theory of elasticity".
We have seen that the frequency approach is only suitable for applications where large numbers of observations are available. Different probability models must be used for statements about unique events. Carnap's approach permits a treatment of statements about unique events. The main objection to his theory is that all relevant experience must be made explicit; intuitive weighing of different kinds of experience is not permitted. If we want to introduce intuitive weighing into our analysis, we must use personalistic probability models.
A personalistic probability model is characterized by a number of consistency

requirements. We cannot expect that our intuition will automatically obey such requirements, but one of the advantages of the model is that it is possible to detect and abandon any inconsistencies in our original intuitive feelings. For the many axiomatic systems dealing with personalistic probabilities, (see R.D. Luce and P. Suppes (1965) for a complete overview), it appears that numercial probabilities can only be derived under the assumption that real-world problems are comparable with hypothetical lotteries.

A personalistic probability model is consistent, but there is no guarantee that our intuitive ideas will correspond to reality. For repetitive events, it is quite possible that the observable relative frequency will be completely different from our original intuitive feelings. Thus it is necessary to extend the subjective probability model by including the possibility of learning by experience. This can be done in several ways. One could redefine the probabilities after each observation, in a purely personalistic way. This is quite unsatisfactory: one would like to have some consistency in the changes of subjective probabilities. This implies that we need a methodology that tells us how to learn from experience. The advantage of Carnap is that he develops such methodology, although it can be applied in a rather limited context. In the world of (personalistic) subjective probabilities, it is quite common to introduce prior distributions and to learn from experience by means of Bayes's theorem. This is what statistical analysis in real-life situations is all about, and in the next chapters we will encounter many of these situations where statistical conclusions can be only justified on the basis of a personalistic concept of probability plus a repeated use of Bayes' theorem.

Suggested Readings

Carnap, R.: 'The two Concepts of Probability', Philosophy and Phenomenological Research 5, 1945, 513–532.

Carnap, R.: Logical Foundations of Probability, Chicago 1950.

Carnap, R. and R. Jeffrey: Studies in Inductive Logic and Probability, Vol. I, Berkeley 1971.

de Finetti: 'La Prevision: ses lois logiques, ses sources subjectives', Annales de l'Institut Henri Poincare 7, 1937 (English translation in: Studies in subjective probability, H. E. Kyburg and H. E. Smokler, eds., New York 1963), 93–158.

B. de Finetti: Probability, Induction and Statistics, London 1972.

Fine, T.: Theories of Probability, New York and London 1973.

Fishburn, P.C.: Decision and Value Theory, New York 1964.

Gottinger, H.W.: Subjektive Wahrscheinlichkeiten, Göttingen and Zürich, 1974 (a).

Gottinger, H.W.: 'Subjective Qualitative Information Structures based on Orderings', Theory and Decision 5, 1974 (b), 69–97.

Halmos, P.R.: Lectures on Boolean Algebras, Princeton 1963.

Jeffreys, H.: Theory of Probability, 3rd edition, Oxford 1961.

Kemeny, J.G.: 'Fair Bets and Inductive Probabilities', Journal of Symbolic Logic 20, 1955, 263–273.

Kemeny, J.G., Snell, J. and G.L. Thompson: Introduction to Finite Mathematics, Englewood Cliffs, 1957.

Kolmogorov, A. N.: Grundbegriffe der Wahrscheinlichkeitsrechnung, Ergebnisse der Mathematik, Berlin 1933 (english translation, Foundations of Probability, Chelsea 1956).
Koopman, B. O.: 'The Axioms and Algebra of Intuitive Probability', Annals of Mathematics 41, 1940, 269–292.
Koopman, B. O.: 'Intuitive Probability and Sequences', Annals of Mathematics 42, 1941, 169–187.
Luce, R. D. and P. Suppes: 'Preferences, Utility and Subjective Probability', Handbook of Mathematical Psychology III, New York 1965.
Richter, H.: 'Eine einfache Axiomatik der subjektiven Wahrscheinlichkeit'. Publ. dell' Institutio Nazionale di Alta Matematica 9, 1972, 95–77.
Savage, L. J.: The Foundations of Statistics, New York 1954. 'Elicitation of personal probabilities and expectations', Journal Am. Statistical Ass. 66, 1971, 783–801.
Uspensky, J. V.: Introduction to Mathematical Probability, New York 1937.
Von Mises, R.: Probability, Statistics and Truth, London 1957.

Appendix A – Chapter 3*

Criticisms of the Classic Conception of Probability

The classic Laplacean conception of probability has been criticized on a number of grounds, we consider six of them.
(1) That probability is defined in terms of a relation of equiprobability and such a definition is circular unless equiprobability is independently defined.
(2) That to define equiprobability one has to appeal to the so-called "principle of insufficient reason". This principle is itself unsatisfactory because

(a) it is only applicable by one who has had no experience relative to the situation at hand,
(b) there is no criterion to determine whether or not it has been correctly applied,
(c) it is difficult to apply in practice,
(d) there are situations in which there is lack of agreement on its correct application.

(3) That, according to the classic conception of probability, numerical probabilities must be rational numbers. But there are cases where irrational numbers occur as probabilities and these cannot be interpreted as ratios of alternatives. It has been noted, for instance, that the probability that two integers chosen at random are relatively prime is $6/\pi^2$. This cannot mean, it is said that there are π^2 equiprobable alternatives of which 6 are favorable to getting relative primes. (This is a criticism which attributes reality to the continuum and fails to recognize that, in relation to practical measurement, it is only a convenient method of approximation. We do not consider it further here).
(4) That there is no logical relation between the number of different ways in which something can happen and the actual relative frequency with which it does happen. Thus probability, as defined, cannot tell us about actual relative frequencies.
(5) That the classic conception of probability does not make it clear whether or not a numerical probability derived from judgements of equiprobability is a measure of what we actually do believe or of what we ought to believe. If the former is meant then it is not clear that the axioms of probability are, in fact, satisfied; whereas if the latter is meant then the source of the imperative is not given.
(6) That, according to the classic conception, probability can be defined only when the underlying situation can be analyzed into a finite set of

equiprobable alternatives. But there are situations where we make numerical probability statements but such an analysis is without meaning. For instance one may make a statement such as "The probability that a thirty-year-old man will live for another year is .945". It has been said that it is absurd to suppose that this statement means there are a thousand possible courses to a man's career, and that exactly 945 of them are favorable to his survival for at least another year.

Appendix B – Chapter 3*

Simultaneous Definition of Utility and Subjective Probability

When dealing with Savage's theory, we have omitted all references to the concept of utility. This could be done very easily, because probabilities are defined by Savage independent of utilities. In the axiomatic system as given in the paper of Pratt, Raiffa and Schlaifer (1964) the concepts of utility and probability are defined simultaneously. We shall restrict ourselves here to those parts, that are relevant for a definition of the probability concept.
The aim of Pratt, Raiffa and Schlaifer is to develop a method to obtain a consistent subjective probability model for real life situations. Essentially, the theory boils down to a comparison of real-life events with a hypothetical canonical experiment. It is supposed that one can imagine an experiment characterized by a *rectangular* distribution on the interval $[0,1]$. Given two consequences c^* and c_*, we can consider the class of lotteries that result in c^* for the interval $[0,\alpha)$ and in c_* for the interval $[\alpha, 1]$. For real-life events E_o one can define lotteries that result in c^* for E_0 and c_* for the complementary event $E - E_o$. It is postulated that for any event E_0 a number $\hat{\alpha}$ exists, such that the two lotteries are equivalent. This number $\hat{\alpha}$ is denoted by $P(E_o)$. In other words, this model can only be used if we feel that the real life problem can be compared with a hypothetical lottery. Before giving the formal postulates we have to introduce the following notation.
Let E be a finite set of real world events. Denote by $X \times Y$ the set of outcomes of a two-dimensional hypothetical experiment; the outcomes are restricted to the generalized interval $[0,1]$. On the Cartesian product $E \times X \times Y$ all sorts of lotteries can be defined. Such lotteries are denoted by

$$\begin{aligned} f(e, x, y) &= c^* \quad \text{if} \quad e \in E_o,\ x \in X_o \quad \text{and} \quad y \in Y_o \\ &= c_* \quad \text{otherwise} \end{aligned}$$

where $E_o \subseteq E$ and where X_o and Y_o are sub-intervals of $[0,1]$. Apparently, if $E_o = E$, the lottery is defined on the hypothetical canonical experiment only; if $X_o \times Y_o = X \times Y$, the lottery is defined on the set of real life events. As far as preferences exist in the class of lotteries, it is supposed that these preferences are transitive. This implies that a partial ordering is defined on the class of lotteries. If f_2 is not strictly preferred to f_1, that is $f_2 \precsim f_1$, and we have

(1) If $f_1 \precsim f_2$ and $f_2 \precsim f_3$, then $f_1 \precsim f_3$.

If both $f_1 \precsim f_2$ and $f_2 \precsim f_1$, this equivalence will be denoted by $f_1 \sim f_2$. Let us now return to the lotteries that are defined on the canonical experiment. Evidently, it is sensible to choose a canonical experiment that is as simple as possible. It is supposed that the canonical experiment is characterized by a two-dimensional rectangular probability distribution.
This is reflected by

(2a) $$\text{If } f_1(e, x, y) = \begin{cases} c^* & \text{if } e \in E_o \quad \text{and} \quad (x, y) \in X_1 \times Y_1 \\ c_* & \text{otherwise} \end{cases}$$

$$f_2(e, x, y) = \begin{cases} c^* & \text{if } e \in E_o \quad \text{and} \quad (x, y) \in X_2 \times Y_2 \\ c_* & \text{otherwise,} \end{cases}$$

if moreover the area of $X_1 \times Y_1$ is equal to the area of $X_2 \times Y_2$, then $f_1 \sim f_2$.
(2b) If $E_o = E$ and the area of $X_1 \times Y_1$ is strictly larger than $X_2 \times Y_2$ then $f_1 \succ f_2$.
The restriction $E_o = E$ in this postulate has to be made because the decision-maker could attach no value to the chance $E_o \times X_o \times Y_o$ whatever area $X_o \times Y_o$ is chosen.
The third postulate asserts that the lottery defined on $E_o \times X \times Y$ may be compared with a lottery defined on $E \times X \times Y_o$. In other words lotteries on real life events may be compared with lotteries on the hypothetical canonical experiment.

(3) For any subset $E_o \subset E$ there exist a value $P(E_o)$ such that

$$f_1(e, x, y) = \begin{cases} c^* & \text{if } e \in E_o \quad \text{and} \quad (x, y) \in X \times Y \\ c_* & \text{otherwise} \end{cases}$$

$$f_2(e, x, y) = \begin{cases} c^* & \text{if } y \in [0, P(E_o)] \quad \text{and} \quad (e, x) \in E \times X \\ c_* & \text{otherwise} \end{cases}$$

are equivalent.
The fourth and last postulate is needed to assure that the property of additivity is not only valid for canonical chances but also for the probability $P(E_o)$.

(4) Let Q be any one of E, X, Y; let q be the corresponding one of e, x, y; let $\{Q_1, \ldots, Q_n\}$ be a partition of Q; for $i = 1, \ldots, n$, let f_i' and f_i'' be lotteries from $E \times X \times Y$ independent of the value of q; let

$$\left.\begin{aligned} f'(e, x, y) &= f_i'(e, x, y) \\ f''(e, x, y) &= f_i''(e, x, y) \end{aligned}\right\} \text{ if } q \in Q_i .$$

Then, if $f_i' \sim f_i''$ for all i, $f' \sim f''$ holds.
From these postulates one can easily derive the existence of a unique finitely additive subjective probability measure on the class of events $\{E_o\}$.
The importance of this approach lies in the fact that it makes explicit a line of thought that is implicitly used by Koopman and Savage. Numerical subjective probabilities only exist if comparisons with hypothetical lotteries can be made. It is quite interesting to mention that the lotteries themselves can be considered as commodities, and in fact, this is a new line of thought, proposed by Savage (1971) to arrive at an economic justification of subjective probabilities in terms of rates of substitution between contingent commodities (lotteries).

Suggested Readings

Pratt, J.W., Raiffa, H., and R. Schlaifer, 'The Foundations of Decision under Uncertainty', *Jour. Amer. Statist. Assoc.* 59, 1964.
Savage, L.J., 'Elicitation of Personal Probabilities and Expectations', *Jour. Amer. Statist. Assoc.* 66, 1971, 783–801.

4.* Utility and Decision Theory

4.*1 Introduction

(a) *History*

Contributions to utility in the context of human values (economic, social and individual values) date back at least three hundred years. The notion of utility arose first in the context of gambling problems, e.g., in decision situations under risk. The notion was used by B. Pascal (1681) ('immortality wager'), by de Montmort (1708) (analyzing card games), and by D. Bernoulli (1738) (to solve the Petersburg game). Here utility was meant essentially as 'utility of a gamble weighted by its probability', other equivalent notions used were 'mean utility', 'average utility', 'moral expection', 'expected utility'.
Independent of this development and much later economists were concerned with 'measuring the degree of satisfaction' derived from consumption of particular commodities. This development bears the names of Gossen, Jevons, Menger, Walras, Antonelli and I. Fisher, (the utilitaristic school), somewhat modified and extended by V. Pareto (around 1900) and followers (the Paretian school). Although there was substantial disagreement between both schools with regard to the form of the utility function and its measurement properties their common point is that the utility function is constructed in a deterministic environment. Most of conventional economic theory has been formulated in this environment and therefore is based on this utility concept. Von Neumann and Morgenstern (1947) gave a rigorous (axiomatic) treatment of Bernoullian utility in the context of game theory.

(b) *Scope of Utility Theory*

Utility theory has many facets comprising economics, psychology, philosophy, statistics and management science. Two approaches are evident: the *normative* (prescriptive) *approach* and the *descriptive approach.* In the *normative approach* one is concerned with the problem of what a 'rational man' *should* do given that his preferences could be represented by utilities. One would like to have a normative guide to help the individual to codify his preferences. For example, if it is true that a person prefers steak to chicken and chicken to hamburger then it is strongly suggested that he complies with the transitivity rule and should prefer steak to hamburger. If his utilities represent preferences he should assign a higher utility to steak than to hamburger. If a person appears to violate consistent preferences, i.e. if he forgets or cannot cope with the complexity of preferences among many alternatives, this approach suggests that he has made a 'computational' error and therefore has to reexamine his preference structure. Even by adopting this approach one is interested to find the weakest set of consistency criteria (in terms of actual behavior) which still permits a representation of preferences by utility. In the *descriptive approach* one is interested in actual choice behavior, e.g. in setting up experimental situations under repetitive conditions where individuals reveal their 'true' preferences in terms of utilities. In many of these situations one has adopted a stochastic approach to choice behavior. In economics, statistics, management science most studies of utility have been normative, whereas psychologists overwhelmingly have pursued a descriptive view.

Because of limited space and the diversity of the subject a concentration on a few aspects of utility theory is necessary. Here we emphasize a normative approach. Many excellent reviews of utility theory are available, some including extensive references on the area under review: we mention Fishburn (1968, 1970) for an overall review, Edwards (1961) and Becker (1967) for reviews covering mainly psychological research, Kauder (1965) on the history of the subject, as far as economics is concerned, Adams (1960) on Bernoullian utility theory and related matters, and Chipman et al. (1971) for an extensive bibliography including over 1000 items.

4.*2 Definition and Existence of Utility Functions

From a mathematical point of view most of utility theory reduces to theories of (binary) order relations, and their representation by functions. In fact, we could think of utility theory in model theoretic terms, e.g., to map a binary relational system isomorphically into a numerical relational system constituted by the order properties of the real numbers. This viewpoint is common in modern measurement theory.

(a) *Assumptions on Preferences*

Let X be a finite set set of alternatives, X could be interpreted as the set of consumption bundles $x \in R^n$ (the n-dimensional Euclidean space). The consumer (or generally the decision-maker) chooses bundles out of the set $X = \{x \in R^n: x_i \geqq 0, i = 1, 2, \ldots, n\}$, the non-negative orthant. The preferences of the consumer can be described by a binary relation R so that xRy means 'x is preferred to or is indifferent to y'. First it is natural to ask what order properties can be imposed on X so that (X, R) forms an order system (preference system). R on X is a *quasi-order* (or *preorder*) if (i) xRx for any $x \in X$ (reflexivity), (ii) xRy, yRz $\Rightarrow$ xRz for any x, y, $z \in X$ (transitivity). R is a *complete quasi-order* (or *complete preorder* or *weak order*) if both (ii)

and (iii) either xRy or yRx (or both) for any $x, y \in X$ hold. (If (iii) holds then automatically (i) holds).
Let R be a weak order on X. Then the relations I (indifference) and P (strict preference) can be derived from R as follows:

(a) xIy is equivalent to xRy and yRx, i.e. I is an equivalence relation (reflexive, transitive, symmetric).
(b) xPy is equivalent to xPy and not yRx.

In terms of interpretation some authors expressed dissatisfaction about (iii), the completeness assumption, and only postulated a quasi-order, others relaxed transitivity of indifference (which is hard to justify even from a normative view-point).
Let $X = X_1 \times X_2 \times \ldots \times X_n$ and $x = (x_1, x_2, \ldots, x_n)$, $y = (y_1, y_2, \ldots, y_n)$ be n-dimensional vectors of numbers, respectively. Let R on X be defined as

$$
\begin{aligned}
&xRy \text{ if and only if} \\
&x_1 > y_1 \text{ or } [x_1 = y_1 \text{ and } x_2 \geqq y_2] \text{ or} \\
&\qquad [x_1 = y_1, x_2 = y_2 \text{ and } x_3 \geqq y_3] \text{ or} \ldots \\
&\qquad [x_i = y_i \text{ for all } i < n \text{ and } x_n \geqq y_n].
\end{aligned}
$$

Then R is called a *lexicographic* order.

(b) *Representation of Preference Orderings*

Let R be a weak order on X. A real-valued utility function u is said to be *order-preserving* if (*) xRy if and only if $u(x) \geqq u(y)$.
Clearly, the assumption of a weak order is necessary for the representation (*) but not sufficient, in particular this is the case if I partitions X into uncountably many equivalence classes. We will develop some sufficiency criteria. R is said to be *order-dense* if there exists a set $S \subset X$ such that for any $x, y \in X$, xPy, and there exists $s \in S$ such that xRs and sRy. X is *separable* if it contains a countable subset S that is R-order dense.
(*) plus separability is *necessary and sufficient* for proving the well-known result, Luce and Suppes (1965), that a weakly ordered set is isomorphic to a subset of the real numbers. Hence there exists a function u that is order-preserving with respect to R.
With the same order assumptions but with different structural assumptions on X (relating to a topology on X) more refined existence theorems have been proved. The relationships between the former and the latter results have been analyzed. In what follows we present a sketch of ideas underlying these results. Let X be a topological space (endowed with an order topology generated by a countable system of disjoint open sets in X), let R be a weak order defined on X. Then R is *continuous* if for any $x \in X$ the sets $M(x) =$

$= \{y \in X : yRx\}$, $N(x) = \{y \in X : xRy\}$ are *closed* in X. It has been shown by Debreu (1954) that for any continuous weak order on X there exists a continuous order-preserving utility function under the following sufficient condition:

X is (topologically) separable, i.e. if the system of *open* sets in X has a countable base. This condition is related to ordinary separability of the previous condition. In fact, it has been proved (see Fleischer (1961)) that both conditions are equivalent under the order topology on X, so that any subset S is topologically dense in X. There is no way to avoid a topological characterization of X in this framework since it can be shown that subsets, like the set of even integers, may order-dense but fail to be topologically dense in the set of all integers.

If X is a metric space then ordinary separability implies topological separability. This fact has some impact on existence proofs of intertemporal utility functions.

The same results with alternative structural assumptions can be obtained. More generally, most measurement theories attempting to imbed an *empirical relational system* in a *numerical relational system* by an isomorphic assignment (measurement scale) are based on linking properties of the order system to structural properties of its underlying topology. The idea is to choose a topology that is compatible with the natural topology of the real numbers. The existence of a continuous order-preserving utility can be proved with more elementary means, dispensing of any topological assumptions, usually by postulating some kind of archimedean assumption on the system of preferences.

Another more ambitious program is attempted by permitting only algebraic assumptions on the order system (X, R) or some subsystem and then to construct a continuous representation based on mathematical results on ordered algebraic structures.

Further remarks are in order regarding the existence of a continuous utility function representing preferences.

(1) *Uniqueness:* Let u be an arbitrary real-valued function defined on X. Then there exists a unique weak order R on X such that u is order-preserving with respect to R.

Conversely, let R be a weak order on X such that an order-preserving function u_0 with respect to R exists on X. Then a real-valued function u on X is orderpreserving with respect to R if and only if

$$u(x) = \phi(u_0(x)), \quad x \in X,$$

where ϕ is any monotonic-increasing transformation. Hence u is uniquely determined up to positive monotone transformations, i.e. u is measurable on an 'ordinal scale'.

(2) *Lexicographic preference:* A lexicographic preference order cannot be represented by a real-valued utility function, technically, it destroys separability in the order topology of X.
However, it can be represented by a vector-valued function in a completely ordered vector space:

(L) xRy if and only if
$$(u_1(x_1), u_2(x_2), \ldots, u_n(x_n)) \geqq (u_1(y_1), u_2(y_2), \ldots, u_n(y_n)),$$

where R is the lexicographic ordering and $\geqq$ indicates the ordering of utility vectors.
A lexicographic utility representation is incompatible with an archimedean assumption of a preference ordering, hence does not permit any compensatory preference structure as exhibited, for example, by ordinary indifference analysis. It is a multiple criteria utility function where the criteria are independent and are ranked strictly according to a priority scheme. Several authors consider lexicographic utility as the core of utility theory, e.g. Chipman (1971). However, applications of lexicographic utilities seem to be limited since people's behavior is more likely to permit trade-offs between preferences than to adopt a strictly hierarchical ranking scheme.

(3) *Additive Utility*

Additive and lexicographic utilities are closely related in so far as they require some independence assumption imposed on the order system (X, R). Both kinds of utility are therefore sometimes considered as 'multidimensional utilities'. One general (qualitative) independence assumption is the following: Let $X = X_1 \times \ldots \times X_m$ and R on X be a weak order. Define an equivalence relation T_m on $X_1 \times \ldots \times X_m$ such that if

(I) $(x_1, \ldots, x_m)\, T_m (y_1, \ldots, y_m)$ and $x_j R y_j$ for $j = 1, 2, \ldots, m-1$

then $y_m R x_m$. Let this be true for arbitrary $m = 2, 3, \ldots$ ad infinitum.
Assumption (I) is crucial for the representation of additive utilities:

(A) xRy if and only if

$$u_1(x_1) + u_2(x_2) + \ldots + u_n(x_n) \geqq u_1(y_1) + u_2(y_2) + \ldots + u_n(y_n).$$

Hence, on the basis of assumption (I), $(x_1, x_2, \ldots, x_m)\, T_m (y_1, y_2, \ldots, y_m)$ implies

$$u_1(x_1) + u_2(x_2) + \ldots + u_m(x_m) = u_1(y_1) + u_2(y_2) + \ldots + u_m(y_m)$$

so that $u_j(x_j) \leqq u_j(y_j)$ for all $j < m$ implies $u_m(y_m) \leqq u_m(x_m)$.
Various independence assumptions have been suggested, the most general ones are given by the Luce-Tukey theory of conjoint measurement (Krantz (1964)), a different approach has been pursued by Debreu (1960) but all

require each X_i to be infinite. Additive utilities go back to ideas of the utilitaristic school, see Wold (1944), they involve measurement of utilities unique up to positive linear transformations, or what economists call 'cardinal utility'. Weaker assumptions with regard to the measurement property but retaining the additive form of utility have gained new reputation in demand and consumer theory. Furthermore, the idea of independence between commodity groups entering the utility function rather than between commodities has led to additive 'separability' of the utility function that permits compensatory preference structures within groups but not between groups.

4*3 Expected Utility

D. Bernoulli's utility concept 'moral expectation' has been revitalized in the context of the theory of games (von Neumann and Morgenstern (1947)) and since then has been used in general situation situations under risk und uncertainty. It is the core concept of modern decision theory, and applies equally well to the foundations of statistics as developed in Blackwell and Girshick (1954). Historically, the first use of expected utility in a decision theoretic formulation has been made by B. Pascal. This situation is known as Pascal's *immortality wager.* This game also involves non-numerical consequences. The treatment of uncertainty is representative for classical decision situations under complete ignorance. Because we don't know anything about immortality of a human being, we may assume with Pascal that his chances are equally distributed, i.e. according to the *principle of insufficient reason* we attach probability 1/2 to any event. The underlying religious conviction is (Pascal was a religious man) that God rewards immortality by a good christian life but punishes a morally bad life by refusing eternity. The decision problem of Pascal's wager can be represented in a simple decision table.

	Act	
Event	a_1	a_2
E	X_{11}	X_{21}
$\bar{E}$	X_{12}	X_{22}

E means 'God exists', $\bar{E}$ means 'God does not exist', the consequences $X_{11}, X_{21}, X_{12}, X_{22}$ are random variables of a given probability distribution. They may be interpreted as X_{11} ('eternity because of good life'), X_{21} ('punishment because of bad life'), X_{12} ('nothing is gained by a good life'), X_{22} ('nothing is lost by a bad life'). The wager may choose – once and for

all – between both strategies. It is assumed that he will choose a strategy which guarantees him maximal expected utility ('moral expectation').
He may compute the expected utility of the first strategy according to

$$E[U(a_1)] \equiv U(a_1) = \tfrac{1}{2}U(X_{11}) + \tfrac{1}{2}U(X_{12})$$

and of the second strategy

$$E[U(a_2)] \equiv U(a_2) = \tfrac{1}{2}U(X_{21}) + \tfrac{1}{2}U(X_{22}).$$

A rational gambler maximizes his expected utility, i.e.

$$U(a_1) > U(a_2) \Leftrightarrow U(X_{11}) - U(X_{21}) > U(X_{12}) - U(X_{22})$$
(utility difference)

and just this will be done by a Pascal wager. The reason is that a religious man feels the utility difference between X_{11} and X_{21} to be much larger than that between X_{12} and X_{22}. In this case a religious man will act as a rational gambler.

(a) *Lotteries and Preferences*

Let X be a non-empty, finite set of sure prospects, define a (discrete) probability distribution f on X such that $0 \leqq f(x) \leqq 1$ and $\sum_{x \in X} f(x) = 1$ for all $x \in X$. Denote the set generated by all probability distributions f, g, h, ... on X by F. Then F is called a *mixture set* the elements of which are referred to as prospects or lotteries. For a specific f on X, suppose $f(x_i) = .1$, $f(x_j) = .2$, $f(x_k) = .7$, then by selecting f a person gets either x_i or x_j or x_k with probabilities .1, .2, .7, respectively where x_i, x_j, x_k could be some monetary amounts. If g and h are two probability distributions on X then also every convex combination (in terms of probabilities p)

$$f = pg + (1-p)h \equiv (pg, \bar{p}h), \; p \in (0, 1)$$

is a probability distribution on X.
First some structural assumptions are imposed of F which turn F into a *mixture space.*

A.1 For $f, g \in F$ and for all $p \in (0, 1)$:
$(pf, \bar{p}g) \in F$ (convexity).
A.2 $(pf, \bar{p}g) = (\bar{p}g, pf)$ (commutativity).
A.3 For $f, g, h \in F$ and for all $p \in (0, 1)$, $q \in (0, 1)$:
$[pf, \bar{p}(qg, \bar{q}h)] = (pf, \bar{p}qg, \bar{p}\bar{q}h)$
(reduction of compound lotteries)
A.4 $(pf, \bar{p}g) = g$ for $p = 0$ and $(pf, \bar{p}g) = f$ for $p = 1$.

Given the structure of the mixture space F a person prefers certain lotteries over others.

0.1 There is a weak order R defined on F.
0.2 (Continuity) For f, g, h $\in$ F and hPg, gPf there exist numbers p, q $\in (0,1)$ such that $(qf, \bar{q}h)$ Pg and gP$(pf, \bar{p}h)$.
0.3 (Independence) If gPf and there exists h $\in$ F then $(pg, \bar{p}h)$ P$(pf, \bar{p}h)$ for all p $\in (0,1]$.

As an immediate consequence of the assumptions further properties can be derived as propositions:

P.1 (Sure-thing Principle) If fPg then fP$(pf, \bar{p}g)$ and $(pf, \bar{p}g)$Pg for all p $\in (0,1)$.
P.2 (Continuity) For some g $\in$ F with fPg Ph there exists a unique p $\in (0,1)$ such that gI$(pg, \bar{p}h)$.
P.3 (Substitution) If fIg then for some p $\in (0,1)$ and h $\in$ F; $(pf, \bar{p}h)$ I $(pg, \bar{p}h)$.

There have been different axiom systems with regard to expected utility, A.1–A.4 and 0.1 are from von Neumann–Morgenstern (1947), 0.2 is an archimedean-type assumption, 0.3 is due to Samuelson (1952), as a modification of a monotony assumption. A further weakening of 0.3 for the countable case is due to Blackwell and Girshick (1954).
There have been extensive discussions about the plausibility and empirical validity of P.1–P.3, see Luce and Raiffa (1957).
Some difficulties in testing the von Neumann–Morgenstern axioms have been encountered, in particular tests show that individuals often cannot cope with the meaning of complex, uncertain prospects. This has led to the formulation of a simple type of uncertain prospects given by *even-chance mixtures* of pairs of sure prospects, Debreu (1959). Let X be the set of sure prospects, let x, y be elements of X. Denote by (x, y) of X $\times$ X the prospect of having x with probability $^1/_2$ or y with probability $^1/_2$. (The chance mechanism can be looked upon as 'flipping a coin' and that the person gets x if 'Heads' turns up or y if 'Tails' appears.) One then defines a preference relation R on X $\times$ X, and xRy is equivalent to (x, x)R(y, y). The following assumptions, structure and order assumptions similar to those presented in Sec. 4.*2 can be used:
A.'1 X is connected and (topologically) separable.
0.'1 R on X $\times$ X is a weak order.
0.'2 The sets $\{(x, y) \in X \times X : (x, y)\, R\, (x', y')\}$ and $\{(x, y) \in X \times X : (x', y')\, R\, (x, y)\}$ are closed for every (x', y') in X $\times$ X.
0.'3 $[(x_1, y_2)\, R\, (x_2, y_1)$ and $(x_2, y_3)\, R\, (x_3, y_2)]$ implies $(y_3, x_1)\, R\, (y_1, x_3)$.

(b) *Representation*

A.1–A.4 and 0.1–0.3 are necessary and sufficient that a utility u can be assigned to every f $\in$ F so that if f, g $\in$ F and p $\in [0,1]$:

$$\text{(E)} \quad \begin{array}{l} fRg \text{ if and only if } u(f) \geqq u(g) \\ u(pf, \bar{p}g) = pu(f) + \bar{p}u(g). \end{array}$$

Hence u is an order-preserving, linear function on F, referred to as *expected utility.*

(The proof of (E) is not as straightforward as it appears but has to use an extension theorem due to Cramer (1956)). Furthermore, a uniqueness result holds for (E). Let u and u′, respectively, be two utilities that exist on F, then for all $f \in F$:

$u'(f) = \alpha u(f) + \beta$ with real numbers $\alpha > 0$, and β, unrestricted in sign, i.e. utility is uniquely determined up to positive linear transformations. Therefore u is measurable on an interval scale (so-called 'cardinal utility').

Now the special case of even chance mixtures can be dealt with. A utility function on an even chance mixture space is a real-valued, order-preserving function u on $X \times X$ such that

$$u[(x, y)] = \tfrac{1}{2}\{u[(x, x)], u[(y, y)]\} = \tfrac{1}{2}u(x) + \tfrac{1}{2}u(y)$$
for every $x, y \in X$.

The assumptions A′1, 0′1–0′3 are necessary and sufficient for the existence of a continuous utility function uniquely determined up to increasing linear transformations.

A proof of this result proceeds according to Debreu (1959, 1960).

In the same way as indicated in Sec. 4*2 you can construct representation theorems on the basis of independence assumptions and lexicographic orderings.

(c) *Interpretation*

A very useful device that has some intuitive appeal is to redefine a lottery by a lottery diagram:

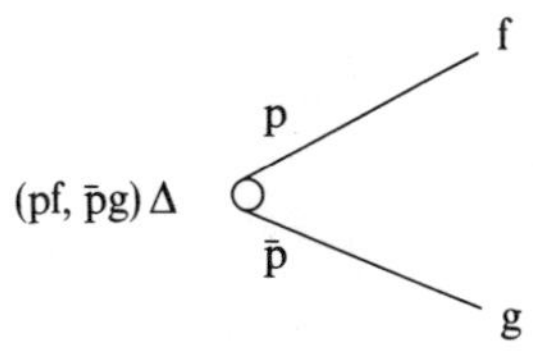

Starting with the structural assumptions, A.2 states simply that the lottery operation is *commutative*, i.e. it is immaterial in which order the elements of the lottery are arranged.

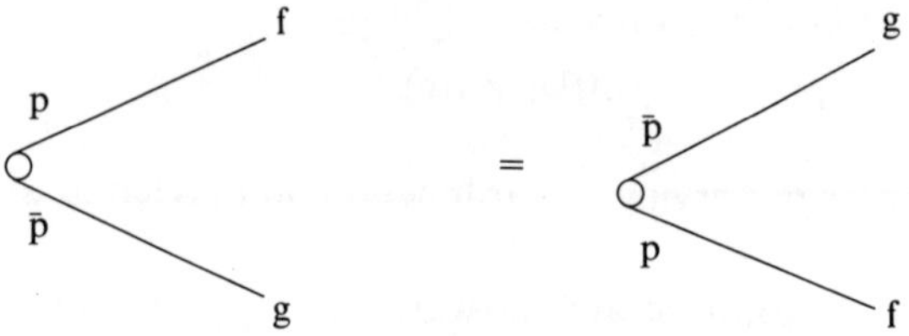

Commutativity of Lottery

A.3, or the reduction of compound lotteries, is virtually some kind of *associativity statement* that in this form involves a series of successive lotteries to be "computationally" reduced to a simple, one-step lottery. The basic motivation for it is that there is no intrinsic reward in lotteries, or 'no fun in gambling' – at least from a normative point of view. In other words, an individual will react to a compound lottery *as if* it were a simple lottery with equivalent probabilities.

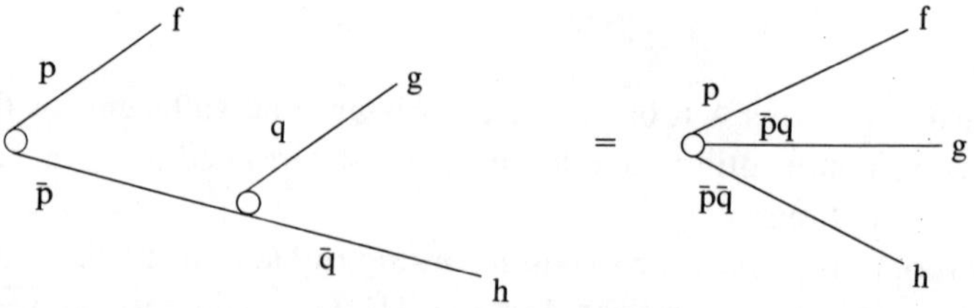

Reduction of a Compound Lottery to a Simple Lottery

Now turning to the ordering assumptions, in particular to 0.2 and 0.3, we first observe that the consequence of 0.2 can be split into two interpretations (a) and (b) which obviously are reflected in the propositions P.1 and P.2. According to P.1 suppose f is preferred to g, then a lottery with even a minimal chance of realizing the more desirable f is preferred to g. Or equivalently, f is preferred to a lottery with even a minimal chance of receiving the less desirable g. Illustrating the two cases, we have

(a)

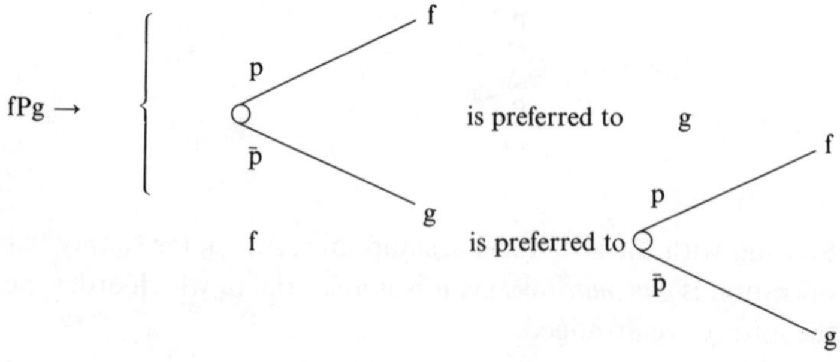

Now suppose, according to P.2, that fPg and gPh. Then given a lottery (p^*f, $\bar{p}^*$h) the *preferential dominance* of f can be made sufficiently small (p^* close to zero) such that g is still preferred to the lottery, i.e. there exists a p^* such that

(b_1)

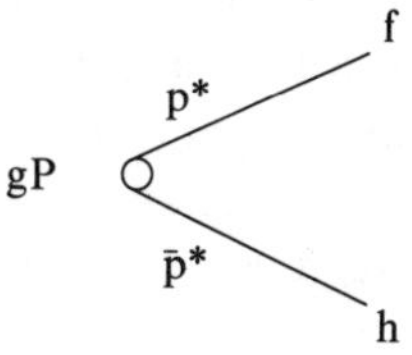

Likewise, there exists a p_* such that

(b_2)

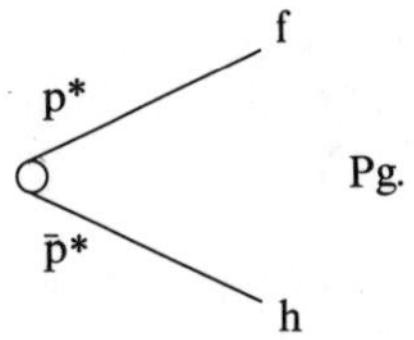

Furthermore, each individual can conceive of some probability p which makes him indifferent between the mid-alternative g, and a lottery involving the extreme alternatives f and h.

(b_3)

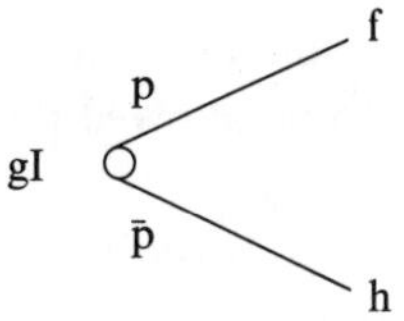

Altogether, parts (a) and (b) imply a reasonable continuity assumption that *no* infinite value is attached to *any* alternatives which cannot be compensated for.

Finally, looking at 0.3 (independence), we find that given the preference of one alternative g over another f and a third alternative h taken into consideration, then the preference over the probability mixtures remains the same irrespective of how we enlarge or restrict the entire mixture space. P.3 is a specific consequence of this statement.

4*4 Bernoullian Utility: The Petersburg Game

D. Bernoulli (1738) gave several examples to show why the expected utility concept is adequate to explain human behavior. Among these examples the Petersburg game attracted most interest. There have been many solutions to this problem which now are primarily of historical interest.

Suppose Peter (normally a Casino) invites Paul (a gambler) on payment of a price Y to participate in a coin-tossing game. They agree that Paul receives 2^n *ducats* if the coin falls 'Heads' on the n-th toss. Obviously, the probability of this occurrence (provided the coin is 'fair') is the probability that in a sequence of $n-1$ tosses 'Tails' occur and on the n-th toss 'Heads', i.e. the probability is $(1/2)^{n-1} 1/2 = 2^{-n}$. To illustrate this we establish a simple decision table.

		Events		
		(H, 1st toss)	(H, 2nd toss) ...	(H, n-th toss) ...
Decisions	Game	$2-Y$	2^2-Y	2^n-Y
	No Game	0	0	0
				outcomes

What is now Paul's monetary expected gain? It is

$$\frac{1}{2}(2-Y)+\frac{1}{4}(4-Y)+\ldots=1+1+\ldots-\frac{Y}{2^n}2^n=1+1+\ldots-Y.$$

and this expectation is infinite.

Thus, according to the principle of expected monetary value one would be willing to pay a price, no matter how large, to be allowed to participate in the game. This is absurd.

Simple examples convince us quickly that for a fairly high price (say 128 ducats) it cannot be rational to participate in the game. There is only one chance in 64 to get the price back (six tails with probability 2^{-6}); otherwise there is always a loss.

Though Bernoulli found some truth in the proposition that people behave according to the expected value, he suggested to take the expected utility for analysis of such situations in order to avoid paradoxical results.

His observations, more or less derived ad hoc, lead to the conclusion of a 'law of diminishing marginal utility', i.e. utility is a concave function, which was later considered by utility theorists (around 1870) as an empirical fact. Let us formulate Bernoulli's latter observation. It means that each 'infinitesimally small' increase in utility (or disutility) dU induced by a corresponding increase in wealth dW is inversely proportional to the endowment of wealth obtained by a person, i.e.

(1) $$dU = \alpha dW/W.$$

Let the the relative increase of wealth be in a certain interval [a, b]. Then integrating (1) we find the total utility

(2) $$U(W) = \int_a^b dW/W + c = \alpha \log W + c. \quad \text{(log is \textit{natural logarithm})}.$$

c is an integration constant which is fixed if we put $U = 0$ so that $c = -\alpha \log W_0$ and W_0 is the initial endowment (present wealth) from which a person starts off. We can assume that U(W) is twice differentiable so that U′(W) is strictly decreasing as W increases (giving rise to the law of diminishing marginal utility) and furthermore $U''(W) < 0$.

From (2) we derive for $W_0 \neq 0$:

(3) $$U(W) = \alpha \log W - \alpha \log W_0 = \alpha \log W/W_0$$

which is zero if $W = W_0$.

Clearly, (3) states (subject to the choice of initial value and utility unit) *that the expected utility of a monetary value is equal to the logarithm of this value.* With this utility function Bernoulli asserts to be able to explain the Petersburg game. From $U(W) = \alpha \log W/W_0$ we can derive:

(4) $$W = W_0 e^{U/\alpha},$$

where e is the base of natural logarithm.

Let us assume that with respect to a certain wealth W_0 there exist n different possibilities in increasing one's wealth, say $B_1, B_2, \ldots, B_n$.

Such increases may occur with probabilities $p_1, p_2, \ldots, p_n$, respectively. Then we may rewrite Bernoulli's moral expectation as:

(5) $$U(W) = \sum_{i=1}^{n} p_i V(W_i) = p_1 \alpha \log \frac{B_1 + W_0}{W_0} + p_2 \alpha \log \frac{B_2 + W_0}{W_0} + \ldots + p_n \alpha \log \frac{B_n + W_0}{W_0}$$

Relating it to the Petersburg game, (5) has the specific form

(5′) $$U(W) = \sum_i 2^{-i} V(W_i) = \frac{\alpha}{2} \log \frac{2 + W_0}{W_0} + \frac{\alpha}{4} \log \frac{4 + W_0}{W_0} + \ldots + \frac{\alpha}{2^n} \log \frac{2^n + W_0}{W_0}$$

unique up to positive linear transformations.

Now, by simple replacement from (5) into (4) we get:

(6) $$W = W_0 e^{p_1 \log \frac{B_1 + W_0}{W_0} + p_2 \log \frac{B_2 + W_0}{W_0} + \ldots + p_n \log \frac{B_n + W_0}{W_0}}.$$

(6) may be called the expected wealth path (on a given set of probability distributions).
Clearly, we can set, taking into account (4) and (6)

$$\text{(7)} \qquad \frac{U}{\alpha} = \sum_{i=1}^{n} p_i \log \frac{B_i + W_0}{W_0} = \log \frac{W}{W_0}$$

and therefore, subject to determining a suitable utility unit, the utility function (5) or 'moral expectation' can be written in terms of (3).
After delogarithmization, (6) may be written as an expansion:

$$\text{(8)} \qquad W = W_0 \left(\frac{B_1 + W_0}{W_0}\right)^{p_1} \left(\frac{B_2 + W_0}{W_0}\right)^{p_2} \cdots \left(\frac{B_n + W_0}{W_0}\right)^{p_n}$$

$$= \frac{W_0}{W_0^{p_1} W_0^{p_2} \cdots W_0^{p_n}} (B_1 + W_0)^{p_1} (B_2 + W_0)^{p_2} \cdots (B_n + W_0)^{p_n}$$

$$= \frac{W_0}{W_0^{p_1 + p_2 + \ldots + p_n}} (B_1 + W_0)^{p_1} (B_2 + W_0)^{p_2} \cdots (B_n + W_0)^{p_n}$$

According to definition, $\sum_i p_i = 1$, we get

$$\text{(9)} \qquad W = (B_1 + W_0)^{p_1} (B_2 + W_0)^{p_2} \cdots (B_n + W_0)^{p_n}.$$

The expected profit path (on a given set of probability distribution) is then the expression

$$\text{(10)} \qquad (B_1 + W_0)^{p_1} (B_2 + W_0)^{p_2} \cdots (B_n + W_0)^{p_n} - W_0.$$

which is called the 'value of the risky proposition'. The next step is to show that this value is approximately equal to the expected profit.
We first note that we can write Bernoulli's 'value of risky proposition' as

$$\text{(11)} \qquad W_0 (1 + B_1/W_0)^{p_1} (1 + B_2/W_0)^{p_2} \cdots (1 + B_n/W_0)^{p_n} - W_0$$

If we compute all exponential terms according to Newton's approximation method, i.e.

$$\text{(12)} \qquad (1 + B_1/W_0)^{p_1} = 1 + \frac{p_1 B_1}{W_0} + \frac{p_1(p_1 - 1)}{2} \cdot \frac{B_1^2}{W_0^2} + \ldots$$

$$(1 + B_2/W_0)^{p_2} = 1 + \frac{p_2 B_2}{W_0} + \ldots$$

$$\cdots\cdots\cdots\cdots\cdots\cdots$$

$$(1 + B_n/W_0)^{p_n} = 1 + \frac{p_n B_n}{W_0} + \ldots$$

then we may write (11) as

$$(13)\qquad W_0\left(1+\frac{p_1 B_1}{W_0}+\ldots\right)\left(1+\frac{p_2 B_2}{W_0}+\ldots\right)\ldots\left(1+\frac{p_n B_n}{W_0}+\ldots\right)-$$
$$-W_0=W_0\left(1+\frac{p_1 B_1}{W_0}+\frac{p_2 B_2}{W_0}+\ldots+\frac{p_n B_n}{W_0}+\ldots\right)-W_0$$
$$\approx p_1 B_1+p_2 B_2+\ldots+p_n B_n=\sum_i p_i B_i,$$

neglecting all terms of higher order.

The last expression in (13) states what Paul will receive from the Petersburg game if he starts off with wealth W_0. If Paul acts according to maximizing 'expected monetary value', than the sum of expected monetary gains goes to infinity as $n \to \infty$. However, by the construction of Bernoulli's utility function as a logarithmic function, $U(\Sigma_i p_i B_i)$ cannot be larger than $U(W)$ and $U(W)$ yields a finite value as can be shown by a simple example.
Suppose Paul is offered a gamble: Paul is a poor fellow and owns only $W_0 = 1$ ducat and let us assume for simplicity that his utility unit is determined for $\alpha = 1$. Peter has to pay $(2^n - 1)$ ducats if 'Heads' is thrown at the n-th toss. In this case we compute

$$(14)\qquad \log\frac{W}{W_0}=\sum_{n=1}^{\infty} p_n \log\frac{B_n+W_0}{W_0}=\sum_{n=1}^{\infty} 2^{-n}\log\frac{(2^n-1)+1}{1}.$$

(14) substituted in the utility function yields:

$$(15)\qquad U(W)=\alpha\log\frac{W}{W_0}=1\sum_{n=1}^{\infty} 2^{-n}\log\frac{(2^n-1)+1}{1}=\sum_{n=1}^{\infty} 2^{-n}\log 2^n$$
$$=\log 2\sum_{n=1}^{\infty} n 2^{-n}=2\log 2.$$

We can compute the value of $\sum_{n=1}^{\infty} n 2^{-n}$ by starting from the sum of the series

$$\sum_{n=0}^{\infty} x^n=\frac{1}{1-x}\quad \text{for}\quad 0<x<1.$$

By differentiation we get

$$\frac{d}{dx}\sum_{n=0}^{\infty} x^n=\sum_{n=0}^{\infty} n x^{n-1}=\frac{d}{dx}\left(\frac{1}{1-x}\right)=\frac{1}{(1-x)^2}.$$

Then

$$\sum_n n x^n=\frac{x}{(1-x)^2}.$$

If we set $x=\frac{1}{2}$, we have

$$\sum_n n 2^{-n}=\sum_n n x^n=\frac{x}{(1-x)^2}=2.$$

Hence, according to earlier considerations, the game would be 'fair' if Paul's 'moral expectation' is equal to the logarithm of the price Y. We compute $\log Y = 2\log 2 = \log 2^2$ or $Y = 4$. If Peter throws the coin infinitely many times the best Paul can win is 4 ducats with a very low probability of winning. Hence, moral expectation can be used to explain why people do not gamble if the price is too high.

4*5 Discussion

As K. Menger (1934) pointed out, the Petersburg game is usually considered paradoxical by the fact 'that the mathematical expectation of the person playing the game is not a finite sum, but infinite'. This discrepancy between infinite mathematical expectation and the observation of people's gambling behavior induced Bernoulli to replace mathematical expectation by moral expectation in such a way that the latter is linked to observed gambling behavior by the construction of a logarithmic utility function.

You may argue that if the logarithmic function were the utility function, one could modify the Petersburg game in such a way that the expected value of utility becomes infinite. For instance, if Peter has to pay to Paul instead of 2^n ducats, 2^{2^n} ducats we get

$$U(W) = \log Y = \sum_{n=1}^{\infty} 2^{-n} \log 2^{2^n} = \log 2 \sum_{n=1}^{\infty} 2^{-n} 2^n = \\ = \log 2\,(1+1+1+\ldots)$$

and this expression is infinite. Nobody would prefer this gamble to the status quo. In order to get around the difficulty that utility assumes an infinite value you have to require *boundedness* of the utility function. However, a logarithmic function is unbounded from above as well as from below, and so it is not suited as a utility function in general. Menger has shown that many other functions do not satisfy the boundedness requirement and that the crucial requirement for any utility function (applied to the Petersburg game) is whether the function $U(\sum_i p_i B_i)$ is bounded. Though boundedness proved to be necessary to solve the Petersburg game adequately, all former approaches for the construction of bounded utility functions were unsatisfactory to explain the occasional occurrence of striking differences between observed human behavior and even a finite expected value. For you can imagine cases where an individual is not even willing to risk a certain finite amount of money corresponding to his expected value of utility. The reason was that up to the time of Menger (1934) all approaches for the construction of bounded utility functions were more or less *ad hoc*; e.g. they were based on some general observations of people's gambling behavior. These approaches did not state gambling behavior in terms of a consistent set of postulates in order to derive a real- or vector-valued utility function reflecting choices under risk. This was first done on an axiomatic basis by von Neumann and Morgenstern.

Menger's paper played a primary role in persuading J. von Neumann to undertake a formal treatment of utility challenged by earlier attempts to construct a bounded utility function in trying to reconcile those with Bernoulli's concept of 'moral expectation' without any ad hoc considerations. So in the context of the Petersburg game and from a utility theorist's point of view the von N. M. type of construction of a bounded utility function seems to be the most satisfactory among all other proposed explanations.

Menger's own treatment of the problem based on psychological considerations with regard to the individual's valuation of small and high probabilities is unsatisfactory. It deals with special cases where individuals violate their expected values of utility and where they do not, but it does not provide a unified formal approach to the whole problem. Some general observations as the monotonicity of risky alternatives with respect to probability ordering, the love of risk or love of danger appearing in the individual valuation of risky alternatives have been discussed later extensively in von Neumann–Morgenstern type approaches.

A second kind of criticism is directed against the underlying concept of 'moral expectation'. The choice of 'moral expectation' as a decision criterion is usually justified by referring to long-run considerations where tosses are repeated many times so that the (weak) law of large numbers applies in the limiting case. This consideration is helpful to an insurance company or casino because they are interested how many events 'on the average' may occur in order to compute their risk of loss. The gambler, on the other hand, might only be interested in what happens if he participates in a gamble only once, or a few times. Consider, for instance, such a desperate gambling situation in which the gambler has to reach a fixed target sum at unfavorable games as quickly as possible.

In case of a favorable game: when a gambler bets his whole fortune on certain events occurring in a random experiment but actually loses his fortune it won't make him happy to tell him that in long sequences of trials his expected value is positive.

The same argument applies, in principle, to von Neumann–Morgenstern's utility theory and the basic difficulty arises from the fact that the use of objective probabilities (derived from the frequency interpretation of probability) might be adequate for probability statements on mass phenomena but proves to be inadequate in dealing with single observations of events which often are relevant for human decision making (see chap. 3*).

4.*6 Subjective Probability and Utility

In the original v. N. M. utility model probability has been taken for granted in the sense that it could be interpreted as long run frequency. Most frequently we encounter situations where the probabilities are not known and can only be estimated on the basis of a few observations regarding uncertain states of nature or events.

When dealing with Savage's theory in chap. 3.* 5, we have omitted all references to the concept of utility, here we restrict ourselves to the interaction of utility and probability.

In principle, there are two main avenues of demonstrating the interaction between subjective probabilities and utilities. One attempt due to Ramsey (1931) is to construct a utility function that is then used to measure subjective probability. Another suggestion due to de Finetti (1937) starts from the opposite point of view: First construct axioms for a measure of subjective probability that can be used to measure utility. More recently, a third avenue has been opened: to axiomatize and measure subjective probability and utility simultaneously.

Savage's model comprises elements of both Ramsey and de Finetti. It describes a decision situation under uncertainty and rests on three main building blocks: (i) a set S of states of nature $s_1, \ldots, s_n$ one of which will occur (is true) but the decision-maker is uncertain about which one is the true state,

(ii) a set of consequences X the elements of which are defined by functions $f(s_1) = x_1$, $f(s_2) = x_2, \ldots$, i.e. mappings from S into the closed unit interval $[0, 1]$.

(iii) a set **F** of decision acts, available to the decision-maker, denoted by **f**, **g**, ... that are technically defined as functions from S into X. The decision-maker would choose that act which maximizes his (subjective) expected utility, given that he assigns subjective probabilities to various states of nature and utilities to the consequences resulting therefrom.

For all states of nature, say n, an act can be represented by an n-tuple of consequences $(x_1, x_2, \ldots, x_n)$ with $f(s_i) = x_i$ one and only one of which will result depending on which state is true. Then the following result can be derived:

Let R be a weak order on the set of decision acts $\mathbf{F} = X_1 x X_2 x \ldots x X_n$, and provided at least two acts in **F** can be ordered (non-triviality). Then

(SE) $(x_1, x_2, \ldots, x_n)\, R\, (y_1, y_2, \ldots, y_n)$ if and only if

$$\sum_{i=1}^{n} p(s_i)\, u(x_i) \geqq \sum_{i=1}^{n} p(s_i)\, u(y_i).$$

Hence, an ordering between decision acts can be represented by a (numerical) ordering of *subjective expected utilities*.

The result can be obtained by using proper independence assumptions similar to those used in additive utility theory. Different necessary and sufficient conditions for (SE) to hold are available depending on whether **F** is finite or infinite. In fact, the assumptions used by Savage imply infinite **F**.

4.*7 Conditional Utility

Let us start with a decision situation under risk where the decision-maker has to choose among various lottery tickets. We will ask what happens to a person's lottery choice if he is given additional information in terms of probabilities on some states of nature which might affect his choice among lottery tickets. In other words, in evaluating his decision situation, a person should not only consider the probability of a certain prospect to be realized but also the problem how and to which extent some state (s) of nature modify the utility of this prospect. This problem has not been dealt with adequately in Bernoullian utility theory.

We show as a main result that it is possible to represent expected utility of decision acts (in Savage's terminology) by conditional expected utility of prospects which preserves well-known properties of expected utility with the exception of linearity.

We suggest a potential application of the notion of 'conditional' utility for the estimation of the 'value of information' as a residual value of prior and posterior utility. A person has to choose between two different lottery tickets. Assume the following decision situation under risk:

1. Let f and g denote the prospects "you will receive $10,000 profit from investments in country X within the next two years" occuring with probability p or "you will have a savings account of $100 next year" with probability $1-p(=\bar{p})$.

2. Let h and k denote the prospects "you will have a savings account of $2,000" with probability q or "a trip around the world" with probability $\bar{q}$.

Now assume that all structural assumptions on a von Neumann–Morgenstern mixture space as well as all order properties on this set hold, so that for some p, $q \in (0,1)$ we have

(1) $(qh, \bar{q}k) < (pf, \bar{p}g)$, and the existence of a v.N.M. utility function can be assured.

Hence the first lottery ticket is preferred to the second. Some complications in this decision might arise, however, if we consider that some additional information is available to the person such as the following:

Let there be states of nature s and t such that s means "within the next two years the government of X will block all foreign profit transfers" and t means "a coin shows heads on the next throw". We assume, in the simplest case, the probabilities of s and t to be known to the person, say $\alpha(s) = 1/10$ and $\alpha(t) = 1/2$, respectively, where $\alpha(s)$ pertains to lottery ticket $(pf, \bar{p}g)$ and $\alpha(t)$ to $(qh, \bar{q}k)$.

What we have in mind here, more generally, is that the states s and t result from an *extraneous chance mechanism* which is not known to the person when making his decision in such gambling situation (but which may be known to somebody else). In order to clarify the notation I refer to these states as "non-generating-states" in the sense that they do not constitute consequences in terms of mappings of the states into the closed unit interval (which corresponds to Savage's terminology).

When talking about what one is faced with as the result of making a decision given that nature is in a certain state usually the term consequence is used because the situation has been brought about in part by making the decision. In the context of v. N. M. utility it is more common to use the term "prospect", without the implication that the future history has necessarily been brought upon by decision – which happens to be the case in decision theory but is not generally so in the theory of utility. In what follows we use the terms "prospect" and "consequence" interchangeably with equivalent meanings. In the above mentioned example we may talk about mixtures of prospects, random prospects, gambles or simply lottery tickets.

Problem: Can one reasonably assume – on the basis of the additional information on s *and* t *– that a person insists on the lottery choice* (1) *which was done without having available this information provided by the extraneous chance mechanism*?

An analysis of the motivational structure of choice behavior is important here. The person knows that in the first gamble he may win the attractive amount of $10,000, however, the additional information on s will tell him how much utility he should reasonably attach to the lottery ticket. In other words, the basic assumption is that f is not *utility independent* of s. Since f and s are independent in a probabilistic sense, we may assume in general that this person does not evaluate his expected utility in terms of

(2) $$u[\alpha(s)pf, \bar{\alpha}(s)\bar{p}g] = \alpha(s)\,pu(f) + \bar{\alpha}(s)\,\bar{p}u(g),$$
(as Bernoullian theory would suggest)

but rather in terms of

(3) $$\alpha(s)\,pu(f|s) + \bar{\alpha}(s)\,\bar{p}u(g|\bar{s}) = p[\alpha(s)\,u(f|s)] + \bar{p}[\bar{\alpha}(s)\,u(g|\bar{s})].$$

This essentially means that the linearity property of Bernoullian utility in the form of (2) can no longer be obtained since we cannot have

(3a) $$\alpha(s)\,pu(f|s) + \bar{\alpha}(s)\,\bar{p}u(g|\bar{s}) = u[\alpha(s)\,p(f|s), \alpha(s)\,\bar{p}(g|\bar{s})]$$

due to the fact that a conditional probability is not defined in the context of an extraneous chance mechanism. We set $\bar{\alpha}(s) = \alpha(\bar{s})$ and $\bar{s}$ denotes the complementary state in S′ (the set of all nongenerating states of nature). Then $u(f|s)$ is called *conditional utility*, i.e. the utility of f conditional on the statement that s is true. Thus, in evaluating this decision situation, a person should consider the problem how and to which extent some state(s) of nature, provided by an extraneous chance mechanism, modify the utility of the prospect. For many decision situations under risk or uncertainty this seems to be a realistic hypothesis. All v. N. M. or Savage type theories do not take care of this kind assumption. Insofar as only generating states are concerned (and only those are considered by Savage) conditionalization or more precisely, achieving utility dependence, seems to be dispensable since, by definition, the consequences are generated by the states. However, the situation changes in case of non-generating states provided by an extraneous chance mechanism.

The following cases show how Savage consistently pursues *utility independence* within his system. As a consequence of showing the equivalence of a qualitative probability ordering of events with a corresponding preference ordering of decision acts Savage's P. 4 assumes implicitly that each of the consequences is utility independent of the states (events). This can easily be derived from the reasoning underlying Savage's decision theory.

P. 4 requires that on which of two events one will stake a prize does not depend on the prize itself. Given this postulate one can define "A is not more probable than B" indeed by the behavior that "the person would not rather stake a prize on A than on B".

This means that personal preferences between consequences are independent (and via an order-preserving utility function also utility-indenpendent) of which state is expected to occur as long as they do not contradict preferences between decision acts. Therefore, it only depends on preferences between decision acts which probability evaluations of events will actually be made. In a certain sense utility independence is already incorporated in Savage's Sure-Thing-Principle (his P. 2) in which he actually requires that conditional preference between acts given the knowledge which state obtains does not alter nonconditional preference.

If we would like to include utility dependence by introducing an extraneous chance mechanism, Savage's theory would be modified and considerably more complicated.

One final remark should be made regarding the potential application of the concept of conditional utility within decision theory.

Let **f** be a decision act reasulting in a set of consequences $\langle f_1, \ldots, f_n \rangle$ and let $s_1, \ldots, s_n$ be the generating states. Then $u(s_i, \mathbf{f})$ is a utility (number), i.e. the utility attached to **f** if it were known that s_i is true. A rational decision-maker should choose the act $\mathbf{f} \in \mathbf{F}$ (the set of decision acts) for which $u(s_i, \mathbf{f})$ is largest, e.g. $\max_{f} u(s(s_i, \mathbf{f}) = u^*(s_i, \mathbf{f})$.

This is the utility which would be obtainable by selecting the "best" decision act given the knowledge of s_i but in ignorance of the existence of any non-generating state (prior utility).
Now assume, by selecting act **f** the consequences are affected by nongenerating states $\langle t_1, \ldots, t_m \rangle = t$ about which the decisionmaker is ignorant at the beginning.
In choosing one particular act for which this is true, we would specify his utility by $u(s_i, [\mathbf{f}|t])$. This describes the utility of having chosen **f**, given that s_i has occurred and knowing that t has obtained (posterior utility).
Setting $u^*(s_i, \mathbf{f}) - u(s_i, [\mathbf{f}|t]) = v(t|s_i) \equiv w(t)$ would yield some measure of the value of information attached to nongenerating states. Thus, in this context, the value of information would be given in terms of the difference between prior and posterior utility or equivalently, between non-conditional and conditional utility.
A reader familiar with statistical decision theory will quickly recognize that the proposed measure leads to the utilization of the regret principle for the evaluation of information relevant to decision-making.

Suggested Readings

Adams, E.W.: 'Survey of Bernoullian utility theory', in Mathematical Thinking in the Measurement of Behavior (H. Solomon, ed.), Glenoce 1960.

Bernoulli, D.: 'Exposition of a New Theory on the Mesurement of Risk', (engl. transl.), Econometrica 22, 1954, 23–36.

Becker, G.M. and C.G. McClintock: 'Value: behavioral decision theory', Annual Review of Psychology 18, 1967, 239–286.

Blackwell, D. and M.A. Girshick: Theory of Games and Statistical Decisions, New York 1954.

Chipman, J.S. et al.: Preferences, Utility and Demand, New York 1971.

Cramer, H.: 'A theorem on ordered sets of probability distributions', Theory of Probability and its Applications 1, 1956, 1–20.

Debreu, G.: 'Representation of a preference ordering by a numerical function', in Decision Processes (R.M. Thrall et al., eds.), New York 1954.

Debreu, G.: 'Cardinal utility of even-chance mixtures of pairs of sure prospects', Review of Economic Studies 71, 1959, 174–177.

Debreu, G.: 'Topological methods in cardinal utility theory', in Mathematical Methods in the Social Sciences (K.J. Arrow, et al., eds.), Stanford 1960, 16–26.

Edwards, W.: 'Behavioral decision theory', Annual Review of Psychology 12, 1961, 473–498.

de Finetti, B.: 'La Prevision: ses lois logiques, ses sources subjectives', Annales de l'Institut Henri Poincare 7, 1937, 1–68.

Fishburn, P.C.: 'Utility Theory', Management Science 14, 1968, 335–378.

Fishburn, P.C.: Utility Theory for Decision Making, New York 1970.

Fleischer, I.: 'Numerical representation of utility', SIAM Journal of Applied Mathematical 9, 1961, 48–50.
Kauder, E.: A History of Marginal Utility Theory, Princeton 1965.
Krantz, D. H.: 'Conjoint Measurement. The Luce-Tukey axiomatization and some extensions', Journal of Mathematical Psychology 1, 1964, 248–277.
Luce, R. D. and H. Raiffa: Games and Decisions, New York 1957.
Menger, K.: 'Das Unsicherheitsmoment in der Wertlehre', Zeitschrift für Nationalökonomie 51, 1934, 459–485.
v. Neumann, J. and O. Morgenstern: Theory of Games and Economic Behavior, Princeton, 2nd ed. 1947.
Ramsey, F. P.: 'Truth and Probability' in The Foundations of Mathematics (R. B. Braithwaite, ed.), New York 1931.
Samuelson, P. A.: 'Probability, utility and the independence axiom', Econometrica 20, 1952, 670–678.
Wold, H. O.: 'A synthesis of pure demand analysis', I, III, Skandinavisk Aktuarietidskrift 26, 1943, 85–118 and 27, 1944, 69–120.

Appendix A – Chapter 4*

Probability of Gambles

What have von Neumann-Morgenstern in mind when they speak of the 'perfectly well founded interpretation of probability as frequency in long runs'? They view the outcomes as specific events or event-types which are realized within a time period.

If we look through the probability numbers to the events on which the outcomes depend, we find that there are specific events (the *next* toss of *this* coin comes up Heads) or event types which are realized during a time period (e.g. it will snow or hail within the next week). Yet according to proponents of the frequency interpretation of probability it does not make sense to speak of the probability of a specific event, or of a specific event-type being realized.

Obviously, von Neumann and Morgenstern mean something different: the outcome of an action a depends upon a specific event E having the property $\mathscr{P}$. E is considered to belong to a reference class R and the probability of an R displaying property $\mathscr{P}$ is p. The outcome of an action is (pf, (1 – p) g), for instance. Consider the following example. Suppose that a coin is produced which is biased on one side, but that after this coin is tossed 1,000 times this inbalance wears off. Suppose that we know further that when such coins have been tossed in the past, the average number of heads in the first 100 tosses was 70. Yet suppose that the limit of the relative frequencies of heads in the infinite sequences of tosses of this coin is one half. If you know that this coin is about to be tossed for the 29th time, if you know all the relevant information about *this* coin, and are given the choice between the following two actions:

(1) Receive $ 10,000 if the coin shows Heads on the 29th toss, otherwise keep the status quo,

(2) Receive $ 10,000 if the coin shows Tails on the 29th toss, otherwise keep the status quo.

Would you be indifferent? The normative conditions suggest that you ought to be indifferent, yet such a statement appears unreasonable in the present situation.

This example shows – despite other arguments to the contrary – that in situations as reported by von Neumann-Morgenstern one cannot rely exclusively on statistical probabilities based on relative frequency.

Let us note another way in which non-statistical probabilities enter into decisions. Koopman has pointed out that some notion of probability,

inductive probability, is needed, since one can never verify that the limit of the relative frequencies in an actual sequence is some definite number.
Carnap also has pointed out that generally one will not know the relative frequency of a property $\mathscr{P}$ in a population or the probability$_2$ that an arbitrarily selected individual (selected from a certain population) will have property $\mathscr{P}$. Yet a decision may depend upon such a frequency or probability$_2$. Since one does not know the frequency or probability$_2$, one will not be able to use it as a basis for decision, and one will have to use probability$_1$, which Carnap interprets as an estimate of probability$_2$.
If we follow the suggestion that normative conditions referring to statistical probabilities with the appropriate reference class are legitimate because the statistical probabilities are tied to inductive probabilities it appears that the normative conditions should be formulated in terms of inductive probabilities in order to make explicit the rationale of the conditions. For example, the well-known v. N. M. monotonicity assumption

> $f \succ g$ implies $(pf, (1-p)g) \succ (qf, (1-q)g)$ *if and only if* $p > q$ with p, q as relative frequencies should be restated as $(f \text{ } if \text{ } h_1, g \text{ } if \text{ } \bar{h}_1) \succ (f \text{ } if \text{ } h_2, g \text{ } if \text{ } \bar{h}_2)$, *if and only if* $c(h_1 | e) > c(h_2 | e)$.

where h_1, h_2 are hypotheses to be true, e is the total evidence available to the person and c is the confirmation function.
If we knew the statistical probabilities we should use them, since they are connected with inductive probabilities. And we should use inductive probabilities because they are estimates of statistical probabilities, and along this line of reasoning we should understand the v. N. M. results.

Appendix B – Chapter 4*

Satisficing Behavior Rules

It is theoretically possible that a person be faced with a set of actions, no one of which has a maximally preferred outcome. For example, suppose that the person prefers outcome f to g, and must choose among actions having as outcomes $(pf, (1-p)g)$ for all p in (0,1). Which of these actions should he choose? There seem to be at least two approaches that might be taken to this problem.

(1) Build the costs of specifying a p into the outcome, e.g. the outcome of

an action may be (for some particular p): [(pf, (1 − p)g), some time spent on specifying the p].
(2) Specify a p, yielding an outcome which is good enough most of the time.

Whether an outcome is *good enough* depends on what you believe is or might be available. In a clearly defined example, you know exactly what else is available, and whether choosing a particular p yields a good enough outcome will depend on how convenient and costly (in time, effort, lost opportunity) it is to find a higher p that enhances the benefits to be gained. So in such a well-defined situation it seems that (2) will collapse into (1).
In this situation you will strike a delicate balance and you will stop, presumably, when intuitively you feel that specifying a higher p is not worth the effort.
H. Simon (1957) has proposed an interesting answer to the question of when to search for an action when the *maximally preferred action* is too costly to pursue. Simon's theory tells the person to search for another action *if he does not think that any of the actions*, scanned so far, *is good enough, and not to search if one of the available actions is good enough.* Clearly, much hinges on the notion of 'good enough'. If the person views an action as good enough if and only if he is willing to do it, and not good enough if and only if he is unwilling to do it, then Simon's rules are trivial.
Simon's considerations, however, are by no means trivial. He interprets 'good enough' in terms of the psychologist's notion of 'level of aspiration'. If the maximally preferred action is such that all its possible outcomes are above the person's level of aspiration, then the person should do it, if not, then he should search for some other action, all of whose possible outcomes are above the person's level of aspiration.
By taking a closer look at the notion of 'level of aspiration', suppose that the set of possible outcomes of a set of actions is simply ordered in the person's preference ordering. Then the indifference class of a member of this set of outcomes such that the person would be satisfied, if his action had an outcome preferred or indifferent to this member, and dissatisfied if it had an outcome to which this member is preferred, is the level of aspiration of the person (in this situation). If an outcome if preferred or indifferent to some member of the level of aspiration (noting that 'level of aspiration' is an indifference class) then it is above the level of aspiration; if some member of the level of aspiration is preferred to it, then it is below the level of aspiration. But it turns out, by sticking to this definition, we need not have required that all of the outcomes be simply ordered.
Most of the psychological literature on the subject of levels of aspiration, apart from related results growing out of the von N.M. approach, makes more specific assumptions about the outcomes. It is assumed that the situa-

tion it self generates a certain order on the outcomes. Consider situations such as (a) a person is shooting at a target and orders the outcomes according to the distance from the center, (b) a person is throwing rings over a stake and orders the outcomes according to the number of rings which go over the stake, (c) the person orders the outcomes according to how quickly he can perform a task or solve a problem, (d) the subject orders outcomes according to salary levels of various job offers etc.

In these outcomes there is already some natural unit between them, e.g. distance from each other, number of rings, difference in number of successful tosses, time interval between them or difference in salary. It would be desirable to have an account of 'level of aspiration' in terms of choice behavior. Let us consider only outcomes that are discrete, rather than based on a continous variable. It seems reasonable then to suppose that there will be a big difference in utility between the first outcome which is at or above the level of aspiration and the outcome which is right below it in the preference ordering. For instance, Siegel (1957) suggests that the level of aspiration is the utility of the outcome c_i such that $u(c_i) - u(c_j) > u(c_k) - u(c_m)$ for all $k \neq i$, where c_j is the outcome immediately below c_i in the preference ordering and c_m is immediately below c_k.

However, this procedure works only for certain kinds of outcomes, e.g. those based on a variable or a natural unit, but it breaks down in case of qualitatively comparable outcomes.

Since we do not yet have an obviously satisfactory account of level of aspiration in terms of choice behavior, we shall continue using notions of satisfaction and dissatisfaction as explaining it. Simon does not introduce his theory only as an answer for the question we are considering, but also to cope with limited computational ability and limited knowledge of possible consequences on the part of the agent. (However, Simon's theory does assume that the person knows all possible consequences of the action to be chosen, or else the person could not know that all of its possible consequences are satisfactory. If we are speaking only of those possible consequences the person knows of, the situation will become far more complicated (see Gottinger (1978)).

Simon seems to be most concerned with situations in which the actions are presented to the agent sequentially. He uses the example of a person who wishes to sell a home. Upon receiving an offer for the home, he must decide whether to accept it, or to reject it and wait for a better offer (which may not be forthcoming). We treat this situation, in a formalized way, in chap. 10. Simon suggests that the person will accept the first satisfactory offer that comes. But depending upon his initial level of aspiration it may be more reasonable for the person to wait for a better offer if the expectation of gain in waiting is greater than the expectation of loss, i.e. the cost of waiting.

It may be that the introduction to dynamical considerations about the level of aspiration handles these difficulties. For example, it may be that if the person's expectation of gain from searching is greater than the cost of searching for another action, then his level of aspiration will go up. If these dynamical factors reflect individual's search activities Simon's theory will provide much more predictive power than standard theories of behavior under uncertainty.

Suggested Readings

Siegel, S., 'Level of Aspiration and Decision Making', *Psychological Review* 64, 1957, 253–262.

Simon, H.A., *Models of Man*, New York 1957.

Gottinger, H.W., 'Complexity and Social Decision Rules', in Gottinger and Leinfellner (eds.), *Decision Theory and Social Ethics*, Dordrecht 1978.

5. Analysis of Probability

5.1 Probability Measures and Random Variables

A probability measure is a function that assigns real numbers to events in such a way that the numbers obey the three axioms of mathematical probability stated in Sec. 2.1. We denote events by A, B, C, ... and the probabilities assigned to the events by P(A). P(B), P(C), ... The symbol $P(\cdot)$ is an abstract notation for a probability measure. The axioms can be expressed as follows:

(1) $P(A) \geqq 0$ for all A in S.
(2) If A and B are incompatible, $P(A \text{ or } B) = P(A) + P(B)$.
(3) $P(S) = 1$.

One technical point is worth brief mention. Axiom (2) says that if A and B are incompatible events, $P(A \text{ or } B) = P(A) + P(B)$. The principle of finite induction implies the extension to any finite number of events, so the axiom is called the axiom of *finite* additivity. In most listing of axioms, axiom (2) is extended to a countably infinite number of events, and is called for this reason the axiom of *countable* additivity.

Technically, a random variable is a function that assigns a real number to each elementary event of a sample space. For example, on the space of two tosses of a coin, we can define the random variable, "the number of heads observed." This random variable can exhibit the values 0, 1, or 2. In some cases, as in the measurement of your weight, the events themselves are described numerically. We can define a random variable that is equal to the observed measurement.

While the underlying sample space is sometimes of interest, in applications we are typically interested in the values that the random variable might exhibit and in the probabilities assigned to various sets of these values. From this point of view it is intuitive to think of a random variable as an unknown or uncertain quantity.

It is often helpful to distinguish between the random variable-uncertain quantity – and specific numbers that it might exhibit. We do this by use of fat print. We speak of the random variable **x**; a particular number that this random variable can exhibit is denoted by x. For example, $P(\mathbf{x} > x)$ means the probability that the quantity we are uncertain about, is larger than the specific number x.

One special random variable, called an indicator, provides a bridge between the concept of random variable and that of event. Consider the events, "the coin comes up heads" (H), and "it does not come up heads" (T). Let the indicator random variable **x** equal 1 for the first event, 0 for the second; then P(H) = P(**x** = 1). Or let A be the event "one head and one tail in two tosses" (including the elementary events "heads followed by tails" and "tails followed by heads"), and $\bar{A}$ be the denial of A. We define **x** = 1 for A and **x** = 0 for $\bar{A}$; again P(A) = P(**x** = 1).

5.2 Sample Space

Suppose we toss a coin twice. The result of such an experiment can be described by a sequence of H's and T's, e.g., (H, T). This particular sequence is an example of an *elementary event*. There are three other elementary events: (H, H), (T, H), (T, T). These four events are incompatible and exhaustive; we refer to this set of events as the *sample space* for this simple experiment:
The reason for this qualification "elementary" can be seen by illustrating a *compound event*: "one H and one T." This event contains two elementary events, (H, T) and (T, H). An elementary event can never be decomposed in this way. A compound event can contain more than one elementary event; it may, however, contain only one elementary event or even no elementary events at all. To illustrate the last possibility, consider the event labelled "three T's": none of the elementary events of the sample space is included in this event. Whenever the word "event" is used without a qualification, it will be understood to mean compound event.

We have explained by example three key concepts: sample space, event, elementary event. More abstractly, these concepts can be defined in terms of sets and subsets. To begin with there is the sample space, a set S consisting of points – elementary events: e_1, e_2, ... The subsets of S, call them A, B, C,..., are the compound events. Two events A and B with no elementary events in common are called *incompatible* or *mutually exclusive*. If all the elementary events of the sample space are contained in at least one event of some particular listing of events, say A, B, and C, then these events are said to be *exhaustive*.

In the sample space consisting of the four events defined by two coin tosses, the elementary events are (H, H), (H, T), (T, H), (T, T). One assignment of probabilities is 1/4, 1/4, 1/4, 1/4, respectively. This defines a probability measure on that sample space. It is, of course, not the only possible probability measure; we can for example, assign the numbers 9/16, 3/16, 3/16 and 1/6, and still be coherent. The probability measure actually assigned is a question of probability assessment.

5.3 Probability and Frequency Distributions

We speak of "$P(\mathbf{x} = x)$," or "$P(x)$," the "probability that **x** exhibits the value x"; or "$P(\mathbf{x} \leqq x)$," the "probability that **x** exhibits the value x or something smaller"; and so on. A tabulation of probabilities $P(x)$ for each possible x is called the *probability distribution* of the random variable. If we think of a set of numbers x and their relative frequencies in an observed sample, the corresponding concept is *frequency distribution*; relative frequencies play the role of probabilities. The following discussion of probability distributions applies to frequency distributions if minor changes of terminology are made.

Table 5–1 gives two ways to display a probability distribution of the discrete random variable, the number of heads in two tosses of a coin. The numerical values of the probabilities are illustrative.

Table 5–1:

x	P(x)	$P(\mathbf{x} \leqq x)$
0	.25	.25
1	.50	.75
2	.25	1.00
Total	1.00	

Columns 2 and 3 of Table 5–1 represent the two commonest ways of displaying the probability distribution. The method of column 2, which gives $P(x)$, is called the *probability mass function* – often called simply *mass function* or *pmf* – of the random variable. The method of column 3 of Table 5–1, $P(\mathbf{x} \leqq x)$, is called the *cumulative distribution function* – often called simply the *distribution function* or *cdf* of the random variable. Note that each entry in column 3 is a cumulation of appropriate entries in column 2; for example, $P(\mathbf{x} \leqq 1) = P(0) + P(1)$. Similarly, entries of column 1 can be obtained by differencing two appropriate entries of column 2; for example, $P(1) = P(\mathbf{x} \leqq 1) - P(\mathbf{x} \leqq 0)$. (For $P(0)$, of course, we have simply $P(0) = P(\mathbf{x} \leqq 0)$.)

When we consider continuous rather than discrete random variables, the pmf is replaced by the *probability density function* – often called simply *density function*, or *pdf*; and instead of $P(x)$ for probability mass we use $D(x)$ for probability density of **x** at x. For continuous distributions a tabular listing is impossible; we must describe them by a mathematical formula or a graph.

5.4 Joint, Conditional, and Marginal Probability

If the model is like one described in Sec. 3*.2, the word "probability" can replace "relative frequency" at every point of this discussion. In particular, we have the terms *marginal probability*, *joint probability*, and *conditional probability.* The general relationship between them is expressed

$$\text{(1)} \qquad \text{conditional probability} = \frac{\text{joint probability}}{\text{marginal probability}},$$

it being assumed that the marginal probability is not zero. Letting D represent dotted and R represent red, an example would be

$$\text{(1a)} \qquad \mathrm{P(D|R)} = \frac{\mathrm{P(D\ and\ R)}}{\mathrm{P(R)}} = \frac{.30}{.40} = .75.$$

Equation (1) serves to *define* conditional probability. The relationship follows from de Finetti's definition of coherence. In terms of the approach to coherence in Chap. 3*, a justification can be given by thinking of an urn with 200 balls. If we are indifferent as to which of the 200 balls, if drawn, would convey a prize, then we assess the joint and marginal probabilities by the relative frequencies of Table 5–2. But if we are indifferent among all 200 balls, we are indifferent among, say, the 80 red balls. Therefore we assess the probability of dotted, *given* a red ball, by the relative frequency of dotted balls among the red ones, i.e., 60/80 = .75.

Table 5–2:

	Pattern		
Color	Dotted	Striped	Total
Red	60	20	80
Green	40	80	120
Total	100	100	200

Table 5–3: Joint and Marginal Distributions

	Pattern		
Color	Dotted	Striped	Total
Red	.30	.10	.40
Green	.20	.40	.60
Total	.50	.50	1.00 (200)

The definition of conditional probability can be rearranged to calculate a joint probability from a marginal and a conditional probability. For events A and B,

(2) $$P(A \text{ and } B) = P(A)P(B|A),$$

which we have encountered as equation (2), Sec. 1.2. The events A and B are independent if $P(A|B) = P(A)$. If so, then (2) becomes

(3) $$P(A \text{ and } B) = P(B)P(A);$$

(3) is known as the multiplication rule for independent events.
If $P(A|B) = P(A)$, then $P(B) = \dfrac{P(A \text{ and } B)}{P(A)}$, assuming $P(A) \neq 0$, by a simple rearrangement of the formula defining $P(A|B)$. But the right hand side is just the definition of $P(B|A)$, so we conclude that $P(A|B) = P(A)$ implies $P(B|A) = P(B)$.
The three events A, B, and C are mutually independent if

(4) $$\begin{aligned} P(A \text{ and } B) &= P(A)P(B) \\ P(A \text{ and } C) &= P(A)P(C) \\ P(B \text{ and } C) &= P(B)P(C) \\ \text{and } P(A \text{ and } B \text{ and } C) &= P(A)P(B)P(C). \end{aligned}$$

The extension to any finite number of events follows the same pattern.
The concept of independence is easily extended to random variables. In the discrete case we say $\mathbf{x}$ and $\mathbf{y}$ are independent if

(5) $$P(\mathbf{x} = x \text{ and } \mathbf{y} = y) = P(\mathbf{x} = x) \cdot P(\mathbf{y} = y),$$

or $$P(x, y) = P(x)P(y),$$

for all x and y in the range of $\mathbf{x}$ and $\mathbf{y}$ respectively. It is obvious from (5) that if $\mathbf{x}$ and $\mathbf{y}$ are independent, and if $\mathbf{z}$ is a function of $\mathbf{x}$ and $\mathbf{w}$ a function of $\mathbf{y}$, then $\mathbf{z}$ and $\mathbf{w}$ are independent.

5.5 Statistical Independence

The ideas of conditional probability happen also to serve as an example of events which are independent in probability, or statistically independent. In intuitive terms, two events are said to be *statistically independent* if information as to one event's occurrence has no impact on the probability of the other event. This statement can be translated, in terms of events A and B, as $P(B|A) = P(B)$ implies independence.
Event B, therefore, bears the same relation in probability to the restricted

sample space A as it does to the original sample space S, when B and A are 'independent'. Independence of two events does not mean the events are mutually exclusive. If two events are mutually exclusive, knowledge that one of them has occurred implies that the other could not possibly have occurred, i.e. if the events A and B are mutually exclusive, $P(A|B) = P(B|A) = 0$. The notion of statistical independence depends on the intersection of the two events containing at least one elementary event.
By making use of the multiplication rule of probability theory, we arrive at an equivalent definition of statistical independence: Two events A and B are statistically independent if

$$P(A \cap B) = P(A)P(B)$$

This definition of independence must also imply that the other possible conditional probability is equal to its appropriate 'unconditional' probability, i.e.: $P(A|B) = P(A)$ when $P(B|A) = P(B)$, and vice verse.
For example, the event 'H on the first toss', H_1, is independent of the event 'H ond the second toss', H_2, since

$$P(H_1 \cap H_2) = \tfrac{1}{4} = P(H_1)P(H_2) = (\tfrac{1}{2})(\tfrac{1}{2}),$$

or by the fact that $P(H_2|H_1) = P(H_2) = \frac{1}{2}$ and $P(H_1|H_2) = P\ (H_1) = \frac{1}{2}$.

5.6 Mathematical Expectation: The Mean

We can give a symbolic definition of expectation of a discrete random variable $\mathbf{x}$. If $\mathbf{x}$ assigns values $x = \mathbf{x}(e)$ with probabilities $P(e)$ for each elementary event e in the sample space, its expected value is

(1) $$E(\mathbf{x}) = \sum_e P(e)\mathbf{x}(e).$$

We always assume, unless explicit mention is made, that the expected value exists in the sense of an absolutely convergent series.
For example, suppose that there are just three elementary events e_1, e_2, e_3 for which $\mathbf{x}$ takes values x_1, x_2, x_3, respectively; then

(2) $$E(\mathbf{x}) = P(\mathbf{x} = x_1)x_1 + P(\mathbf{x} = x_2)x_2 + P(\mathbf{x} = x_3)x_3.$$

We can follow the notation of this example in defining expectation without reference to the e's:

(3) $$E(\mathbf{x}) = \sum_x P(\mathbf{x} = x)x,$$

the summation being understood to include all possible x's.
If the random variable is continuous, the summation must be replaced by integration. You can think intuitively of a continuous variable as a discrete

variable that can take a very large number of values, these values being very close together. All properties of expectation given in this section apply to continuous as well as discrete variables.

It is an immediate consequence of the definition of expectation that if $\mathbf{x}(e) = k$, a constant, for all e in the sample space, then

$$E(\mathbf{x}) = k. \tag{4}$$

The expression *arithmetic mean* can be used either as a synonym for the expected value of a random variable, or for the ordinary mean of the numbers in a sample. For any n such numbers, $x_1, x_2, \ldots, x_n$, we define the mean $\bar{x}$ by

$$\bar{x} = \sum_{i=1}^{n} x_i \Big/ n \tag{5}$$

To see the analogy between this definition and the definition of $E(\mathbf{x})$, note that

$$\sum_{i=1}^{n} x_i/n = \sum_{i=1}^{n} \left(\frac{1}{n}\right) x_i. \tag{6}$$

The relative frequency $\frac{1}{n}$ plays the role played by probability in the definition of $E(\mathbf{x})$. Always an expectation can be called a mean. A sample mean is ordinarily not thought of as an expectation, although it could be so regarded with respect to a drawing of one member of the sample in which probability $\frac{1}{n}$ is assigned to each of the n members.

All these definitions apply to qualitative data for which there are just two possible values, such as heads-tails, success-failure, male-female, etc. We use the indicator random variables mentioned in Sec. 5.1 to label one of the categories by the symbol "1" and the other by "0" and proceed as above. For example, if we label H in the toss of a coin as "1" and T as "0", and if $P(H) = p$, then the expected number of H's in a single toss, the expected value of the indicator, is

$$\begin{aligned} P(\mathbf{x}=1)\cdot 1 + P(\mathbf{x}=0)\cdot 0 &= P(H)\cdot 1 + P(T)\cdot 0 \\ &= P(H) = p \end{aligned} \tag{7}$$

In general the expected value of the indicator of an event is the probability of an event. In this way we interpret a probability as an expectation.

Often we are concerned with random variables that are *sums*, or more generally, *linear combinations* of other random variables. Thus if $\mathbf{z} = \mathbf{x} + \mathbf{y}$, $\mathbf{z}$ is the *sum* of $\mathbf{x}$ and $\mathbf{y}$; if

(8) $\mathbf{z} = a\mathbf{x} + b\mathbf{y}$,

where a and b are any real numbers, then **z** is said to be a *linear combination* of **x** and **y**. If $a = b = 1$, the concept of linear combination specializes to the concept of sum.

The following theorem relates the expectation of a linear combination to the expectations of the component random variables. If $\mathbf{z} = a\mathbf{x} + b\mathbf{y}$, then

(9) $E(\mathbf{z}) = aE(\mathbf{x}) + bE(\mathbf{y})$.

In words the theorem says that the expectation of a linear combination of random variables is that linear combination of the expectations. If in (9), $a = b = 1$, then the theorem says that if $\mathbf{z} = \mathbf{x} + \mathbf{y}$, then

$$E(\mathbf{z}) = E(\mathbf{x}) + E(\mathbf{y}),$$

i.e., the expectation of the sum equals the sum of the expectations.

The theorem is easily proved for the discrete case by recalling that a random variable **x** assigns a particular number $x = \mathbf{x}(e)$ to each elementary event e in the sample space, and a probability measure $P(\cdot)$ assigns a number $P(e)$ to each elementary event. Then

(10) $E(a\mathbf{x} + b\mathbf{y}) = \sum_{e} P(e)[a\mathbf{x}(e) + b\mathbf{y}(e)]$

where the summation is taken over all elementary events e in the sample space. It then follows that the right hand side equals

(11) $a\sum_{e} P(e)\mathbf{x}(e) + b\sum_{e} P(e)\mathbf{y}(e)$

and this is just $aE(\mathbf{x}) + bE(\mathbf{y})$. If the transition from (10) to (11) is troublesome, take the simple case in which there are just two elementary events e_1 and e_2 and write out the summation as follows:

$$\begin{aligned}\sum P(e)[a\mathbf{x}(e) + b\mathbf{y}(e)] &= P(e_1)[a\mathbf{x}(e_1) + b\mathbf{y}(e_1)] + P(e_2)[a\mathbf{x}(e_2) + b\mathbf{y}(e_2)] \\ &= a[P(e_1)\mathbf{x}(e_1) + P(e_2)\mathbf{x}(e_2)] + b[P(e_1)\mathbf{y}(e_1) + \\ &\quad + P(e_2)\mathbf{y}(e_2)] = aE(\mathbf{x}) + bE(\mathbf{y}).\end{aligned}$$

For example, in many applications it is important to know that the theorem does *not* assume that the random variables **x** and **y** are independent; if you re-examine the proof, you will see that it was not necessary to assume independence.

As an application of the theorem, we compute the expected number of H's in two tosses of a coin. Letting **x** be the indicator for H on the first toss and **y** the indicator for H on the second, then $\mathbf{z} = \mathbf{x} + \mathbf{y}$ is the number of H's in two tosses. If we assume $E(\mathbf{x}) = E(\mathbf{y}) = p$, we have $E(\mathbf{z}) = p + p = 2p$. Thus, if $p = .6$, the expected number of H's in two tosses is 1.2.

Suppose now that we find the expected *relative frequency or fraction* of H's in two tosses, i.e.,

$$\frac{\mathbf{z}}{2} = \frac{\mathbf{x}+\mathbf{y}}{2} = \frac{1}{2}\mathbf{x} + \frac{1}{2}\mathbf{y}.$$

We compute

$$\mathrm{E}\left(\frac{\mathbf{z}}{2}\right) = \frac{1}{2}\mathrm{E}(\mathbf{x}) + \frac{1}{2}\mathrm{E}(\mathbf{y})$$

$$= \frac{1}{2}\mathrm{p} + \frac{1}{2}\mathrm{p} = \mathrm{p}.$$

Equation (9) generalizes (by finite induction) to linear combinations of any finite number of random variables. For example, if $\mathbf{z} = a\mathbf{x} + b\mathbf{y} + c\mathbf{w}$, then

$$\mathrm{E}(\mathbf{z}) = a\mathrm{E}(\mathbf{x}) + b\mathrm{E}(\mathbf{y}) + c\mathrm{E}(\mathbf{w}).$$

We state one other theorem on expectation. If **x** and **y** are *independent*, then

$$\mathrm{E}(\mathbf{xy}) = \mathrm{E}(\mathbf{x})\mathrm{E}(\mathbf{y}).$$

In words, the expectation of the product of two *independent* random variables is the product of the expectations of the individual variables. A proof is:

$$\begin{aligned}\mathrm{E}(\mathbf{xy}) &= \sum_{e} \mathrm{P}(e)\mathbf{x}(e)\mathbf{y}(e)\\ &= \sum_{x}\sum_{y} \mathrm{P}(\mathbf{x}=x, \mathbf{y}=y)xy\\ &= \sum_{x}\sum_{y} \mathrm{P}(\mathbf{x}=x)\mathrm{P}(\mathbf{y}=y)xy\\ &= \Big(\sum_{x} \mathrm{P}(\mathbf{x}=x)x\Big)\Big(\sum_{y} \mathrm{P}(\mathbf{y}=y)y\Big)\\ &= \mathrm{E}(\mathbf{x})\mathrm{E}(\mathbf{y}).\end{aligned}$$

Expectation is defined for a conditional distribution as for any other. We denote the *conditional expectation of* **y** *given* x (i.e., given $\mathbf{x} = x$) by $\mathrm{E}(\mathbf{y}|x)$; in the discrete case this is

$$\mathrm{E}(\mathbf{y}|x) = \sum_{y} \mathrm{P}(y|x)y.$$

All the rules of this section apply to conditional expectations.

An alternative notation for $\mathrm{E}(\mathbf{y}|x)$ is $\mathrm{E}_{y|x}(\mathbf{y})$, the subscript to the operator E denoting the probability measure relevant in computing the expectation. In this same notation the ordinary expectation of **y** is written $\mathrm{E}_{y}(\mathbf{y})$. It is useful to know that the ordinary expectation of **y** is the expected value of $\mathrm{E}(\mathbf{y}|x) = \mathrm{E}_{y|x}(\mathbf{y})$ with respect to the marginal distribution of **x**:

$$\mathrm{E}(\mathbf{y}) = \mathrm{E}_{x}[\mathrm{E}_{y|x}(\mathbf{y})]. \tag{12}$$

(The expression in square brackets is a random variable with respect to E_x.)

5.7 Measures of Dispersion: Variance and Standard Deviation

The *variance* of a random variable **x**, denoted $\sigma^2(\mathbf{x})$, is a special kind of expectation. In words, it is the expected squared deviation from the expected value. In symbols:

(1) $$\sigma^2(\mathbf{x}) = \mathrm{E}[\mathbf{x} - \mathrm{E}(\mathbf{x})]^2.$$

The standard deviation $\sigma(\mathbf{x})$ is the square root of the variance:

(2) $$\sigma(\mathbf{x}) = \sqrt{\mathrm{E}[\mathbf{x} - \mathrm{E}(\mathbf{x})]^2}$$

Whenever the explicit mention of the random variable can be omitted without loss of clarity, we write σ^2 or σ in place of $\sigma^2(\mathbf{x})$ or $\sigma(\mathbf{x})$. As for expected value, we assume the variance exists unless otherwise stated.
As an example we compute in Table 5–4, the expectation, variance and standard deviation of the distribution shown in Table 5–1.

Table 5–4:

x	$P(\mathbf{x} = x)$	$x \cdot P(\mathbf{x} = x)$	$x - E(\mathbf{x})$	$[x - E(\mathbf{x})]^2$	$[x - E(\mathbf{x})]^2\, P(\mathbf{x} = x)$
0	.25	.00	−1.00	1.00	.25
1	.50	.50	.00	.00	.00
2	.25	.50	1.00	1.00	.25
Total	1.00	$1.00 = E(\mathbf{x})$	0	–	$.50 = \sigma^2(\mathbf{x})$

$\sigma(\mathbf{x}) = \sqrt{\cdot 50} = .707$

Simply think of the variance and standard deviation as measures of dispersion or variability; their usefulness will become apparent in the applications.
Now to certain important facts about variances. We note immediately that if $\mathbf{x}(e) = k$, a constant, for all e, then

(3) $$\sigma^2(\mathbf{x}) = E(k - k)^2 = E(0) = 0.$$

In words: the variance of a constant is zero.
We need a basic theorem about the variance of linear combinations of random variables: for random variables **x** and **y** and constants a and b,

(4) $$\sigma^2(a\mathbf{x} + b\mathbf{y}) = a^2\sigma^2(\mathbf{x}) + b^2\sigma^2(\mathbf{y}) + 2ab\sigma(\mathbf{x}, \mathbf{y}),$$

where $\sigma(\mathbf{x}, \mathbf{y}) = E[(\mathbf{x} - E(\mathbf{x}))(\mathbf{y} - E(\mathbf{y}))]$ is called the *covariance* of **x** and **y**. If **x** and **y** are independent, then $\sigma(\mathbf{x}, \mathbf{y}) = 0$ and the theorem reduces to

(5) $$\sigma^2(a\mathbf{x} + b\mathbf{y}) = a^2\sigma^2(\mathbf{x}) + b^2\sigma^2(\mathbf{y}).$$

To present the proof in simple notation, let $\mathbf{z} = \mathbf{x} - E(\mathbf{x})$ and $\mathbf{w} = \mathbf{y} - E(\mathbf{y})$.

Then $E(\mathbf{z}) = E(\mathbf{w}) = 0$ and $E(a\mathbf{z} + b\mathbf{w}) = 0$, so $\sigma^2(\mathbf{x}) = E(\mathbf{z}^2), \sigma^2(\mathbf{y}) = E(\mathbf{w}^2)$, and $\sigma^2(a\mathbf{x} + b\mathbf{y}) = E[(a\mathbf{x} + b\mathbf{y}) - E(a\mathbf{x} + b\mathbf{y})]^2 = E[a(\mathbf{x} - E(\mathbf{x})) + + b(\mathbf{y} - E(\mathbf{y}))]^2 = E(a\mathbf{z} + b\mathbf{w}).^2$ Using elementary algebra we write

(6) $$(a\mathbf{z} + b\mathbf{w})^2 = a^2\mathbf{z}^2 + b^2\mathbf{w}^2 + 2ab\mathbf{z}\mathbf{w}.$$

Taking the expectation of both sides, we have

(7) $$\begin{aligned} E(a\mathbf{z} + b\mathbf{w})^2 &= a^2E(\mathbf{z}^2) + b^2E(\mathbf{w}^2) + 2abE(\mathbf{z}\mathbf{w}) \\ &= a^2\sigma^2(\mathbf{x}) + b^2\sigma^2(\mathbf{y}) + 2ab\sigma(\mathbf{x}, \mathbf{y}), \end{aligned}$$

as the theorem states, since $E(a\mathbf{z} + b\mathbf{w})^2 = \sigma^2(a\mathbf{x} + b\mathbf{y})$. If $\mathbf{x}$ and $\mathbf{y}$ are independent, $\sigma(\mathbf{x}, \mathbf{y}) = E(\mathbf{z}\mathbf{w})$ is shown to be zero as follows. By Sec. 5.4 (5) independence of $\mathbf{x}$ and $\mathbf{y}$ implies independence of $\mathbf{z}$ and $\mathbf{w}$. But by Sec. 5.6 independence of $\mathbf{z}$ and $\mathbf{w}$ implies $E(\mathbf{z}\mathbf{w}) = E(\mathbf{z})E(\mathbf{w})$. The conclusion follows since $E(\mathbf{z}) = E(\mathbf{w}) = 0$.

If we wanted the variance of the *mean* number of heads in two tosses, then $a = b = \frac{1}{2}$ and we calculate

(8) $$(\tfrac{1}{2})^2 p(1-p) + (\tfrac{1}{2})^2 p(1-p) = \tfrac{1}{2} p(1-p).$$

The theorem expressed in (5) can be specialized, e.g.,

(9) $$\sigma^2(a\mathbf{x}) = a^2\sigma^2(\mathbf{x}).$$

It can be generalized by finite induction to more than two random variables. For example, if $\mathbf{x}$, $\mathbf{y}$, and $\mathbf{w}$ are mutually independent,

(10) $$\sigma^2(a\mathbf{x} + b\mathbf{y} + c\mathbf{w}) = a^2\sigma^2(\mathbf{x}) + b^2\sigma^2(\mathbf{y}) + c^2\sigma^2(\mathbf{w}).$$

For *each* pair of variables that are *not* independent, e.g., $\mathbf{x}$ and $\mathbf{w}$, we must modify the right hand side by adding an appropriate covariance term, e.g., $2ac\sigma(\mathbf{x}, \mathbf{w})$.

If we refer not to a random variable $\mathbf{x}$ but simply to a set of n known numbers $x_1, x_2, \ldots, x_n$, as in a sample, there are two common definitions of variance (and standard deviation). The first is analogous to that just given for a random variable:

(11) $$\sum_{i=1}^{n} \frac{1}{n}(x_i - \bar{x})^2.$$

The second is a slight variation:

(12) $$\sum_{i=1}^{n} \left(\frac{1}{n-1}\right)(x_i - \bar{x})^2.$$

There is no deep reason for preferring one definition to the other, and consistency points to the first, but the second turns out to be more convenient because of the way in which certain distributions happen to have been tabulated. And so, to standardize, we use (12); we define

$$s^2(x) = \sum_{i=1}^{n} \left(\frac{1}{n-1}\right)(x_i - \bar{x})^2$$

for the sample variance, and

$$s(x) = \sqrt{s^2(x)}$$

for the standard deviation.

5.8 Problems

(1) Verify *statistical independence* in the following cases:
  (a) A card is drawn from a standard deck and a die is rolled. A is the event of drawing a three from the deck, B is the event of rolling a three with the die.
  (b) Two dice are rolled. C is the event of rolling a one-spot on the first die, D is the event of rolling a one-spot on the second die.
  (c) Can you prove that if two events, A and B, neither of which is impossible, are mutually exclusive, then they cannot be independent?

(2) Take the following table of joint probabilities:

	B_1,	B_2,	B_3,	B_4
A_1	.15	.05	.10	.00
A_2	.10	.10	.15	.05
A_3	.10	.05	.15	.05

(3) Compute the marginal probabilities $P(A_1)$, $P(A_2)$, $P(A_3)$, the marginal probabilities $P(B_1) \ldots P(B_4)$, the conditional probabilities of the B's given A_1, A_2, A_3.

(4) It is confirmed by reports that 70 percent of all thefts committed in state C are committed by residents of this state, whereas the rest is committed by residents in state D. Suppose that only 5 percent of the residents in state C wear black neckties, whereas 20 percent of the residents in state D do the same. A theft is reported in state C by a person wearing a black necktie. What is the probability that he is a resident of state C?

(5) Show that if $\mathbf{x}_i$ and $\mathbf{x}_j$ are independent, then the variance σ_{ij} is zero.

(6) Each time a coin falls Heads, your wealth is doubled, each time it falls Tails, your wealth is halved. What is your expected wealth after two tosses if the probability of Heads is $\frac{2}{5}$?

(7) If a card is drawn from an ordinary pack of 52 playing cards, what is

the probability that the card will be (a) either an ace or a spade, (b) neither a black card nor a picture?

(8) If a coin has been tossed twenty times and has come up Tails all twenty times, what is the probability that it will come up Tails on the 21st toss, if it is a fair coin?
If you have no knowledge about the coin other than the history of these twenty tosses what would you expect the next toss to yield? Explain.

(9) What is the probability of finding exactly three defectives when a random sample of six is drawn from a process producing 40 percent defectives?

(10) Suppose your probability that the U.S. has a fusion reactor for cheap energy provision running by the year 2000 is .6, the probability that the USSR has the same kind of reactor by 2000 is .5, and your probability that both nations have it by 2000 is .30. What is your probability that neither nation has it by 2000?

(11) (a) In the sample space consisting of the outcomes of two coin tosses, are the events "at least one H" and "at least one T" mutually exclusive? Explain.
(b) Are the events "at least one H" and "at least one T" collectively exclusive? Explain.

(12) Consider the following probability distribution:

x	0	1	2
$P(\mathbf{x} = x)$	.16	.48	.36

(a) Graph the distribution in all the ways you know.
(b) Calculate the mean, variance, and standard deviation.
(c) Can you guess how the distribution of **x** was constructed? If so, use the theorems of Secs. 5.6 and 5.7 to make an alternative calculation of the mean, variance, and standard deviation.

(13) Examine the following tables:

Color	Dotted	Striped	Total
Red	.25	.75	1.00
Green	.50	.50	1.00

Color	Prob.
Red	.80
Green	.20

Assuming that all the entries are probabilities, calculate the joint probabilities, the marginal probabilities for dotted and striped, and the conditional probabilities for color given pattern.

(14) You assess each of the six sides of a die as equally probable and the successive rolls as independent. Calculate the probabilities of the following events in three trials. Explain your reasoning in each case
(a) An ace followed by two non-aces.
(b) Non-ace, ace, non-ace.
(c) Two non-aces followed by an ace.
(d) Exactly one ace in three trials.
(e) At least one ace in three trials.

(15) Calculate the two sets of conditional distributions corresponding to the joint distribution in Table (5–3).

(16) Consider a six-sided die with sides 1, 2, 3, 4, 5, 6. Let $\mathbf{x}_1$ be the random variable for the first trial, $\mathbf{x}_2$ for the second. You judge that $\mathbf{x}_1$ and $\mathbf{x}_2$ are independent and that all of the six outcomes for each trial are equally probable.
(a) Give the joint and marginal distributions of $\mathbf{x}_1$ and $\mathbf{x}_2$.
(b) Give the conditional distributions of $\mathbf{x}_1$ for each possible value of $\mathbf{x}_2$.
(c) Give the conditional distribution of $\mathbf{x}_2$ for each possible value of $\mathbf{x}_1$.
(d) Give $E(\mathbf{x}_1 + \mathbf{x}_2)$ and $\sigma^2(\mathbf{x}_1 + \mathbf{x}_2)$.
(e) Give $E(\mathbf{x}_1 | x_2)$ for $x_2 = 6$, and $E(\mathbf{x}_2 | x_1)$ for $x_1 = 6$.
(f) Give $E(\mathbf{x}_1 + \mathbf{x}_2 | \mathbf{x}_1 = 6)$.

(17) Consider an ideal urn with six balls numbered 1, 2, 3, 4, 5, 6. One ball is drawn and replaced, and a second ball is drawn after very thorough stirring of all six balls. Let $\mathbf{x}_1$ represent the random variable for the first draw, $\mathbf{x}_2$ for the second. Same requirements as (16).

(18) Same as (17) except that the first ball is *not* replaced; the remaining five balls are stirred very thoroughly before the second ball is drawn.

(19) (Due to William Feller.) Two symmetrical six-sided dice are thrown independently. Event A includes all odd numbers for the first die; B includes all odd numbers for the second die; C includes all outcomes for the two dice such that the sum is odd. Are the following events deependent or independent?
(a) A and B (b) A and C (c) B and C (d) A, B, and C.

(20) (a) Prove that $\sigma^2(\mathbf{x} - a) = \sigma^2(\mathbf{x})$. Use this result to obtain a short computation of the $\sigma^2(\mathbf{x})$ for the distribution.
(b) Prove that $s^2(x - a) = s^2(x)$. Use this result to obtain a short cut computation of $s^2(x)$ for the x's.

(21) (a) Prove that $\sigma^2(\mathbf{x}) = E(\mathbf{x}^2) - [E(\mathbf{x})]^2$. Use this result as an alternative way of doing the final step in the computation of the variance.
(b) Prove that $(x - 1)s^2(x) = \sum_{i=1}^{n} x_i^2 - n\bar{x}^2 = \sum_{i=1}^{n} x_i^2 - \frac{(\sum_{i=1}^{n} x_i)^2}{n}$.

(22) Calculate the mean and variance of the total number of H's in 3 independent tosses of a coin with $P(H) = p$.

(23) A vaccine is given to three children. If your probability that the vaccine results in immunization is $\frac{2}{3}$ for each child, and you assume that the vaccine reacts on each child independently, find your probability that exactly two children are immune.

(24) Take a family with two children. Assume (a) $P(\text{Boy}) = \frac{1}{2}$, $P(\text{Girl}) = \frac{1}{2}$, (b) the sex of either child is independent of that of the other child. What is the probability that both children are girls, given that at least one child is a girl?

(25) A man plans to ask a young lady for a date. He believes that the probability that she is interested in him is $\frac{1}{3}$. He further believes that if she is interested, he will fail to get the date with probability $\frac{1}{2}$ (the reasons are not disclosed to him). If she is not interested he will fail to get the date with probability 1.

(i) what is his probability that she is interested and he fails to get the date?

(ii) what is his probability that she is not interested and he fails to get the date?

Suggested Readings

Zehna, P. W.: Finite Probability, Boston (Mass.), 1969.
Dixon, W. J. and F. J. Massey: Introduction to Statistical Analysis, 3rd ed., New York 1969.
Guenther, W. C.: Concepts of Probability, New York 1968, Chaps. 2 and 3.
Lindgren, B. W. and G. W. McElrath: Introduction to Probability and Statistics, 2nd ed., New York 1966.
Savage, R.: Statistics: Uncertainty and Behavior, Boston 1968.
Feller, W.: An Introduction to Probability Theory and its Applications, Vol. I, 2 nd. ed., New York, 1957.
Parzen, E.: Modern Probability Theory and its Applications, New York, 1960.
Pratt, J., Raiffa, H., and R. Schlaifer: The Foundations of Decision under Uncertainty, Jour. of the American Statistical Association 59, 1964, 353–375.
Savage, L. J.: Foundations of Statistics, New York, 1954.
Schlaifer, R.: Probability and Statistics for Business Decisions, New York, 1959.

Part II.
Simple random processes and probability distributions

6. Bernoulli Trials

6.1 Binomial Distributions

Take a sequence of success S and failure F that is a random sequence. Now consider the sample space consisting of all possible sequences of S's and F's in n Bernoulli trials. If $n = 5$, for example, we can use a series of S's and F's ... to illustrate the realization of events in this sample space:

$$(F, F, F, S, S),\ (F, F, F, F, F),\ (F, F, F, F, S),\ (F, S, F, F, F),\ \ldots$$

Now define the random variable **r** as the number of S's in n Bernoulli trials. In the example just given we find that **r** takes the values 2, 0, 1, 1, ...
In general **r** must equal some integer r from 0 to n. The distribution of **r** is called a *binomial distribution*, for a reason that will be mentioned in a moment. The probability assigned to any elementary event is, by the multiplication rule for independent events, the product of factors p and $q = 1 - p$, there being one p for each S and one q for each F. Hence the probability of an elementary event with r S's and $n - r$ F's is $p^r q^{n-r}$.,
regardless of the sequence in which the r S's and $n - r$ F's appear. The compound event ($\mathbf{r} = r$) comprises all elementary events with precisely r S's and $n - r$ F's. That is, $\mathbf{r} = r$ for any sequence of n trials in which r S's appear, regardless of *where* they appear in the sequence. By the addition axiom for incompatible events, the probability of the compound event is the sum of the probabilities of these elementary events. Since the probability of each elementary event is $p^r q^{n-r}$, we multiply this number by the number of elementary events that have r S's in n positions.
It is shown in elementary algebra that the desired number of elementary events is

$$C_r^n = \frac{n!}{r!\,(n-r)!} = \binom{n}{r}$$

where

$$n! = n(n-1)(n-2)\ldots 1,$$

n! is read "n-factorial," and C_r^n is read "the combinations of n things taken r at a time." (It is convenient to define $0! = 1$ and $C_r^n = 0$ whenever $r > n$.) Essentially C_r^n is just an easy counting device for accomplishing what can be done, with greater effort, by direct enumeration.

Thus we write for the pmf

$$f_b(\mathbf{r} = r \mid n, p) = C_r^n p^r q^{n-r},$$

where $r = 0, \ldots, n$, and the subscript "b" denotes "binomial". The symbols n and p remind us that a binomial distribution is not fully specified until n and p are. The name "binomial" arises because the individual terms of the binomial expansion of $(p+q)^n$, called the binomial expansion, give the binomial probabilities $f_b(\mathbf{r} = r \mid n, p)$. For the cdf the notation is, for left-tail and right-tails distribution, respectively,

$$F_b(\mathbf{r} \leq r \mid n, p) = \sum_{i=0}^{r} C_i^n p^i q^{n-i}$$

$$G_b(\mathbf{r} \geq r \mid n, p) = \sum_{i=r}^{n} C_i^n p^i q^{n-i}.$$

It is helpful to visualize the dependence of binomial distributions on the parameter p for fixed n, and Fig. 6.1 illustrates what goes on by showing the special case for $n = 5$ and $p = .1, .3, .5, .7, .9$.

Fig. 6.1

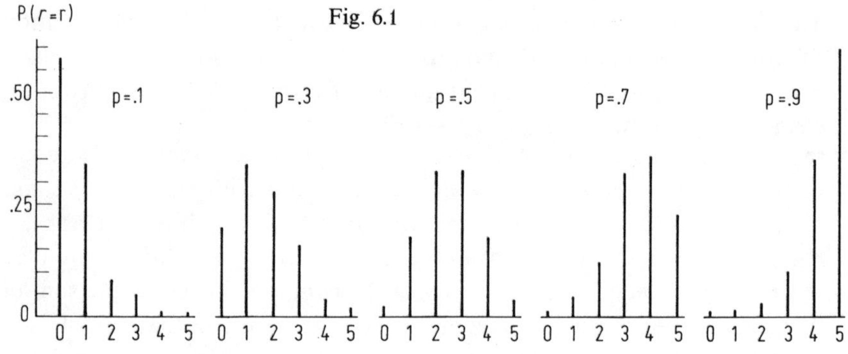

Notice the following: (1) There is always either one or two *modes*. A mode is a value of r for which $P(\mathbf{r} = r)$ is at least as large as for adjacent values of r. It can be shown that a mode will always be found in the interval from

$$np - q \quad \text{to} \quad np + p.$$

If $np + p$ and $np - q$ are integers, then both $np + p$ and $np - q$ are modes; otherwise there will be a unique mode between $np - q$ and $np + p$. (2) The distribution for $p = .5$ is *symmetrical* about $np = 5(.5) = 2.5$. That is, for $p = .5$, $f_b(r \mid n, p) = f_b(n - r \mid n, p)$. (3) For all other p's, the distribution is *asymmetrical*. For $p < .5$, the long tail of the distribution points to the right. For $p > .5$, illustrated by $p = .7$ and $p = .9$, the long tail of the distribution points to the left. (4) The lack of symmetry becomes more pronounced the further p is from .5 in *either* direction. (5) The distribution for any p is the mirror image of the distribution for parameter $1 - p$. (6) The distribution is less dispersed the further p is from .5 in either direction.

The expectation or mean of a binomial distribution is easy to calculate using the indicators $\mathbf{x}_i = 1$ for success and $\mathbf{x}_i = 0$ for failure on the i-th trial. We know that

$$E(\mathbf{x}_i) = p$$

The total number of successes r is defined by

$$r = x_1 + x_2 + \ldots + x_n.$$

Furthermore,

$$\begin{aligned} E(\mathbf{r}) &= E(\mathbf{x}_1) + E(\mathbf{x}_2) \ldots + E(\mathbf{x}_n) \\ &= p + p + \ldots + p = np. \end{aligned}$$

Thus in the example of Fig. 6.1, the means are respectively .5, 1.5, 2.5, 3.5, 4.5. Compare with the modes (read from the graph): 0, 1, 2 and 3, 4, 5.
The variance of a binomial distribution is also easy to calculate. By Sec. 5.7 we derive

$$\sigma^2(\mathbf{x}_i) = pq$$

for all i. Since the trials of a Bernoulli process are independent, Sec. 5.7 (5) gives

$$\begin{aligned} \sigma^2(\mathbf{r}) &= \sigma^2(\mathbf{x}_1) + \sigma^2(\mathbf{x}_2) + \ldots + \sigma^2(\mathbf{x}_n) \\ &= pq + pq + \ldots + pq \\ &= npq, \end{aligned}$$

and $$\sigma(\mathbf{r}) = \sqrt{npq}.$$

In the example of Fig. 6.1, the variances are .45, 1.05, 1.25, 1.05, .45, while the standard deviations are .67, 1.02, 1.12, 1.02, .67. We see again that for fixed n, the dispersion of a binomial distribution is smaller as p is farther from .5 in either direction.
The facts about the distribution of **r**, the *total number* of S's in n Bernoulli trials, can be readily extended to the distribution of **r**/n, the fraction of S's in n Bernoulli trials. Since the event ($\mathbf{r} = r$) is exactly the same as the event ($\mathbf{r}/n = r/n$), we have

$$P\left(\frac{\mathbf{r}}{n} = \frac{r}{n} \,|\, n, p, \text{binomial sampling}\right) = f_b(\mathbf{r} = r \,|\, n, p)$$

so in Fig. 6.1 we relabel the horizontal axis by 0, 1/5, 2/5, 3/5, 4/5 and 1 instead of 0, 1, 2, 3, 4, 5. The mean and variance of the distribution of **r**/n are derived from the corresponding parameters of the distribution of **r** by application of Sec. 5.6 (9) and Sec. 5.7 (9)

$$E\left(\frac{\mathbf{r}}{n}\right) = \frac{1}{n} E(\mathbf{r}) = \frac{1}{n}(np)$$
$$= p$$
$$\sigma^2\left(\frac{\mathbf{r}}{n}\right) = \frac{1}{n^2}\sigma^2(\mathbf{r}) = \frac{1}{n^2}(npq)$$
$$= pq/n.$$

6.2 Bernoulli Process

The process of repeatedly tossing a "well-behaved" coin illustrates a particular kind of data-generating process known as a *Bernoulli process*, named after James Bernoulli (1654–1706). On each *Bernoulli trial*, the sample space consists of just two elementary events, called, for example, success and failure, or H and T (heads and tails). The coin "has no memory." Regardless of the history of the process, the conditional probability p of success – whatever it is numerically – is always the same on each trial. Similarly, the probability of failure is always $1 - p$ on each trial.

We speak of a *Bernoulli process with parameter p.* The word *parameter* used for p means that one Bernoulli process can be distinguished from another by the numerical value of p. A Bernoulli process has only one parameter.

We can describe the Bernoulli process (and other processes to be discussed later) as *independent.* (More precisely, the *trials* of the process are independent.) For example, in two tosses of the coin, the probability of H and T is

(1) $$P(H, T \mid p) = P(H \mid p) P(T \mid p) = p(1 - p).$$

Equation (1) makes clear that the independence in this sense is conditional upon the parameter p. To have independence unconditional of p, p would have to be some known number. Then we could write

(2) $$P(H, T) = P(H) P(T) = p(1 - p).$$

This second, stronger sense of independence can be conveyed by the expression, "independent with known parameter p." In the usual sampling-theory notation, the independence of the Bernoulli process is expressed in the notation of (2), but the precise meaning requires the notation of (1). For a Bernoulli process, of course, equations (1) and (2) or their obvious extensions apply to any possible sample outcome, not just the sequence H, T.

We now digress to explain the Bayesian interpretation of "known p." Suppose a Bayesian observing a Bernoulli process assesses a discrete prior distribution P(p) for **p**. The probability of H on the first trial is

$$P(H) = \sum_p P(p)P(H|p) = \sum_p P(p)p = E(\mathbf{p}).$$

That is, the assessment is the mean of the prior distribution. (Compare Table 1–5 Sec. 1.3.) Now suppose that H is actually observed on the first trial. Application of Bayes' theorem yields a new distribution for **p**, call it $P(p|H)$. The probability of T on the second trial is

$$\begin{aligned} P(T|H) &= \sum_p P(p|H)P(T|p) = \sum_p P(p|H)(1-p) \\ &= 1 - E(\mathbf{p}|H) \end{aligned}$$

(Note that $P(T|p) = P(T|p, H)$ by the Bernoulli assumption.)
Since

$$P(H, T) = P(H)P(T|H),$$

we do not have independence unless $P(T|H) = P(T)$, i.e., unless $E(\mathbf{p}) = E(\mathbf{p}|H)$. The latter condition can hold only if the H on trial one does not alter the prior distribution of **p** when Bayes' theorem is applied, i.e., $P(p) = P(p|H)$ for all p. But this can happen only if $P(p)$ has no dispersion at all, that is, if it assigns probability of unity to one value of p, the "known p." In practice this would be true to a close approximation if we could base the assessment of **p** on an extremely large prior sample from the process; the known p would be the relative frequency of H in this sample. Further samples of moderate size from the process would not change the assessment perceptibly.

Consider now a process for which (1) the sample space at the i-th trial consists of just two elementary events and (2) the unknown conditional probabilities p_i and $1 - p_i$ of the two events do not depend on outcomes of the previous trials of the process. Such a process is independent (given p_i), but it is not necessarily a Bernoulli process because the description of the process leaves open the possibility that the probability p_i may change from trial to trial *in a way that does not depend on the outcomes of previous trials.* For example, the probability of success might be p_1 on odd numbered trials and p_2 on even numbered trials, $p_1 \neq p_2$, regardless of previous outcomes. A Bernoulli process is not only independent given p_i but the same $p_i = p$ governs each trial. This last requirement is an instance of *stationarity*, so that a Bernoulli process is both *independent and stationary.*

If we have a Bernoulli process, *independence* means that for any observed sample $(x_1, x_2, \ldots, x_n)$,

$$P(x_1, x_2, \ldots, x_n | p_1, p_2, \ldots, p_n) = P(x_1|p_1)P(x_2|p_2) \cdots P(x_n|p_n).$$

Stationarity means that for all i, $p_i = p$, i.e., $P(\mathbf{x}_i = 1|p_i) = p$. If stationarity holds in the presence of independence, it is often said that the random variables $\mathbf{x}_1, \mathbf{x}_2, \ldots$ are *identically distributed.* Thus, we can define a Bernoulli process as a process generating mutually independent and identically distributed random variables, each of which takes the value 1 or 0.

We can avoid mention of an unknown p by giving de Finetti's purely subjectivistic definition of a Bernoulli process. Consider, for example, the events H and T for tosses of a coin. The following equivalent definitions can be given, assuming that r is an integer from 0 to n.

(1) For all r and n, the (subjective) probability of r H's and n-r T's in the first n trials is the same *regardless of the sequence* of the r H's and n-r T's.

(2) The statement of (1) holds for any n trials, not necessarily the first n.

(3) The (subjective) probability that any n trials whatever (not necessarily the first n) will all give H's is the same.

(4) The (subjective) probability of H on any trial given that there have been r H's and n-r T's on any other n trials depends only on r and n, and not on the particular trials involved.

That these definitions are equivalent is proved by de Finetti. What is important here is that they provide alternative ways of introspection in deciding whether or not we judge data to arise "as if from a Bernoulli process with unknown p." Instead of referring to a process, de Finetti would say simply that the events are *exchangeable.* The aptness of this term is best brought out by examining the generalization of the concept of exchangeability to random variables. If the random variables are indicator variables, the concept of exchangeable events would be a special case. Consider the random variables $\mathbf{x}_1, \mathbf{x}_2, \ldots, \mathbf{x}_n, \ldots$. These random variables are said to be exchangeable if for any given n, the probability that any given condition is satisfied by a subset of n of them is the same for all subsets of n. That is, any set of n subscripts can be *exchanged* for any other without altering the probability that the condition holds. The case of exchangeable random variables corresponds to the sampling theory concept of a stationary, independent process, or alternatively, of independent, identically-distributed random variables.

In order to assign probabilities to observations of designated random variables, numerical assessments of subjective probabilities are needed. Exchangeability simply means, for example, that

$$P(\mathbf{x}_{i_1} = x_{i_1}, \mathbf{x}_{i_2} = x_{i_2}, \ldots, \mathbf{x}_{i_n} = x_{i_n})$$

is the same regardless of the n subscripts involved. The numerical assessment must be made subjectively. In Chap. 8 we study some of the standard ways of easing the task of making such assessments. De Finetti shows an interesting direct approach for Bernoulli processes. We assess directly $E(\mathbf{x}_i)$, $E(\mathbf{x}_i\mathbf{x}_j)$, $E(\mathbf{x}_i\mathbf{x}_j\mathbf{x}_k), \ldots$, where i, j, k, ... are all different. Since the x's are indicator variables and we are assuming exchangeability, these expectations can be interpreted as probabilities: $E(\mathbf{x}_i)$ is the probability that any one trial will give success, $E(\mathbf{x}_i \mathbf{x}_j)$ is the probability that any two trials will both give successes, etc. All other numerical probability assessments for observable samples from the process are implied by these.

6.3 Geometric Distributions

Let examine a Bernoulli process from a different point of view. In Sec. 6.1 the sample space was so defined that n was fixed and **r** was a random variable. Now we define it in such a way that r is fixed and **n** is a random variable. Now set r = 1 and consider the number of trials required to produce a success. The elementary events can be listed according to the following scheme:

$$(S), (F, S), (F, F, S), (F, F, F, S), (F, F, F, F, S), \ldots$$

Since the individual trials are Bernoulli trials, we use the multiplication rule for independent events to assign probabilities

$$p, qp, q^2p, q^3p, q^4p, \ldots$$

to these events. In general, the probability that n trials are required to produce a success is given by

$$f_g(\mathbf{n} = n \mid p) = q^{n-1}p,$$

where $n = 1, 2, \ldots$. This is the pmf for a geometric distribution, as the subscript "g" suggests. Even though the number of events is infinite, it can be shown that these probabilities add to 1. That is,

$$\begin{aligned}\sum_{n=1}^{\infty} f_g(\mathbf{n} = n \mid p) &= p + qp + q^2p + \ldots \\ &= p(1 + q + q^2 + \ldots) \\ &= p\left(\frac{1}{1-q}\right) = p/p = 1.\end{aligned}$$

We have here used the fact that the sum of the infinite geometric series $1 + q + q^2 + \ldots$ is $1/(1-q)$ for $|q| < 1$.

One geometric distribution is distinguished from another by p alone, hence we have a one parameter family of distributions.

Since successive Bernoulli trials are independent given the unknown p, a geometric distribution can also be interpreted as the conditional distribution of the number of trials from "now" through the next success. Even if we have just observed a long string of failures, this will be true. In subjectivistic terms, of course, the string of failures would modify the assessment of **p** and therefore the distribution for the number of trials necessary for the next success.

It is intuitively plausible that if the long-run frequency of S's per trial, E(**x**), is p, then the long-run frequency of trials per S, E(**n**), is 1/p. A proof can be given using elementary calculus:

$$(*)\ E(\mathbf{n}) = \sum_{n=1}^{\infty} n q^{n-1} p = p \sum_{n=1}^{\infty} n q^{n-1}.$$

The last summation is the derivative of the series

$$q + q^2 + \ldots = q(1 + q + q^2 + \ldots) = q/(1-q).$$

We evaluate it in closed form by taking the derivative of the sum of the series, i.e.,

$$\frac{d\left(\frac{q}{1-q}\right)}{dq} = \frac{1}{(1-q)^2} = \frac{1}{p^2}.$$

Substituting back in (*) we conclude

$$E(\mathbf{n}) = p \cdot \frac{1}{p^2} = \frac{1}{p}.$$

The variance of a geometric distribution is $\sigma^2(\mathbf{n}) = q/p^2$. To show this, we use the easily verified fact that

$$\sigma^2(\mathbf{n}) = E(\mathbf{n}^2) - [E(\mathbf{n})]^2.$$

Since we know E(**n**), we need only evaluate $E(\mathbf{n}^2)$ and substitute in this formula. We calculate

$$\begin{aligned} E(\mathbf{n}^2) &= \sum_{n=1}^{\infty} n^2 q^{n-1} p \\ &= pq \sum_{n=1}^{\infty} n(n-1)\, q^{n-2} + p \sum_{n=1}^{\infty} n q^{n-1}. \end{aligned}$$

The first of these summations is the second derivative of a geometric series. Following our previous approach we evaluate

$$\frac{d^2\left(\frac{1}{1-q}\right)}{dq^2} = \frac{2}{(1-q)^3} = \frac{2}{p^3}.$$

Remembering that $\sum_{n=1}^{\infty} n q^{n-1}$ is $1/p^2$, we substitute back in the formula for $\sigma^2(\mathbf{n})$ to obtain

$$\sigma^2(n) = \frac{2q}{p^2} + \frac{1}{p} - \frac{1}{p^2} = \frac{1}{p^2}[2(1-p)+p-1]$$
$$= \frac{1}{p^2}(1-p) = \frac{q}{p^2}.$$

A geometric distribution always has a unique mode at $n = 1$ since

$$p > qp > q^2 p > \ldots \text{ for } p > 0.$$

Now we study the distribution of the number of trials to the r-th success, where r can be 1, 2, 3, ... We are led to a two parameter family of distributions to which the name *Pascal* had been applied. (The name *negative binomial* family is used if r is allowed to take any non-negative value, not necessarily an integer.) The two parameters are p and r. For $r = 1$, the Pascal family specializes to the geometric family.

The sample space is now more complicated, but for $r = 2$, we can begin a systematic listing with

$$(S, S), (F, S, S), (S, F, S), (F, F, S, S), (F, S, F, S), (S, F, F, S), \ldots$$

Each interval necessarily ends with S. An interval of length n must have $n - r$ F's and r S's. The probability of any one sequence of $n - r$ F's and r S's is $p^r q^{n-r}$ since the individual trials are independent. The number of sequences ending in S with a total of r S's and $n - r$ F's is slightly tricky. Since S is always in the final position, we count only the number of ways $r - 1$ S's can be fitted into the first $n - 1$ positions, that is C^{n-1}_{r-1}. So we conclude

$$f_{Pa}(\mathbf{n} = n \mid r, p) = C^{n-1}_{r-1} p^r q^{n-r},$$

where $n = r, r + 1, \ldots$

6.4 Problems

(1) Two evenly-matched baseball teams A and B play a four-game series – exactly four games are to be played. On any game you judge $P(A) = P(B) = .5$, and the games are unconditionally independent. The event "A wins the series" means that A wins more games than B during the four games.

(a) Before the series starts, what is your probability that A will win the series?

(b) After the first game, which A loses, what is the probability that A will win the series?

(c) After the first two games, both of which are lost by A, what is the probability that A will win the series?

(2) Again consider the two evenly-matched teams A and B of prob. (1).

This time they are to play until first one team wins four games, at which time that team will be declared the winner and the series is over.

(a) Before the series starts, what is your probability that A will win the series?

(b) A loses the first game. What is your probability that A will win the series? The second game? The seventh game?

(c) A loses the first two games. What is your probability that A will win the series? The third game? The seventh game?

(d) A loses the first three games. What is your probability that A will win the series? The fourth game? The seventh game?

(3) You judge the events of a two-valued process to be exchangeable. You assess $P(S_i) = .5$, $P(S_i, S_j) = P(S_i)\,P(S_j)$, $P(S_i, S_j, S_k) = P(S_i)\,P(S_j)\,P(S_k)$, etc., for any distinct subscripts i, j, k, ...

(a) How would such a process be described in relative-frequency language?

(b) Is the process independent conditional on p?

(c) Is the process unconditionally independent?

(4) There are 3 urns with fraction black balls .1, .5, .9 respectively. You will decide which urn to draw from by tossing a fair coin 2 times: 0 heads designates the first urn; 1 head, the second; 2 heads, the third. When you have decided which urn to draw from, you will draw 3 balls *with replacement.* This means, that the sample of 3 will, in effect, be drawn from a Bernoulli process.

(a) What is the probability you will draw 3 black balls?

(b) What is the expected fraction of black balls in the urn chosen by the preliminary coin-tossing?

(c) What would be the probability of 3 black balls in drawing with replacement from an urn with the fraction black equal to the answer to (b)?

(d) Answer (a) and (c) for 0, 1, and 2 black balls. Tabulate your results concisely and comment on the differences.

(5) Compute the binomial distribution for $n = 5$, $p = .50$.

(a) Calculate $E(\mathbf{r})$, $\sigma^2(\mathbf{r})$, and $\sigma(\mathbf{r})$ directly from the distribution.

(b) Same as (a) but use formulas np, npq, and $\sqrt{npq}$.

(6) Compute the geometric distribution for $p = .50$.

(a) Approximate $E(\mathbf{n})$, $\sigma^2(\mathbf{n})$, and $\sigma(\mathbf{n})$ by using the distribution of $\mathbf{n}$ from $n = 1$ to $n = 16$.

(b) Calculate $E(\mathbf{n})$, $\sigma^2(\mathbf{n})$, and $\sigma(\mathbf{n})$ from the general formulas given in Sec. 6.3.

(7) Given a Bernoulli process with $p = \frac{1}{2}$, how can you use it to simulate a Bernoulli process for any p in the unit interval? (Hint: Apply what you may know about binary numbers.)

(8) A multiple-choice exam is given, each question having six responses

listed with only one correct response. There are 90 questions, and 60 questions must be answered to get a passing grade. If a student merely guesses the answer to each question, and is completely ignorant about the subject what is the probability that he will get a passing grade?

(9) In a sequence of Bernoulli trials let **x** be the length of the run (of either successes and failure) started by the first trial. Find the distribution of **x**, $E(\mathbf{x})$, $\sigma^2(\mathbf{x})$.

(10) In a certain population 30 percent of the voters are Republicans. Suppose that you could fix a sample size n, and that the number of voters will be selected at random (with replacement) from the population. Someone offers you a prize if there are exactly 6 Republicans in the sample. What value of n gives the best chance and what is the chance for this value of n?

(11) In a production lot of N items, there are R defectives and N − R non-defectives.

Show that the distribution of **r**, the number of defectives in a random sample of n items from the batch, is given by the hypergeometric pmf

$$P(\mathbf{r} = r) = \binom{R}{r}\binom{N-R}{n-r} \bigg/ \binom{N}{n} \quad (r = 0, 1, \ldots, n)$$

If R is a binomial random variable with parameter p, use Bayes' theorem to show that, given $\mathbf{r} = r$, the distribution of $R - r$ is independent of r.

(12) (R. Schlaifer, 1959) The prior distribution in the following table is based on the average fraction defective of a machine which can be regarded as a Bernoulli process:

p:	.10	.25	.30
P(p):	.50	.30	.20

A sample of 100 pieces is taken from the process and 15 defectives are found. What is the posterior probability of **p**?

(13) In casts of a fair die what is the probability of observing the sequence 1, 2, 3, 4, 5, 6?

Suggested Readings

Cramer, Harold: Mathematical Methods of Statistics, Chap. 13, Princeton, 1946.
Feller, William: An Introduction to Probability Theory and Its Applications, Chaps. 3,6, Vol. I, 2nd ed., New York, 1957.
de Finetti, Bruno: Foresight: Its Logical Laws, Its Subjectives Sources. In: Kyburg and Smokler, op. cit., Chap. 3.
Parzen, Emanuel: Modern Probability Theory and Its Applications, Chap. 3, New York, 1960.
Raiffa, Howard, and Robert Schlaifer: Applied Statistical Decision Theory, Boston: Division of Research, Harvard Business School, 1961.

Schlaifer, R.: Probability and Statistics for Business Decisions, New York, 1959.
Lindley, D. V.: Introduction to Probability and Statistics, Part I and II, Cambridge 1965.
Dixon, W. J. and F. J. Massey: Introduction to Statistical Analysis, 3rd ed., New York 1969, Chaps. 1–6.
Mosteller, F. et al.: Probability with Statistical Applications, Reading (Mass.), 1970, Chaps. 1–4.
De Finetti, B.: Probability, Induction and Statistics, London 1972.

7. Gaussian Analysis

7.1 Characteristics of a Gaussian or Normal Process

Conditional on parameters μ and σ, a normal process independently generates continuous random variables $\mathbf{x}$ with identical densities $f_N(x|\mu, \sigma)$ on all trials. A normal process is stationary and independent; its random variables are exchangeable.

Paralleling the earlier discussions of Bernoulli processes, we list the behavior of samples from a normal process.

(a) The plot of the observations in time sequence, x versus trial number, should suggest stationary independent variation: no persistent trends or cycles, no sharp shifts of level, no systematic change of variability, etc.

(b) If we plot x_i versus x_{i-1} for $i = 2, 3, \ldots, n$, the resulting scatter diagram tends to be densest in a central area and less dense as we move away from the central area in any direction. There is no tendency for the location of the dots to change systematically as we move from small to large i.

(c) The sample cdf of x's should tend to approximate an underlying normal cdf, such as Fig. 7.2.

(d) The sample histogram of x's should tend to approximate an underlying normal pdf, such as Fig. 7.1.

(e) Suppose the description of x's is simplified by reporting simply whether x was above or below some fixed number x_a. The resulting observations would be distributed by a Bernoulli process with probability $F_N(x_a|\mu, \sigma)$ of being below x_a, and $G_N(x_a|\mu, \sigma)$ of being above. All the earlier remarks about the behavior of Bernoulli processes, Chap. 6, are pertinent.

7.2 Gaussian Distributions

A continuous random variable $\mathbf{x}$ is said to be distributed by the (non-degenerate) normal distribution with parameters μ and σ if its density is

$$\begin{aligned} D(x) &= \frac{1}{\sqrt{2\pi}\sigma} e^{-\frac{1}{2}\left(\frac{x-\mu}{\sigma}\right)^2} \\ &= f_N(x|\mu, \sigma), \end{aligned}$$

where $\sigma > 0$, $-\infty < \mu < \infty$, $-\infty < x < \infty$. It can be shown by elementary calculus that the two parameters μ and σ have the following interpretation:

$E(\mathbf{x}) = \mu$ and $\sigma(\mathbf{x}) = \sigma$.

We speak of the normal distribution with mean μ and standard deviation σ. (Instead of the standard deviation σ, we may refer to variance σ^2 or the reciprocal of the variance, $h = \sigma^{-2}$, which is called the *precision.* Thus $f_N(x|\mu, \sigma)$, $f_N(x|\mu, \sigma^2)$, and $f_N(x|\mu, h)$ denote the same density in different parametrizations. The parametrization $f_N(x|\mu, \sigma)$ seems most convenient for present purposes.

With the choice of vertical scaling usually used, this density function (pdf) graphs as a "bell-shaped" curve as shown in Fig. 7.1.

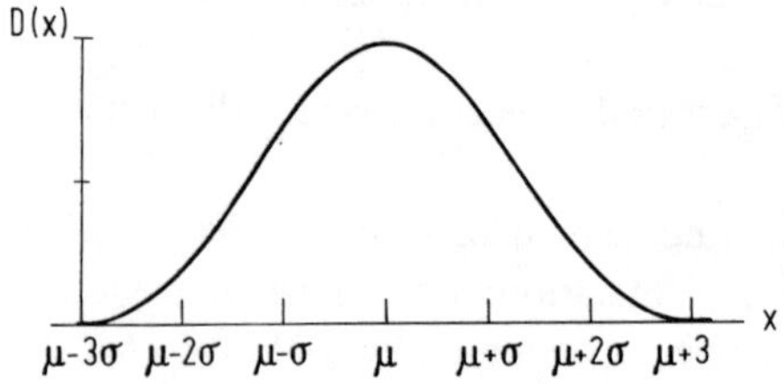

Fig. 7.1

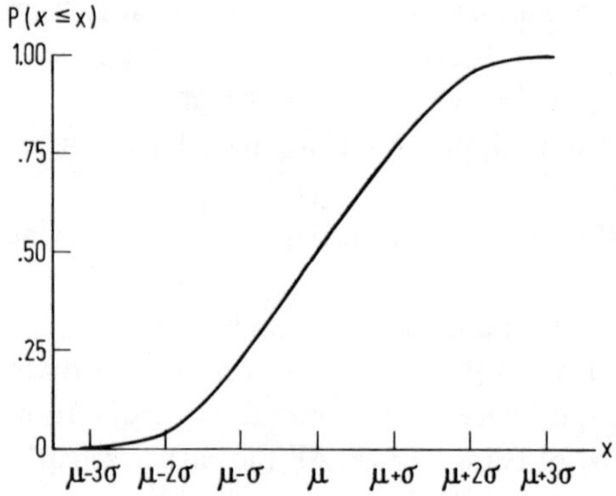

Fig. 7.2

We see that the pdf is symmetrical about $E(\mathbf{x}) = \mu$; that is, the half of the curve to the right of μ is the mirror image of the half to the left. The mode is unique and occurs at μ. Thus as we move away from μ in either direction the height of the pdf declines. The *absolute* rate of decline is slow at first but increases until we are one standard deviation away from μ, that is, at $\mu + \sigma$ or $\mu - \sigma$. At either of these points the height of the curve is about .6 of the maximum. As we move still further away the height continues to decline but at a continuously slower absolute rate.

The pdf never gets to zero. At $\mu + 5\sigma$ or $\mu - 5\sigma$ the pdf has only a very small fraction of its height at μ.

The normal cdf will be denoted $F_N(x|\mu, \sigma)$ in line with our notation. We have

$$P(\mathbf{x} \leq x) = F_N(x|\mu, \sigma) = \int_{-\infty}^{x} f_N(t|\mu, \sigma)dt.$$

This definite integral must be evaluated numerically, and we shall learn to read the relevant tables. The cdf plots in a characteristic "S-shape" as shown in Fig. 7.2.

We want to be able to calculate probability densities (heights on the pdf) and tail areas (heights on the cdf). The normal family is a two parameter family of distributions; that is, two parameters, say μ and σ or μ and σ^2, distinguish one normal distribution from another. The binomial family was also a two parameter family, and we see that a separate table is needed for each combination of n and p. To avoid the impossible task of providing a separate table for each μ and σ, the device of *standardization* is needed to obtain heights or tail areas for *any* normal distribution. Define the standardized variable

$$\mathbf{u} = \frac{\mathbf{x} - \mu}{\sigma}.$$

The mean and standard deviation of **u** are given by

$$E(\mathbf{u}) = \frac{1}{\sigma}\,[E(\mathbf{x} - \mu)] = 0$$

and

$$\sigma(\mathbf{u}) = \frac{1}{\sigma}\,\sigma(\mathbf{x} - \mu) = \frac{1}{\sigma}\cdot\sigma = 1.$$

The distribution of **u** is called the *standardized normal distribution.* The connection between the density of **x** and that of **u** is given by

$$f_N(x\,|\,\mu, \sigma)\cdot\sigma = f_N(u\,|\,0,1) = D(u)$$

or

$$f_N(x\,|\,\mu, \sigma) = \frac{1}{\sigma}\,f_N(u\,|\,0,1),\ u = \frac{x - \mu}{\sigma}.$$

The relation between cdf's is simpler since $P(\mathbf{x} \leqq x) = P(\mathbf{u} \leqq u)$ for $\mathbf{u} = (\mathbf{x} - \mu)/\sigma$:

$$F_N(x\,|\,\mu, \sigma) = F_N(u\,|\,0,1), \qquad u = \frac{x - \mu}{\sigma}.$$

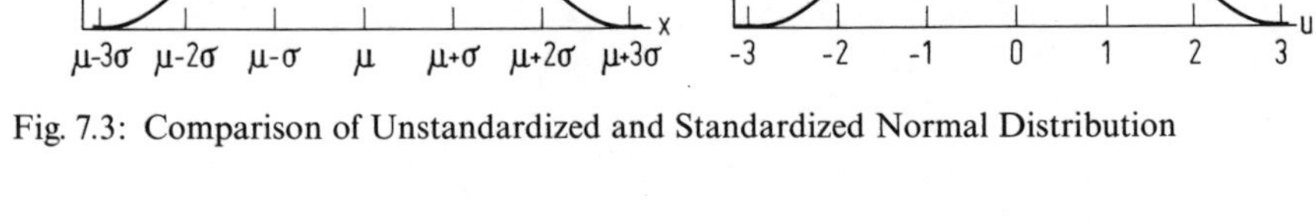

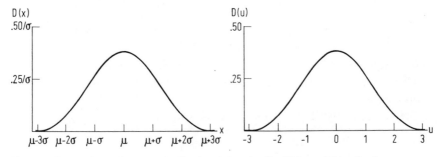

Fig. 7.3: Comparison of Unstandardized and Standardized Normal Distribution

The vertical axis of Fig. 7.2 (cdf) is unchanged; the vertical axis of Fig. 7.1 (pdf) is relabelled by multiplying each previous density by σ. The comparison of densities is given in Fig. 7.3.

Most statistical tables give heights, $f_N(u|0,1)$, and upper or right tail areas, $G_N(u|0,1) = 1 - F_N(u|0,1)$, respectively, for the standardized normal distribution.

7.3 Sampling Distributions

Suppose we have normal random variables $\mathbf{x}_1, \mathbf{x}_2, \ldots, \mathbf{x}_n$, and consider a linear combination $a_1\mathbf{x}_1 + \ldots + a_n\mathbf{x}_n$ of these variables. From Secs. 5.6 and 5.7 we know that the expectation and variance of this linear combination are

$$\sum_{i=1}^{n} a_i E(\mathbf{x}_i) = E(\mathbf{x})$$

and

$$\sum_{i=1}^{n} a_i^2 \sigma^2(\mathbf{x}_i) + \sum_{i \neq j} a_i a_j \sigma(\mathbf{x}_i, \mathbf{x}_j). = \sigma^2(\mathbf{x})$$

If the $\mathbf{x}_i$ are mutually independent, the variance is simply $\sum_{i=1}^{n} a_i^2 \sigma^2(\mathbf{x}_i)$ since all the covariances are zero. The facts about expectation and variance are true so long as all the $E(\mathbf{x}_i)$ and $\sigma^2(\mathbf{x}_i)$ "exist" in the sense of an absolutely convergent sum or integral.

If in addition the $\mathbf{x}_i$ are all normal, as we assume in this section, it can be proved that the distribution of $\sum_{i=1}^{n} a_i \mathbf{x}_i$ is also normal.

Two important special cases are the following. Let the $\mathbf{x}_i$ be independent, normal, with identical mean μ and variance σ^2. In other words the $\mathbf{x}_i$ are generated by a normal process. What about the distribution of $\bar{\mathbf{x}}$, the sample mean of $\mathbf{x}_1, \mathbf{x}_2, \ldots, \mathbf{x}_n$, and $n\bar{\mathbf{x}}$, the sample total? By comparison with the general results just stated, we see that the distribution of $\bar{\mathbf{x}}$ is normal with

$$E(\bar{\mathbf{x}}) = \mu$$

and

$$\sigma^2(\bar{\mathbf{x}}) = \sigma^2/n \quad \text{or} \quad \sigma(\bar{\mathbf{x}}) = \sigma/\sqrt{n}.$$

For example, if $n = 4$, $\sigma/\sqrt{n} = \sigma/2$, and we have the situation in Fig. 7.4. where there is a corresponding sharpening of the distribution of $\mathbf{x}$ by the distribution of $\bar{\mathbf{x}}$.

Similarly, the distribution of $n\bar{\mathbf{x}}$ is normal with

$$E(n\bar{\mathbf{x}}) = n\mu$$

and

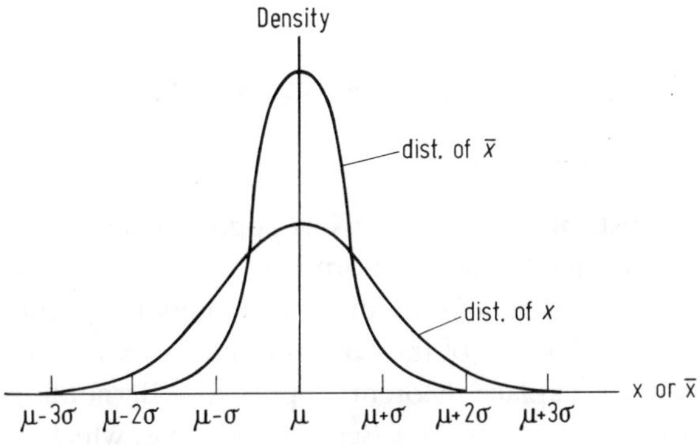

Fig. 7.4: Distribution of **x** and $\bar{\mathbf{x}}$

$$\sigma^2(n\bar{\mathbf{x}}) = n\sigma^2 \quad \text{or} \quad \sigma(n\bar{\mathbf{x}}) = \sqrt{n}\,\sigma.$$

We often refer to the distribution of $\bar{\mathbf{x}}$ or $n\bar{\mathbf{x}}$ as a *derived distribution* or *sampling distribution* (the distribution of **x** is sometimes called the *parent distribution* or *parent population*). Most of these can be regarded as the sampling distributions of sums of independent, identically-distributed random variables. The normal sampling distribution of $\bar{\mathbf{x}}$ or $n\bar{\mathbf{x}}$, however, has a unique and interesting property. Standardize $\bar{\mathbf{x}}$ or $n\bar{\mathbf{x}}$ by

$$\mathbf{u} = \frac{\bar{\mathbf{x}} - \mu}{\sigma/\sqrt{n}} \quad \text{or} \quad \mathbf{u} = \frac{n\bar{\mathbf{x}} - n\mu}{\sqrt{n}\,\sigma};$$

the distribution of **u** is a unique distribution (not just a member of a family of distributions) that we have called the *standardized normal distribution*. The property is this: among all possible identically distributed random variables **x** with finite variances, only for normal variables is it possible to standardize $\bar{\mathbf{x}}$ or $n\bar{\mathbf{x}}$ by a location and a dispersion parameter (μ and $\sigma/\sqrt{n}$ or $n\mu$ and $\sqrt{n}\,\sigma$ in the normal case) to get a unique sampling distribution regardless of n. Roughly, only for the normal distribution is the shape of the sampling distribution of $\bar{\mathbf{x}}$ or $n\bar{\mathbf{x}}$ the same regardless of n.

7.4 The Central Limit Theorem

Now consider any stationary, independent process generating random variables $\mathbf{x}_i$ with $E(\mathbf{x}_i) = \mu$ and $\sigma^2(\mathbf{x}_i) = \sigma^2$, where σ^2 is finite. We define the standardized variable

$$\mathbf{u}_n = \frac{\bar{\mathbf{x}} - \mu}{\sigma/\sqrt{n}} = \frac{n\bar{\mathbf{x}} - n\mu}{\sqrt{n}\,\sigma},$$

where $n\bar{\mathbf{x}} = \sum_{i=1}^{n} \mathbf{x}_i$. Let u_f be the f *fractile* of the standardized normal distribution*. For all f, $0 < f < 1$, it can be proved that

$$\lim_{n\to\infty} P(\mathbf{u}_n \leqq u_f) = f.$$

Roughly, the distribution of $\bar{\mathbf{x}}$ or $n\bar{\mathbf{x}}$ is approximately normal for large n even if the individual $\mathbf{x}_i$'s are not normal.

This is a brief statement of one form of the famous *central limit theorem.* An important special case of the central limit theorem (known historically as the De Moivre-Laplace theorem) applies to a Bernoulli process. It says that the distribution of **r** from a Bernoulli process, which we have seen in Chap. 6 to be a binomial distribution, can be approximated by a normal distribution. That is, we consider a sum $\mathbf{r} = \mathbf{x}_1 + \ldots + \mathbf{x}_n$ of underlying Bernoulli random variables, and set

$$\mathbf{u}_n = \frac{\mathbf{r} - np}{\sqrt{npq}};$$

the limiting distribution of $\mathbf{u}_n$ as $n \to \infty$ is the standardized normal distribution. Consider an example. We consider a fixed p and illustrate how the distribution of **r** changes as n increases.

Now if we fit a normal distribution to the binomial distribution for n and p by setting $\mu = E(\mathbf{r}) = np$ and $\sigma = \sigma(\mathbf{r}) = \sqrt{npq}$, we can get a normal pdf that approximates the outline of the binomial pmf, and a normal cdf that approximates the binomial cdf. The central limit theorem simply says, roughly, that these approximations tend to be better for larger n.

For illustration, we now look at the approximation for $p = .4$, $n = 8$. It is convenient to choose the scale in such a way that the horizontal axis is scaled in units of

$$\mathbf{u} = \frac{\mathbf{r} - E(\mathbf{r})}{\sigma(\mathbf{r})} = \frac{\mathbf{r} - np}{\sqrt{npq}}.$$

This enables us to use the standardized normal distribution directly. If we were considering a series of n's as before, the tendency for the distribution to move to the right and flatten out is just offset by this standardization. That is, $E[\mathbf{r} - E(\mathbf{r})] = E(\mathbf{r}) - E(\mathbf{r}) = 0$, locating the distribution at 0; by then dividing by $\sigma(\mathbf{r}) = \sqrt{npq}$, we obtain

$$\sigma^2\left(\frac{\mathbf{r} - E(\mathbf{r})}{\sigma(\mathbf{r})}\right) = \frac{1}{\sigma^2(\mathbf{r})} \cdot \sigma^2(\mathbf{r}) = 1,$$

so the dispersion, as measured by the variance, does not change.

---

* In terms of the probability distribution of a continuous random variable **x**, the f fractile is defined by solving for **x** in the following equation: $P(\mathbf{x} < x) = P(\mathbf{x} \leqq x) = f$.

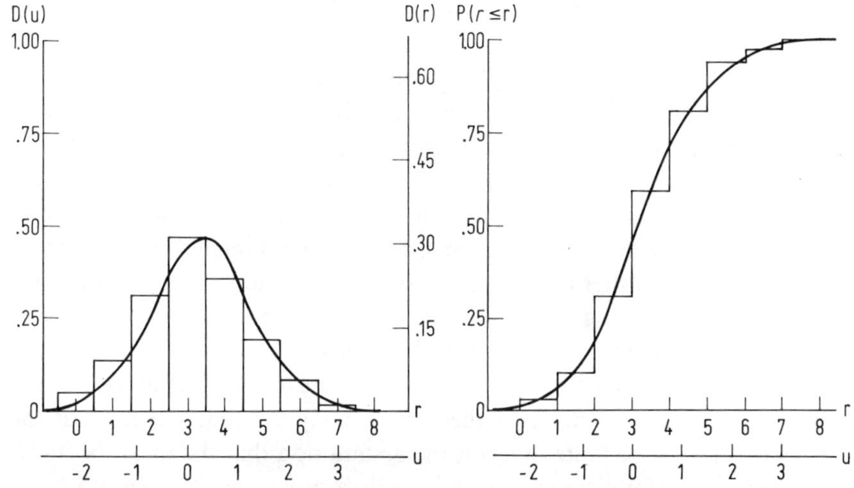

Fig. 7.5: Normal Approximation to Binomial pmf and cdf.

Fig. 7.5 shows the example for $p = .4$, $n = 8$. Look first at the cdf, the right hand graph. Both the original scale (r) and the transformed scale (u) are shown at the bottom. The smooth curve is the standardized normal cdf, and it is seen to follow the binomial cdf fairly closely. If we were to show similar graphs for $p = .4$ and other values of n, holding the u-scale constant, it would be seen that the fit is better for $n > 8$, poorer for $n < 8$.

Now look at the left hand graph, which requires special explanation of a technical point. While it is easy to compare a smooth curve with a step function, as with the cdf's, graphic comparison of a pdf and a pmf raises problems. To circumvent these problems, we represent the pmf by a histogram, in which the areas of appropriate rectangles measure probabilities. Now this convention commits us to a standardization of the vertical as well as the horizontal scale so that the areas of the rectangles sum to unity. The vertical axis will have to measure density for the standardized normal pdf. If we fix a vertical scale for **u**, D(u), we get the corresponding vertical scale for **r**, D(r), by multiplying the numbers on the D(u) scale by $du/dr = 1/\sigma(\mathbf{r}) = 1/\sqrt{8(.4)(.6)} = .72$. That is, we think of the histogram as a density for **r**. The result is the left hand graph of Fig. 7.5. Again, it is seen that the Gaussian approximation is fairly good.

Thus by keeping the u-scale constant and scaling the vertical axis appropriately, we can approximate the binomial pmf by the standardized normal pdf. Of course, the quality of the approximation depends on n; and, it depends also on p.

In essence one can say:

(1) For fixed n, the approximation is better the closer p is to 1/2.

(2) For fixed p, the approximation improves the larger is n.

7.5 Chebychev's Inequality and Law of Large Numbers

We know that under certain conditions the distribution of $(\bar{\mathbf{x}} - E(\bar{\mathbf{x}}))/\sigma(\bar{\mathbf{x}})$ is approximately a standardized normal distribution. Whenever these conditions hold, the distribution of $\bar{\mathbf{x}}$ centers more tightly around $E(\bar{\mathbf{x}}) = E(\mathbf{x}) = \mu$ as n increases since $\sigma(\bar{\mathbf{x}}) = \sigma(\mathbf{x})/\sqrt{n}$. Thus, a sample mean $\bar{\mathbf{x}}$ is close to the process (or population) mean μ with high probability for large n. More precisely, we can always find a sample size N large enough so that the probability that $\bar{\mathbf{x}}$ will differ from μ by any specified amount, however small, will be as close to zero as we specify. In technical language it is said that $\bar{\mathbf{x}}$ *converges in probability* to μ, or that the *probability limit* of $\bar{\mathbf{x}}$ is μ.

It can be proved that this statement will hold even if we relax one of the conditions of the central limit theorem, namely the requirement that the process variance be finite, but not the assumption that the mean be finite. In other words, for a stationary, independent process with mean μ, $\bar{\mathbf{x}}$ has μ as probability limit as n gets large. This statement is known as the *weak law of large numbers.* Applied to a Bernoulli process, the weak law says that $\mathbf{r}/n$ converges in probability to p, and this is the basis for the longrun frequency interpretation of probability.

The weak law can be proved easily if we assume that the variance is finite. We first demonstrate the Chebychev inequality: if $\mathbf{x}$ has finite mean μ and finite variance σ^2, then for any k,

$$(1) \qquad P[(\mathbf{x} - \mu)^2 \geqq k^2] \leqq \frac{\sigma^2}{k^2},$$

or equivalently,

$$(1a) \qquad P[|\bar{\mathbf{x}} - \mu| \geqq k] \leqq \frac{\sigma^2}{k^2} \qquad \text{for} \quad k > 0.$$

We show this for the discrete case; the extension to the continuous case is straightforward. The variance is defined by

$$(2) \qquad \sigma^2 = \sum_{x} P(\mathbf{x} = x)(x - \mu)^2.$$

Deleting from the sum all terms with squared deviations $(x - \mu)^2 < k^2$, we have

$$(3) \qquad \sigma^2 \geqq \sum_{(x-\mu)^2 \geqq k^2} P(\mathbf{x} = x)(x - \mu)^2.$$

This last summation, in turn, is at least equal to

$$(4) \qquad k^2 \sum_{(x-\mu)^2 \geqq k^2} P(\mathbf{x} = x) = k^2 P[(\mathbf{x} - \mu)^2 \geqq k^2]$$

hence

(5) $$\sigma^2 \geqq k^2 P[(\mathbf{x}-\mu)^2 \geqq k^2],$$

as desired conclusion. Note that the Chebychev inequality shows *that the maximum probability of any given large deviation from the mean is proportional to the variance*, so in this sense the variance can be regarded as a measure of dispersion. Note also that for $k^2 < \sigma^2$ the inequality gives no useful information.

Now apply this result to the random variable $\bar{\mathbf{x}}$, whose variance is σ^2/n:

(6) $$P[(\bar{\mathbf{x}}-\mu)^2 \geqq k^2] \leqq \frac{\sigma^2}{nk^2}.$$

No matter how small $k>0$ is chosen, the maximum probability that $|\bar{\mathbf{x}}-\mu|$ equals or exceeds it can be made as small as we please by selecting a sufficiently large n.

De Finetti has shown that the weak law can be expressed and proved in terms of subjective probability, using the concept of exchangeable random variables. We now outline his statement and proof. Suppose that the random variables $\mathbf{x}_1, \mathbf{x}_2, \ldots$ are exchangeable. Let $\bar{\mathbf{x}}_{n_1}$ and $\bar{\mathbf{x}}_{n_2}$ denote the average of n_1 and n_2 of them respectively, where $\bar{\mathbf{x}}_{n_1}$ and $\bar{\mathbf{x}}_{n_2}$ have r terms in common (r is possibly 0). Assume that we *assess* $E(\mathbf{x}_i)=\mu_1'$ and $E(\mathbf{x}_i^2)=\mu_2'$ for all i, and $E(\mathbf{x}_i\mathbf{x}_j)=\mu_{11}'$ for all i and j. Then

(7) $$\lim_{n_1, n_2 \to \infty} P(|\bar{\mathbf{x}}_{n_1}-\bar{\mathbf{x}}_{n_2}|>\epsilon)=0.$$

To prove (7), first note that $E(\bar{\mathbf{x}}_{n_1}-\bar{\mathbf{x}}_{n_2})=\mu_1'-\mu_1'=0$, so $\sigma^2(\bar{\mathbf{x}}_{n_1}-\bar{\mathbf{x}}_{n_2})= E(\bar{\mathbf{x}}_{n_1}-\bar{\mathbf{x}}_{n_2})^2$. If we can show $\lim_{n_1, n_2 \to \infty} \sigma^2(\bar{\mathbf{x}}_{n_1}-\bar{\mathbf{x}}_{n_2})=0$, the conclusion will follow from the Chebychev inequality. Note that

(8) $$E(\bar{\mathbf{x}}_{n_1}-\bar{\mathbf{x}}_{n_2})^2 = E(\bar{\mathbf{x}}_{n_1}^2)+E(\bar{\mathbf{x}}_{n_2}^2)-2E(\bar{\mathbf{x}}_{n_1}-\bar{\mathbf{x}}_{n_2}).$$

Examine each of the right hand expectations in turn:

(9) $$E(\bar{\mathbf{x}}_{n_1}^2)=\frac{1}{n_1^2}[n_1 E(\mathbf{x}_i^2)+n_1(n_1-1)E(\mathbf{x}_i\mathbf{x}_j)]$$
$$=\frac{1}{n_1}\mu_2'+\frac{n_1-1}{n_1}\mu_{11}'$$

(10) $$E(\bar{\mathbf{x}}_{n_2}^2)=\frac{1}{n_2}\mu_2'+\frac{n_2-1}{n_2}\mu_{11}'.$$

(11) $$-2E(\bar{\mathbf{x}}_{n_1}\bar{\mathbf{x}}_{n_2})=\frac{-2}{n_1 n_2}[rE(\mathbf{x}_i^2)+(n_1 n_2-r)E(\mathbf{x}_i\mathbf{x}_j)]$$
$$=\frac{-2r}{n_1 n_2}\mu_2'-2\left(1-\frac{r}{n_1 n_2}\right)\mu_{11}'$$

Substituting (9), (10), (11) in (8) and simplifying:

(12) $$E(\bar{\mathbf{x}}_{n_1} - \bar{\mathbf{x}}_{n_2})^2 = \left(\frac{1}{n_1} + \frac{1}{n_2} - \frac{2r}{n_1 n_2}\right)(\mu_2' - \mu_{11}').$$

Since

$$\left(\frac{1}{n_1} + \frac{1}{n_2} - \frac{2r}{n_1 n_2}\right) \leqq \left(\frac{1}{n_1} + \frac{1}{n_2}\right),$$

we have

(13) $$E(\bar{\mathbf{x}}_{n_1} - \bar{\mathbf{x}}_{n_2})^2 \leqq \left(\frac{1}{n_1} + \frac{1}{n_2}\right)(\mu_2' - \mu_{11}'),$$

and the limit of the right hand side of (13) as $n_1, n_2 \to \infty$ is zero, as required. For comparison of (7) with (6) consider the case in which the n_1 terms of $\bar{\mathbf{x}}_{n_1}$ are the first n_1 terms of $\bar{\mathbf{x}}_{n_2}$. Then $r = n_1$ and (12) becomes

(14) $$E(\bar{\mathbf{x}}_{n_2} - \bar{\mathbf{x}}_{n_1})^2 = \left(\frac{1}{n_1} - \frac{1}{n_2}\right)(\mu_2' - \mu_{11}').$$

In this case, the subjective version of the weak law, (7), says roughly that the probability of large deviations of successive averages is small, if the successive averages are based on large sample sizes. The frequency version, (6), says that the probability of a large deviation of an average from an unknown μ is small if the average is based on a large sample. The subjective version is free of reference to an unknown parameter.

7.6 Problems

(1) If 100 balls are drawn at random with replacement from an urn in which 20 percent of the balls are black, what is the probability that at least 30 of the balls drawn are black?

(2) Use the normal approximation to evaluate the following binomial probabilities for $n = 3000$, $p = .25$

(a) $P(\mathbf{r} = 650)$, (c) $P(\mathbf{r} > 650)$

(b) $P(\mathbf{r} \geqq 650)$, (d) $P(\mathbf{r} < 650)$.

(3) (Oil-Drilling) For a wild-cat the cost of drilling is a normal random variable with expected value \$ 200,000 and standard deviation \$ 20,000. The wild-catter estimates his prior probability to be .9 that no oil will be found. If there is oil its value is estimated at \$ 200,000 with a standard deviation of \$ 100,000. What is the probability of making a profit if he drills. What is the expected net profit? For \$ 30,000 the wild-catter can make a survey. The survey is highly reliable and gives a correct answer 99 percent

of the time. What is the probability of making a profit if the survey is used? What is the expected profit if the survey is used

(4) Suppose that we are sampling from a normal process, $\mu = 0$, $\sigma = 1$. How big does n have to be so that the probability is only .01 that $\bar{x}$ will be more than .002 from its expected value? What would be the answer if we did not assume sampling from a normal process but only that the process variance was finite?

(5) Suppose that the distribution of heights of males in Tribe A can be well approximated by a normal distribution with mean 70" and standard deviation 3". In Tribe B, the corresponding approximation has mean 72" and a standard deviation 4". If we draw one member from each tribe "at random" (e. g., by using balls in a well-stirred urn to represent individuals, and drawing one out blindfolded), what is the probability that the man from Tribe B will be taller than the one from Tribe A?

(6) Verify the following facts about the normal pdf mentioned in Sec. 7.2: mode at μ, concavity and convexity, inflection points at $\mu \pm \sigma$, the proportional rate of decline of the density is proportional to $|x - \mu|$.

(7) For a normal distribution the following approximation gets better as $u > 0$ gets larger:

$$1 - F_N(u|0, 1) \cong \frac{1}{u} f_N(u|0, 1).$$

Verify this approximation in Tables II and III of Schlaifer (1959) for $u = 1, 2, 3, 4, \ldots$.

(8) Two millionaires A and B match pennies with "fair coins." Assuming that each has 10^8 pennies to begin with, what is the probability that one or the other will have lost at least 10^8 pennies at the end of $4 \cdot 10^{20}$ trials? (Assume that either one can borrow an unlimited amount if he loses his initial 10^8 pennies.) If millionaire A loses his last cent at trial number $4 \cdot 10^{20}$, what will be the fraction of trials he has won?

(9) Suppose certain intelligence tests are designed in such a way that the test applied to a certain individual selected at random shows a score which is a normal random variable with expectation 100 and variance 49. What is the probability that a person to be tested will score above 110?

(10) A town has 5000 people. Each resident either likes swimming or engages in some other activity during his spare time. The city council has to decide on how big a new public swimming center has to be built. Let $\mathbf{x}_i = 1$ if the i-th resident likes swimming in his spare time, and let $\mathbf{x}_i = 0$ if the same person engages in some other activity. Let $\mathbf{z} = \sum_{i=1}^{5000} \mathbf{x}_i$ be the number of persons who actually will prefer swimming and $\bar{\mathbf{x}}$ be the percentage of those persons $\bar{\mathbf{x}} = \sum_{i=1}^{n} \mathbf{x}_i/n$. Assume the swimming habits of the residents to be

mutually independent and that the council's initial probabilities that a randomly selected person will swim is about .70. The probability of satisfying the demand is required to be at least 80 percent most of the time. How 'big' should the public swimming center be designed; in which way is the use of the central limit theorem helpful in providing a solution? Sketch.

(11) (Flood control – modified after R. Savage) A dam is to be built high enough to contain a prospective flood height of either 60 or 70 feet. For the higher dam exactly three million dollars have to be appropriated in addition. Previous experience over the past ten years suggests that the flood height is a normal random variable with mean 55 feet and variance 16. Whenever the flood exceeds the capacity of the dam, there will be a minimum damage of at least $ 500,000 because of flooding:

(a) What is the probability of flooding with each dam?

(b) What is the expected number of floodings within fifty years or within a century?

(12) Assume $\mathbf{u}$ is a standard normal rv. Then $\varepsilon^2 P(|\mathbf{u}| \geqq \varepsilon)$ will be the ratio of the probability that $|\mathbf{u}| \geqq \varepsilon$ to the Chebychev inequality bound for that probability. Compute the expression for integer values $\varepsilon \geqq 3$ up to 10. How does the Chebychev inequality behave for large values?

(13) Show why the following theorem is true: if $\mathbf{z} = \sum_{i=1}^{n} x_i$ is the sum of n independent rv's of a Bernoulli process all having the same probability distribution, then as n increases the distribution of $\mathbf{z}$ becomes more closely approximated by a normal distribution with mean $E(\mathbf{z})$ equal to the expectation of the sum and with variance $\sigma^2(\mathbf{z})$ equal to the variance of the sum.

(14) Consider all towns that have populations not exceeding 3000. If x stands for the number of males in such a town, then $\mathbf{u} = (\mathbf{x} - 1500)/50$ is a standard normal variable. Find the probability that there will be more than 1600 females in such a town.

(15) Suppose that $\mathbf{x}$ is a rv with normal distribution which has expected value $E(\mathbf{x}) = 200$, and standard deviation $\sigma = 4$. Find the corresponding values of $\mathbf{u}$, the standardized normal variable, for the following values of $\mathbf{x}$: (a) $x = 202$, (b) $x = 96$, (c) $x = 94$, (d) $x = 107$, (e) $x = 200$.

(16) Suppose that a sample of size n is to be taken from a normal distribution with mean and standard deviation 4. Determine the smallest value of n such that $P(|\bar{x}_n - \mu| < .05) \geqq .95$.

Suggested Readings

De Finetti, B.: Introduction to Probability Theory, London 1973, Chaps. 2–6.
Dixon, W.J. and F.J. Massey: Introduction to Statistical Analysis, 3rd ed., New York 1969, Chaps. 1–6.
Feller, W.: An Introduction to Probability Theory and its Applications, 2nd ed., New York 1957, Chaps. 7, 10.
Mosteller, F. et al.: Probability with Statistical Applications, Reading (Mass.), 1970, Chaps. 3–8.
Raiffa, H. and R. Schlaifer, Applied Statistical Decision Theory, Boston 1961.
Schlaifer, R.: Probability and Statistics for Business Decisions, New York 1959, Chaps. 17, 18.
Savage, R.: Statistics: Uncertainty and Behavior, Boston 1968, Chap. 7.

Part III.
Topics in statistical inference, information and decision

8. Statistical Inference

8.1 An Application of Bayes' Theorem to Genetic Risks

The following application of Bayes' theorem to the calculation of genetic risks is presented in research by K. Tanaka (1967).
Genetic counselors are requested to tell genetic risks not only before marriage or before birth of the first child, but also after births of one or several children. Collected information about *phenotypes* of these children may affect the estimate of genetic risk for subsequent children.
If any child already born to given parents is affected, the parents obviously have *genotypes* which can produce affected children.
However, if several children already born to given parents are all unaffected, the parents are less likely to have genotypes, which could produce affected children than can be expected before the birth of the first child.
A Bayesian analysis of the genetic risk supports the findings that the risk of getting affected children would decrease with the increase of the number of unaffected children already born. The genetic risk in a child subsequent to his unaffected siblings can be estimated according to Bayes' theorem. Suppose that an event S is linked to k mutually exclusive causes $C_1, C_2, \dots C_k$. Suppose further that the cause C_i has a probability c_i occurring in the general population and that when C_i is known to have occurred, the event S has a probability s_i assigned. Then if we observe that S did happen, the probability that it was caused by C_i is the conditional probability

$$P(C_i|S) = \frac{c_i s_i}{\sum_{j=1}^{k} c_j s_j}$$

For simplicity, suppose that two mutually exclusive events C and $\bar{C}$ can occur with probabilities c and $\bar{c}$, respectively ($c + \bar{c} = 1$).
Let an affected child be born with a *chance* q given the event C, and with no such chance in the event $\bar{C}$. Let $p = 1 - q$ which is the chance of getting unaffected children in the event C.
If the case is C, the probability that (say) all x children already born are unaffected would be p^x, and if the case is $\bar{C}$, the probability would be unity. Therefore, in a sample of kinships in which all children are unaffected (event S), the proportion of kinships through C would be

$$P(C|S) = \frac{cp^x}{cp^x + \bar{c}} \quad \text{or} \quad \frac{cp^x}{cp^x + 1 - c}$$

And the risk that a couple, whose x already born children are all unaffected, may produce an abnormal child in a subsequent birth would be

$$R_x = \frac{cp^x q}{cp^x + 1 - c} \quad \text{or} \quad \frac{cp^x(1-p)}{cp^x + 1 - c}$$

The actual figures of the risk for various values of c and p are given in the following table.

c	p = 1/2, q = 1/2				p = 3/4, q = 1/4			
	x				x			
	0	1	2	3	0	1	2	3
1	1/2	1/2	1/2	1/2	1/4	1/4	1/4	1/4
1/2	1/4	1/6	1/10	1/18	1/8	3/28	9/100	27/364
1/4	1/8	1/14	1/26	1/50	1/16	3/60	9/228	27/876
1/8	1/16	1/30	1/58	1/114	1/32	3/124	9/484	27/1900
1/16	1/32	1/62	1/122	1/242	1/64	3/252	9/996	27/3948
1/36	1/72	1/142	1/282	1/562	1/144	3/572	9/2276	27/9068
1/100	1/200	1/398	1/794	1/1585	1/400	3/1596	9/6372	27/25452
1/200	1/400	1/798	1/1594	1/3186	1/800	3/3196	9/12772	27/51052

Table 8–1: Genetic risk for a child subsequent to x previous nonaffected offsprings.

The decrease of the risk by the births of nonaffected children is confirmed by the calculations. As can be derived from the table, the smaller the values of c and p, the larger is the amount of decreasing risk. In particular, if c is small the risk is roughly proportional to p^x.
Taking up a numerical example, let it be confirmed by experiments that the frequency of the albino gene is 5/1000 so that the prior probability of one *heterozygous* carrier is 1/100 (= c). Then the risk of producing an albino-affect child is 1/200 before the birth of the first child, 1/398 after the birth of one unaffected child, 1/794 after the birth ot two unaffected children etc. making the risk decreasing roughly by half for each unaffected child (see Table for c = 1/100 and p = 1/2).

8.2 Bayes' Theorem Reconsidered

All computations leading to Bayes' theorem simply represent manipulations of the definition of conditional probability. For example,

$$(1)\qquad P(R \mid S) = \frac{P(R \text{ and } S)}{P(S)}, \qquad P(S) \neq 0$$

is the conditional probability of R given S. The numerator of the right hand side can be expressed

$$(2)\qquad P(R \text{ and } S) = P(R)\,P(S \mid R).$$

Here P(R) is the prior probability of R; P(S|R) is the conditional probability of the evidence S given the event R. The denominator can be expressed

$$(3)\qquad \begin{aligned} P(S) &= P(R \text{ and } S) + P(G \text{ and } S) \\ &= P(R)\,P(S \mid R) + P(G)\,P(S \mid G). \end{aligned}$$

Substituting (2) and (3) in (1), we have

$$(4)\qquad P(R \mid S) = \frac{P(R)\,P(S \mid R)}{P(R)\,P(S \mid R) + P(G)\,P(S \mid G)}.$$

Formula (4) is one way to write out Bayes' theorem in this application; P(R|S) is the posterior probability of R given the sample evidence S.
In terms of the tabular computational layout introduced in Chap. 1, Sec. 3, this algebraic formula, and the corresponding one for P(G|S), can be displayed as follows:

Table 8–2:

Event	Prior Probability	Likelihood	Joint Probability	Posterior Probability
R	P(R)	P(S|R)	P(R) P(S|R)	P(R) P(S|R)/P(S)
G	P(G)	P(S|G)	P(G) P(S|G)	P(G) P(S|G)/P(S)
Total	1	–	P(S)	1

Next we turn to an illustration that will give additional computational practice. Consider a hypothetical test for the presence of cancer. The event "you have cancer" is denoted by C; the complementary event "do not have cancer" is denoted by $\bar{C}$. The event "positive diagnosis by the test" is denoted by "+"; "negative diagnosis," by "–". Suppose that you are in a middle age group for which the incidence of cancer has been about.005, and no special information about your health is available. You decide to assess your *prior* probabilities by this relative frequency, that is, $P(C) = .005$ and $P(\bar{C}) = .995$. The diagnostic test is assumed to be a relatively cheap one, suitable for use in a large scale cancer screening program. It is hypothetical, and purely for illustration, its reliability is assumed to be higher than for any existing test. The reliability is expressed in terms of conditional probabilities, as follows: $P(+|C) = .95$ and $P(-|C) = .05$; $P(+|\bar{C}) = .05$ and $P(-|\bar{C}) = .95$. Note that $P(+|C) + P(-|C) = 1$, $P(+|\bar{C}) + P(-|\bar{C}) = 1$, necessarily, but that no significance is to be attached to the sums $P(+|C) + P(+|\bar{C})$ or $P(-|C) + P(-|\bar{C})$. These latter two both *happen* to add to one in this example, but would not typically do so. We might have set $P(+|\bar{C}) = .10$ and $P(-|\bar{C}) = .90$, and worked through the problem from that starting point.

Suppose that you take the test and get the diagnosis "+." How now do you assess the probability that you have cancer, $P(C|+)$? Many people are tempted to give the quick answer, ".95." Their reasoning goes something like this: "The test has reliability .95, since $P(+|C) = P(-|\bar{C}) = .95$. It has given a positive reading, so the probability of cancer must be .95." By seeing why this analysis is wrong, one is led to a deeper understanding of Bayes' theorem.

We now apply Bayes' theorem formally:

$$P(C|+) = \frac{P(C) \cdot P(+|C)}{P(C)\,P(+|C) + P(\bar{C})\,P(+|\bar{C})}$$

$$= \frac{(.005)\,(.95)}{(.005)\,(.95) + (.995)\,(.05)} = \frac{.00475}{.05450} = .087.$$

The calculation can also be done in tabular form:

Table 8–3:

Event	Prior Probability	Likelihood	Joint Probability	Posterior Probability
C	.005	.95	.00475	.087
$\bar{C}$	.995	.05	.04975	.913
Total	1.000	–	.05450	1.000

The probability that you have cancer is now .087. While this is substantially higher than the prior probability of .005, it is very much lower than the intuitive answer, .95. It is helpful to see why .95 is wrong and .087 is right. The relative-frequency interpretation of probability can be used to advantage. Visualize the prior probabilities as follows: you are one of a group of 100,000 people who are taking the screening test. Of this group, 99,500 are free of cancer while 500 have cancer. The test gives false positives for 5 per cent of the 99,500 people without cancer; this makes 4,975 false positives. It gives true positives for 95 per cent of the 500 people with cancer; this makes 475 true positives. Altogether there are 4,975 + 475 = 5,450 positives, and you are one of this uneasy group. Your anxiety is reduced, however, if you realize that only 475 of the 5,450 actually have cancer. The ratio 475/5,450 is the number .087. The posterior probability .087 reconciles both your prior information and the evidence of the diagnostic test. If you still feel that it is incorrect, your only recourse is to go back over the inputs of the computation – the prior probabilities and the likelihoods.

Whatever the numerical assessments of the prior probabilities and likelihoods, Bayes' theorem blends them correctly in arriving at posterior probabilities.

Had the test given a negative rather than a positive reading, you should verify that $P(C|-) = .00026$ as compared with $P(C) = .005$. The negative reading makes cancer 20-fold less probable than it was *a priori.*

8.3 Application to Bernoulli Processes

In general, we were concerned directly with the probabilities of events such as R and G and C and $\bar{C}$. We can sometimes reinterpret events in terms of possible values taken by the parameter(s) of a data-generating process. In the cancer diagnosis example, assume that repetitions of the diagnosis on the same individual can be regarded as a Bernoulli process generating a sequence of +'s and −'s. If we denote $p_1 = P(+|C) = .95$, then the event C is the same as the event $(\mathbf{p} = p_1)$. That is, we can interpret the event "has cancer" as the event "we are observing a Bernoulli process with $\mathbf{p} = p_1 = .95$." Similarly, the event "does not have cancer" can be interpreted as the event "we are observing a Bernoulli process with $\mathbf{p} = p_2 = .05$," where $p_2 = P(+|\bar{C})$.

Now consider situations in which the prior distribution refers to $\mathbf{p}$, where p is a possible value of the parameter of a Bernoulli process. The information consists of a *sample* from the process, that is, an elementary event in the sample space. We assume that either n or r is fixed in advance of sampling. According to Sec. 6.1, the conditional probability or likelihood for any such elementary event is $p^r q^{n-r}$, where n is the number of trials, r is the number of successes, and $q = 1 - p$. For simplicity think of p as discrete, ranging over $p_1, p_2, \ldots, p_m$. For each such value we have prior probabilities $P(p_1)$, $P(p_2), \ldots, P(p_m)$. Then Bayes' theorem says

$$P(\mathbf{p} = p_i | \text{sample}) = \frac{P(\mathbf{p} = p_i)\, p_i^r q_i^{n-r}}{\sum_{j=1}^{m} P(\mathbf{p} = p_j)\, p_j^r q_j^{n-r}}, \qquad i = 1, 2, \ldots, m. \tag{1}$$

Note that

$$\sum_{j=1}^{m} P(\mathbf{p} = p_j)\, p_j^r q_j^{n-r} = P(\text{sample}), \tag{2}$$

which is the marginal probability, in the light of the prior distribution of **p**, of the particular sequence of + 's and − 's actually observed.
But while P (sample) has a useful interpretation, it is more or less incidental in the application of Bayes' theorem. By looking only at the joint probabilities, and remembering that these joint probabilities must be rescaled to add to 1 in order to obtain the corresponding posterior probabilities, we can avoid writing the common denominator explicitly each time. Bayes' theorem can then be written more compactly

$$\text{(3)} \qquad P(\mathbf{p} = p_j \mid \text{sample}) \propto P(\mathbf{p} = p_j)\, p_j^r q_j^{n-r}, \qquad j = 1, 2, \ldots, m,$$

where the symbol "$\propto$" means "is proportional to." In the cancer example we can write

$$\text{(4)} \qquad P(C \mid +) \propto P(C)\, P(+ \mid C) = (.005)\,(.95) = .00475.$$

Similarly,

$$\text{(5)} \qquad P(\bar{C} \mid +) \propto P(\bar{C})\, P(+ \mid \bar{C}) = (.995)\,(.05) = .04975.$$

We then calculate .00475 + .04975 = .05450, the marginal probability of the diagnosis "+", which is then divided into the right hand side of (4) and (5), respectively, to obtain

$$\text{(6)} \qquad P(C \mid +) = \frac{.00475}{.05450} = .087$$

and

$$\text{(7)} \qquad P(\bar{C} \mid +) = \frac{.04975}{.05450} = .913.$$

If the prior distribution of **p** is continuous, we can write

$$D(p \mid \text{sample}) \propto D(p)\, p^r q^{n-r}.$$

The essential modification is that $\sum P(\mathbf{p} = p)\, p^r q^{n-r}$ in the discrete case is replaced by $\int_0^1 D(p)\, p^r q^{n-r} dp$ in the continuous case. The integral, like the sum, is interpreted as the prior probability of the observed sample, P (sample). Thus the posterior density of **p** is expressed as

$$D(p \mid \text{sample}) = \frac{D(p)\, p^r q^{n-r}}{\int_0^1 D(p)\, p^r q^{n-r} dp}.$$

We simply use our best judgment to assess a discrete or continuous prior distribution for **p**, P(p) or D(p), and then carry out Bayes' theorem to get P(p | sample) or D(p | sample).

8.4 The Likelihood Function

In sampling from a Bernoulli process with either n or r fixed in advance, the likelihood can be written $p^r q^{n-r}$. We may think of $p^r q^{n-r}$ either as a conditional probability *given* p that a particular sequence of r successes will be observed in n trials, or a function of the variable p given n and r. In the second interpretation, $p^r q^{n-r}$ is the *likelihood function* of p given the sample. Frequently the likelihood function is defined in a broader sense as $k\,p^r q^{n-r}$, where k is any positive constant (constant with respect to p). In this terminology, for example, we can equally well speak of a binomial probability $C^n_r p^r q^{n-r}$ (or a Pascal probability $C^{n-1}_{r-1} p^r q^{n-r}$) as the likelihood function. The constant k simply cancels out in application of Bayes' theorem. For example,

$$P(p\,|\,\text{sample}) = \frac{P(p)\,k p^r q^{n-r}}{\sum P(p)\,k p^r q^{n-r}} = \frac{P(p)\,q^r q^{n-r}}{\sum P(p)\,p^r q^{n-r}}.$$

At this point we discuss stopping rules, a subject introduced more generally in Chap. 10. The stopping rule determines the stopping probability, which we express by $P(n\,|\,x_1,\ldots,x_n, p, \theta)$. This notation shows that the probability that n random variables will be observed may depend on the actual *values* of the observations, on the parameter of interest p, and on other possible parameters summarized by the symbol θ. The likelihood function can be written

$$P(n, x_1,\ldots,x_n\,|\,p,\theta) = P(n\,|\,x_1,\ldots,x_n, p,\theta)\cdot P(x_1,\ldots,x_n\,|\,p, n,\theta).$$

Now consider special types of stopping rules* First, the stopping probability is conditional only on the values of the observations, so we may write it as $P(n\,|\,x_1,\ldots,x_n)$. Since this is a constant with respect to p, it cancels out in application of Bayes' theorem. We say that the stopping rule is *non-informative*, in that it tells us nothing is needed in order to reach the posterior distribution.

Second, the rule may depend only on p. In effect, n is determined by a probability distribution that is conditional upon p, $P(n\,|\,p)$. The likelihood is

$$P(n\,|\,p)\,P(x_1,\ldots,x_n\,|\,p, n).$$

Since $P(n\,|\,p)$ obviously affects the posterior distribution, the stopping rule is said to be *informative.*

Third, the stopping probability may be conditional both on the observations

---

* For an extensive discussion of stopping processes, see I. H. Lavalle, An Introduction to Probability, Decision and Inference, New York 1970, chap. 9. See also Raiffa and Schlaifer op. cit. Sec. 2.3.

and on p, $P(n|x_1, \ldots, x_n, p)$. This rule is informative, as the general rule that assigns stopping probabilities $P(n|x_1, \ldots, x_n, p, \theta)$.

Fourth, the stopping rule may be $P(n|x_1, \ldots, x_n, \theta)$. This is noninformative if **p** and $\boldsymbol{\theta}$ are independent *a priori*, but not otherwise.

Actually, in the vast majority of applications, the stopping rule is either simply $P(n) = 1$ (that is, the sample size is fixed in advance) or else one of the non-informative rules given above. In these cases the likelihood is written without explicit mention of the stopping probability.

To determine the *predictive distribution*, however, the stopping rule must be specified even if it is non-informative. In binomial sampling, the stopping probability is simply $P(n|p) = 1$, and we can write the likelihood as $p^r(1-p)^{n-r}$. We can equally well write it as $C_r^n p^r(1-p)^{n-r}$, since C_r^n does not involve p; in this form the likelihood can be interpreted as the conditional probability of r successes in n trials, when n is fixed in advance. The predictive probability of r successes in n trials (that is the probability unconditional on p) is

$$\sum_p P(p)\, C_r^n p^r (1-p)^{n-r}.$$

What is the importance of the likelihood function? From Bayes' theorem it is immediate that the likelihood function (including the stopping rule, if informative) constitutes the entire evidence of the sample. This fact, an immediate consequence of Bayes' theorem, has been called the *likelihood principle***. Why should one accept the likelihood principle? Because it is an immediate consequence of Bayes' theorem, since the posterior probability function of the unknown parameters is proportional to the product of the likelihood function and the prior pdf or pmf. But this truism requires acceptance of prior probabilities and hence a new outlook towards a consistent subjectivistic interpretation of data.

The likelihood principle has important consequences for statistics. One is that the stopping is irrelevant to the calculation of the posterior distribution so long as it is non-informative.

Another facet of the irrelevance of a non-informative stopping-rule is that we get the same answer whether we analyze a sample sequentially, say item by item, or simply carry out one single analysis on the whole sample. This is an immediate consequence of the following basic probability relationship:

$$P(x_1, x_2, \ldots, x_n|p) = P(x_1|p)\, P(x_2|p, x_1) \ldots P(x_n|p, x_1, \ldots, x_{n-1}).$$

** The likelihood principle has also been supported by some statisticians without reliance on Bayes' theorem, as a consequence of the *principle of conditionality*. See Birnbaum, "On the Foundations of Statistical Inference," *Journal of the American Statistical Association*, 57, 1962, 269–306.

It is *not* generally true, however, that in designing a sample we are indifferent between a sequential sampling plan and one that fixes the sample size in advance. Nor, as we expect, is it true that the stopping rule is irrelevant for predicting the outcomes of samples from the process.

The likelihood principle also has implications for the reporting of data. We have seen that statistical inference (for discrete priors and posteriors) can be expressed verbally by

(*) Posterior probability ∞ (prior probability) (likelihood).

All three elements of (*) are ultimately subjective. Sometimes, however, many people would make virtually the same judgements about the likelihood. A description of a data-generating process, for example, may lead almost anyone to agree that the process is a Bernoulli process (conditional on p). If so, then there will be general agreement that the likelihood function may be written $p^r q^{n-r}$.

There may be substantial disagreement on the prior probabilities. Some people are unwilling to assess prior probabilities even though they are quite willing to make a specific judgment about the data-generating process. To complete a Bayesian analysis *formally*, prior probabilities must be assessed. But it is a misunderstanding to think that anyone *must* ever accept someone else's prior probabilities or that any researcher should try to impose his prior probabilities on anyone else.

When a researcher wishes to communicate to someone else, he should keep prior probabilities and likelihoods separate. His first task is to report the data. The likelihood principle says that a likelihood function, in our example $p^r q^{n-r}$, suffices for this. In this example, the likelihood function can be further condensed by reporting only r and n, which are called *sufficient statistics*. The idea of sufficient statistics is this. Any person knowing the sufficient statistics can reconstruct a likelihood function. This likelihood function, when fed into a prior distribution and processed by Bayes' theorem, gives a posterior distribution. Another person who knows the *exact sequence* in which the r S's and $n-r$ F's occurred, that is, who knew all the data, would arrive at exactly the same posterior distribution if his prior probabilities are the same.

8.5* Prior and Posterior Distributions

We begin with an improper prior distribution that serves as an approximate representation for an "informationless" prior distribution – a prior distribution that is extremely sensitive to revision by even a small amount of data. Specifically consider the improper prior for $\boldsymbol{\mu}$ that has uniform "density" k for all values μ, $-\infty<\mu<\infty$. Starting from this point, we postulate a hypothetical prior sample from the process of size n′ with sufficient statistic $\bar{x}'$. The likelihood function for such a sample can be written as $f_N(\bar{x}'|\mu, \sigma/\sqrt{n'})$ Bayes' theorem can be applied to this hypothetical sample very simply, as follows.

$$(1) \qquad D(\mu|\bar{x}', \sigma/\sqrt{n'}) = \frac{k f_N(\bar{x}'|\mu, \sigma/\sqrt{n'})}{\int_{-\infty}^{\infty} k f_N(\bar{x}'|\mu, \sigma/\sqrt{n'}) d\mu} = f_N(\mu|\bar{x}', \sigma/\sqrt{n'}).$$

In this argument, the facts that $\int_{-\infty}^{\infty} f_N(\bar{x}'|\mu, \sigma/\sqrt{n'})\, d\mu = 1$ and that of re-writing $f_N(\bar{x}'|\mu, \sigma/\sqrt{n'})$ as $f_N(\mu|\bar{x}', \sigma/\sqrt{n'})$ are consequences of the symmetry in $\bar{x}'$ and μ of $f_N(\bar{x}'|\mu, \sigma/\sqrt{n'})$:

$$(2) \qquad f_N(\bar{x}'|\mu, \sigma/\sqrt{n'}) = \frac{1}{\sqrt{2\pi}\sigma/\sqrt{n'}} e^{-\frac{1}{2\sigma^2/n'}(\bar{x}'-\mu)^2} = \frac{1}{\sqrt{2\pi}\sigma/\sqrt{n'}} e^{-\frac{1}{2\sigma^2/n'}(\mu-\bar{x}')^2}$$

We can interpret this function either as the density of a normal sampling distribution of $\bar{x}'$ given μ or of a normal distribution of $\boldsymbol{\mu}$ given $\bar{x}'$. In this way we are then led to a normal prior distribution of $\boldsymbol{\mu}$ with mean $\bar{x}'$ and standard deviation $\sigma/\sqrt{n'}$ as equivalent to an "informationless" state followed by a hypothetical sample of n′ from the process giving mean $\bar{x}'$. The parameter n′ need not be an integer. For example, $n' = \frac{1}{2}$ can be interpreted as a single observation from another process with mean μ but variance $2\sigma^2$.
Given this interpretation of the prior distribution, we see immediately what the posterior distribution must be, given an *actual* sample of n with mean $\bar{x}$. Conceptually, we simply pool the hypothetical prior sample with the actual sample to get a combined sample of size $n'' = n' + n$ with mean $\bar{x}'' = (n'\bar{x}' + n\bar{x})/n''$. The likelihood function can therefore be written as

$$(3) \qquad f_N(\bar{x}''|\mu, \sigma/\sqrt{n''}).$$

Going back to the improper uniform "density" prior to the hypothetical sample, we see from (3) that the posterior density is given by

$$(4) \qquad f_N(\mu|\bar{x}'', \sigma/\sqrt{n''});$$

the reasoning is the same as in (1).
The key relations between prior and posterior distributions are

$$(5) \qquad n'' = n' + n$$

and

(6) $$\bar{x}'' = \frac{n'\bar{x}' + n\bar{x}}{n''}.$$

We can interpret $\bar{x}''$ as a *weighted average* of the sample mean $\bar{x}$ and the prior mean $\bar{x}'$, the weights being n'/n'' and n/n'' respectively. If n' is very small compared to n, the sample approximately determines the parameters of the posterior distribution as $\bar{x}$ and $\sigma/\sqrt{n}$.

8.6* Sufficient Statistics

Let us turn to analysis of samples from a normal process of unknown mean μ and known variance σ^2. When we speak of „unknown" μ, we mean that the distribution of $\boldsymbol{\mu}$ has dispersion that is not negligible for some problem being analyzed. In the same way, „known" σ^2 means that information about σ^2 is so extensive that the distribution of $\boldsymbol{\sigma}^2$ has negligible dispersion for the problem being analyzed; we can replace the distribution by some known number σ^2 in pursuing the analysis.

Consideration of the case of known variance serves as an easy step to the more difficult problem that arises when both variance and mean are unknown. For large n, uncertainty about $\boldsymbol{\sigma}^2$ becomes of second-order importance in making inferences about $\boldsymbol{\mu}$, and the results of the subsequent part serve as good approximations if we simply pretend that the sample variance s^2 *is* the true variance σ^2. Moreover, it is possible that n may not be large, yet there may be extensive prior information bearing on $\boldsymbol{\sigma}^2$ but not on $\boldsymbol{\mu}$. As an example, consider a laboratory balance for which n_i repeated measurements of a given object i have sample variance s_i^2 and appear to be normally distributed. Past evidence of this sort for many different objects $i = 1, 2, \ldots, k$ suggests that the observed $s_1^2, s_2^2, \ldots, s_k^2$ are all estimates of a single underlying variance σ^2, which measures the intrinsic error of the balance, regardless of the object being weighed. We define the *pooled sample variance* s^2 as

(1) $$s^2 = \frac{\sum_{i=1}^{k} (n_i - 1)s_i^2}{\sum_{i=1}^{k} (n_i - 1)} = \frac{\sum_{i=1}^{k} (n_i - 1)s_i^2}{n - k},$$

where $n = \sum_{i=1}^{k} n_i$. For analysis of a sample of measurements of a *new* object, for which μ is unknown, we may treat s^2 as if it were σ^2, so long as $n - k$ is large.

In at least two circumstances, then, the assumption of known σ^2 leads to a satisfactory analysis.

We observe a sample of n random variables $\mathbf{x}_1, \mathbf{x}_2, \ldots, \mathbf{x}_n$ from a Gaussian process of known σ. Conditional on the unknown parameter μ (σ is now to be thought of as a known number), the joint density of the sample is

$$(2) \qquad D(x_1, x_2, \ldots, x_n | \mu, n) = f_N(x_1 | \mu, \sigma) \cdot f_N(x_2 | \mu, \sigma) \ldots f_N(x_n | \mu, \sigma)$$

$$= \left(\frac{1}{\sqrt{2\pi}\sigma}\right)^n e^{-\frac{1}{2\sigma^2}\sum_{i=1}^{n}(x_i - \mu)^2}$$

The expression (2) serves as the likelihood function of μ given the sample; any positive constant multiple will serve just as well. We rewrite the summation in the exponent of e as

$$(3) \qquad \sum_{i=1}^{n}(x_i - \mu)^2 = \sum_{i=1}^{n}[(x_i - \bar{x}) + (\bar{x} - \mu)]^2$$

$$= \sum_{i=1}^{n}(x_i - \bar{x})^2 + n(\bar{x} - \mu)^2 + 2(\bar{x} - \mu)\sum_{i=1}^{n}(x_i - \bar{x})$$

$$= \sum_{i=1}^{n}(x_\cdot - \bar{x})^2 + n(\bar{x} - \mu)^2,$$

the final step following because $\sum(x - \bar{x}) = \sum x - n\bar{x} = 0$. Substituting (3) in (2) and rearranging, we obtain

$$(4) \qquad D(x_1, x_2, \ldots, x_n | \mu, n) = k\, e^{-\frac{1}{2\sigma^2/n}(\bar{x} - \mu)^2}$$

where

$$k = \left(\frac{1}{\sqrt{2\pi}\sigma}\right)^n e^{-\frac{1}{2\sigma^2}\sum_{i=1}^{n}(x_i - \bar{x})^2}$$

Thinking of (4) as the likelihood function we replace k by $\dfrac{1}{\sqrt{2\pi}\sigma/\sqrt{n}}$ to obtain

$$(5) \qquad D(x_1, x_2, \ldots, x_n | \mu, n) \propto \frac{1}{\sqrt{2\pi}\sigma/\sqrt{n}}\, e^{-\frac{1}{2\sigma^2/n}(\bar{x} - \mu)^2}$$

$$= f_N(\bar{x} | \mu, \sigma/\sqrt{n}),$$

We see that $f_N(\bar{x} | \mu, \sigma/\sqrt{n})$, considered as a function of μ for observed $\bar{x}$ and n and known σ, serves as the likelihood function.

An immediate consequence of (5) is that the sample mean $\bar{x}$ and n are *sufficient statistics.* That is, if the process is a normal process with known σ^2, as alleged, everything to be learned from the sample of n is expressed in $\bar{x}$. The individual observations $x_1, x_2, \ldots, x_n$, and the sequence in which they occurred, are irrelevant. In other words, sufficient statistics conveniently summarize a likelihood function.

8.7* Vague Priors (Savage's Theory of Stable Estimation)

Sometimes a partial assessment of a prior distribution may suffice to fix the posterior distribution with sufficient accuracy. A leading example of this is provided by L. J. Savage's *theory of stable estimation or precise measurement*. The following sketch of the theory follows closely an exposition by Savage (1962).

You are holding a potato, or some other irregular object, in your hand and need to know something of its weight. You can, in principle, assess your own prior probability density $D(\mu)$ for the unknown weight of the potato, but in practice the self-interrogation may not work very well and you may be vague about $D(\mu)$. There is a temptation to say that $D(\mu)$ does not exist or that you know nothing about the weight of the potato. Actually, it has proven impossible to give a satisfactory definitionof the tempting expression "know nothing." Still more, you do know a great deal about your opinions about the weight of the potato, and these can be quite well expressed in terms of *partial* specifications of $D(\mu)$. If, for example, it were necessary to mail the potato without weighing it, you could put enough postage to be reasonably sure that it would not be returned to you nor be 500 per cent overpaid.

More important, you are almost sure to have a certain kind of knowledge about $D(\mu)$ that will be very useful after you have a chance to weigh the potato on a good balance. To illustrate, suppose that you found out, as a result of some experiment, that the weight of the potato to the nearest gram was either 146 or 147 grams. Given this knowledge, you would probably be willing not to accept odds slightly more favorable than one-to-one in favor of either of the two possibilities, 146 grams or 147 grams. This may be interpreted to mean that, for you, the average value of $D(\mu)$ near 146 is almost the same as its average value near 147. Continuing along this line, you might arrive at the conclusion that $D(\mu)$ varies by at most a few per cent in *any* 10-gram interval included between, say, 100 and 300 grams. You might also conclude that $D(\mu)$ is nowhere enormously greater, say 100 times greater, than even the smallest value that it attains between the bounds of 100 grams and 300 grams. This illustrates a *diffuse* or *locally uniform* prior distribution. With such knowledge, what could you conclude after weighing the potato on a balance known to have a normally distributed error with a standard deviation of 1 gram? The balance, of course, is a normal data-generating process. It has standard deviation σ of 1 gram. If we averaged two readings, then $\bar{\mathbf{x}}$ would have standard deviation $\sigma(\bar{\mathbf{x}}) = \sigma/\sqrt{n} = 1/\sqrt{2} = .707$, and so on for averages of any number of readings. Here we assume $n = 1$, so $\bar{\mathbf{x}}$ and $\mathbf{x}$ are the same and $\sigma(\bar{\mathbf{x}}) = \sigma(\mathbf{x}) = 1$. Suppose, for definiteness, that $\bar{x} = 174.3$ grams. We can write Bayes' theorem as

$$D(\mu|\bar{x}, n) = \frac{D(\mu) f_N(174.3|\mu, 1)}{\int_{-\infty}^{\infty} D(\mu) f_N(174.3|\mu, 1) d\mu}.$$

By the assumption of diffuseness $D(\mu)$ varies little within any interval of 10 standard errors, or 10 grams, from 100 to 300 grams, and is never enormously greater outside the interval than within it. The likelihood function $f_N(174.3|\mu, 1)$, on the other hand, has a maximum at $\mu = \bar{x} = 174.3$, at which its height is about .40. At $\mu = 174.3 - 5.0 = 169.3$ or $\mu = 174.3 + 5.0 = 179.3$, the height is very low and it drops sharply as we go further away. This suggests that we can replace $D(\mu)$ by a constant, say $D(\boldsymbol{\mu} = \bar{x})$ to arrive at an approximate posterior density $f_N(\mu|174.3, 1)$.
This happens essentially for two reasons: (1) For $169.3 < \mu < 179.3$, $D(\mu)$ varies so gently that its value at $\bar{x}$, $D(\boldsymbol{\mu} = \bar{x})$ serves well to approximate it. (2) For μ outside the interval (169.3, 179.3), the variations of $D(\mu)$ can be substantial but never so great that the products $D(\mu) \cdot f_N(174.3|\mu, 1)$ will amount to anything, even in aggregate, since $f_N(174.3|\mu, 1)$ is so small. This is suggested schematically in Fig. 8.1.

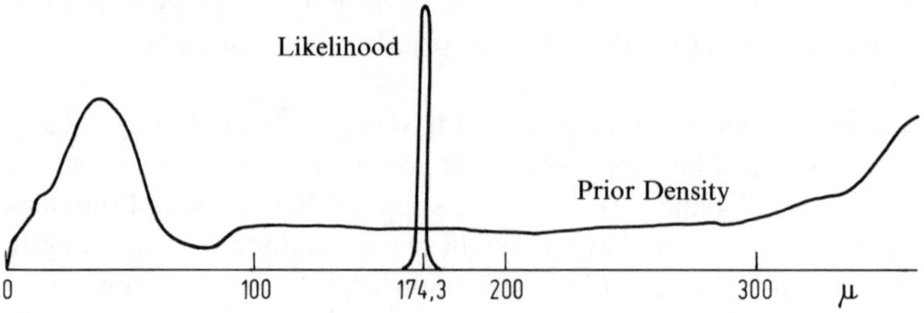

Fig. 8.1: Illustration of Bayes' Theorem for Vague Prior Knowledge.

The scales are *not* the same for the prior and posterior densities. The prior density may continue to be substantial far beyond $\mu = 300$, while the posterior density is concentrated close to $\mu = 174.3$. While the prior density is sketched for specificity from $\mu = 0$ to values larger than 300, it need not be actually assessed. All that is needed are the *partial* assessments described above: these lead to $f_N(\mu|174.3, 1)$ as an approximating posterior distribution without making more detailed commitments. A diffuse prior distribution is not tantamount to "complete ignorance," whatever that expression may mean. First, diffuseness refers only to *local near-uniformity* of the prior distribution. Second, even a strictly uniform distribution of $\boldsymbol{\mu}$ over a very wide interval does not represent complete ignorance. For example, to say that $\boldsymbol{\mu}$ is uniform over the interval .000001 to 1,000,000 is to say that $1/\boldsymbol{\mu}$ is almost surely between one and zero, hardly a statement of ignorance. The key points are these: (1) a diffuse prior distribution is sharply altered by data by comparison to which the prior can be reckoned as diffuse; (2) the shape of the posterior distribution is mainly determined by the likelihood function.

A traditional criticism of the use of a uniform prior distribution goes like this. If μ is uniform, the simple transformations such as μ^2, $1/\mu$, or $\log \mu$ cannot be uniform. In situations in which we feel "diffuse" about one of these, it is argued, we may also feel diffuse about the others. This is true. But "diffuseness" refers to uniformity that is *local* and *approximate*, and the force of the criticism is largely lost. Within short intervals, several plausible functions of μ fall within the range of oscillation specified by a diffuse prior of μ. Or, to put it differently, starting from diffuse priors of μ and several transformations thereof, the posterior distributions would differ only slightly, and the practical differences among these posterior distributions are unimportant.

It is sometimes regarded as a shortcoming of the Bayesian approach that different people may assess prior distributions differently and arrive at different conclusions from the same sample evidence. From the Bayesian point of view this is simply a formal way of describing an inevitable fact of life. The importance of prior judgment is reflected in scientific controversies over the interpretation of what is essentially the same body of statistical evidence.

The theory of stable estimation gives a posterior distribution that can be accepted as a good approximation by all with vague prior judgments, but it is relevant even when no interested party's opinions are vague compared with a given body of evidence, for it gives one possible way to define an open-minded or unprejudiced observer.

8.8 Problems

(1) The following questions refer to the cancer-diagnosis problem. Assume that repeated measurements on the same individual conform to the model of a Bernoulli process.

(a) For what prior probability of cancer $P(C)$ would the intuitive answer $P(C|+) = .95$ be in fact correct?

(b) Using $P(C|+) = .087$ as the prior probability before a second measurement, calculate $P(+|+)$ and $P(C|+,+)$.

(c) In the light of the original prior probabilities, calculate $P(+)$ for the first measurement and $P(+,+)$. Verify that $P(+,+) = P(+) \cdot P(+|+)$.

(d) In the light of the original prior probabilities, calculate $P(C|+,+)$ in one single step and compare with the second result of (b). What general feature of the working of Bayes' theorem is illustrated by this comparison?

(2) A family has two children. As a rough approximation you regard the probability of a male birth in this family as $\frac{1}{2}$ independently of the sex of any previous children. What is the probability that both children are boys under the following conditions?

(a) Given only the probability assessments just stated.
(b) Given that the younger child is a boy.
(c) Given that the older child is a boy.
(d) Given that someone has seen both children and reported that at least one child is a boy.
(e) Given that someone has seen both children and reported that exactly one child is a boy.
(f) Given that someone has seen both children and reported that both children are of the same sex.

(3) The following sampling inspection plan is proposed for an expensive industrial item produced by a process assumed to behave as a Bernoulli process with probability p of a defective item on each trial. If the first item is defective, sampling is to be terminated immediately. Otherwise two additional items will be tested and sampling then terminated.

(a) Is the stopping rule informative or uninformative? Explain.
(b) What is the sampling distribution of **r**, the number of defectives – that is, the distribution of **r** conditional on p?
(c) What is the *unconditional* distribution of **r** given a prior distribution for **p** with parameters $r' = 1$, $n' = 12$?
(d) What is the expected value of the distribution in (c)?
(e) What is the posterior distribution of **p**, if $r = 1$, $n = 1$?

(4) In 25 test runs of a certain plane, 2 gross malfunctions have occurred. Assume that you are willing to regard successive runs as realizations of a Bernoulli process and to regard other evidence as negligible compared to the results of the 25 runs.

(a) How do you assess **p**, the probability of gross malfunction?
(b) What is the probability that there will be a gross malfunction on the next firing?
(c) What is the expected number of trials to the next gross malfunction?
(d) What is the probability that the next three runs will be without gross malfunction?

(5) A certain production process has been in control for a long time, behaving as a Bernoulli process with probability p of a defective item equal to .05. An engineer suggests a modification of the process that he hopes will reduce p below .05. He expresses his judgment about **p** *for the modified process* by a prior distribution with $r = 3$, $n = 100$.

(a) What is the probability that the first unit produced after the modification will be defective?

(b) Suppose now that the first units is in fact defective. What now is the distribution of the post-modification **p**?

(c) What is the posterior probability that the modification has really improved the process?

(d) What is the probability of a defective unit on the second trial?

(6) You will draw nails, with replacement, from a wooden box and measure them in order to obtain information about their average size $\bar{x}$. You will continue measuring until quitting time. Is the stopping informative or noninformative?

(7) A quality controller has assessed a prior pdf $f_b(\mathbf{p}|1,4)$ for the proportion **p** of defective parts in a production lot and plans to take a random sample of five parts with replacement:

(a) indicate his posterior pdf of p given that $\mathbf{r}=0$, $\mathbf{r}=1$, $\mathbf{r}=2$ and $\mathbf{r}=5$ defectives are found?

(b) suppose he has decided not to deliver the part unless his posterior probability that $p \geqq .20$ were less than .25. For what values or **r** would be deliver?

(8) A doctor's inference process can proceed according to Bayes' theorem. The following table is borrowed from Lindley (1971),

Diseases	Prior probabilities $p(\theta_j\|H)$	Likelihoods $p(X\|\theta_j \text{ and } H)$	Prior times likelihood	Posterior probabilities $p(\theta_j\|X \text{ and } H)$
θ_1	.6	.2	.12	.33
θ_2	.3	.6	.18	.50
θ_3	.1	.6	.06	.17
	1.0		.36	1.00

where H represents initial knowledge about a disease, and X denotes the set of symptoms associated with a particular disease.

Discuss the table and show what kinds of inference statements can be drawn.

(9) An economic forecaster predicts that next year's Gross National Product (GNP) will be 1250 billion dollars, adding the qualification that he thinks there is only an even chance that he will be within 10 billion dollars of the correct figure. If his distribution can be adequately described by a normal distribution, what would the parameters of the distribution be?

(10) An economist assesses the prior distribution of the marginal propensity to consume in his country by a normal distribution with mean .90 and standard deviation .05. On the basis of a subsequent small-scale econometric

study in this country, it turns out that for a person whose prior distribution was diffuse, marginal propensity to consume is approximately normally distributed with mean .95 and standard deviation .10. What is the economist's posterior distribution?

(11) You start with a diffuse prior distribution and obtain statistical evidence from a pilot study on a normal process from which you assess a posterior distribution. Then a full-scale study is done. In analyzing the results of this study, can your prior distribution be diffuse? Discuss.

(12) As a result of a large sample survey it is estimated that unemployment this month is 6 per cent of the labor force with a standard error of 0.4 per cent.

(a) If the prior distribution of true unemployment was diffuse, what would be the approximate posterior distribution?

(b) Do you think a diffuse prior distribution would be realistic for a labor economist?

(13) For which particular experimental situations would you consider the configurations illustrated below pertinent?

(a)

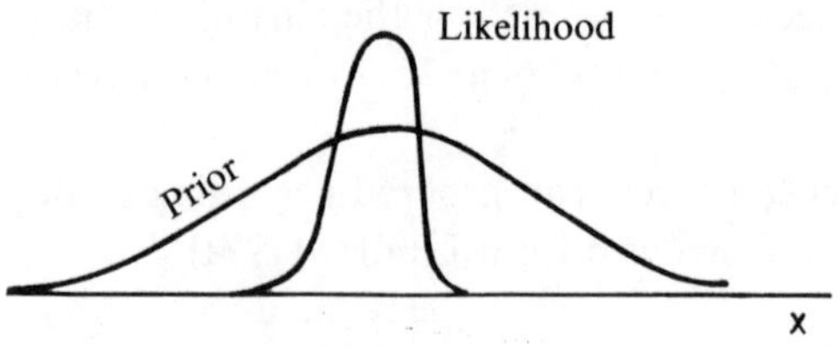

(b)

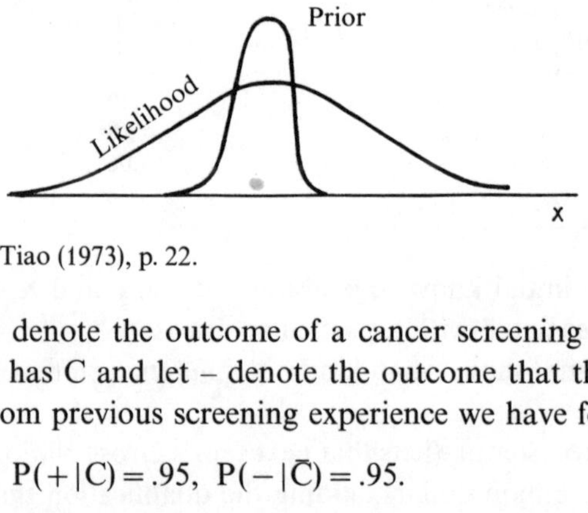

See Box and Tiao (1973), p. 22.

(14) Let + denote the outcome of a cancer screening program reporting the patient has C and let – denote the outcome that the patient does not have C. From previous screening experience we have found

$$P(+|C)=.95, \quad P(-|\bar{C})=.95.$$

Evaluate $P(C|+)$ and $P(C|-)$. For a given prior probability $P(C)=.005$, and after a positive result has been obtained, what is the probability that an individual does not have cancer?

(15) Suppose 1 percent of the population of a country suffers from lung cancer. Let A be the event 'has lung cancer', let $\bar{A}$ be 'has not lung cancer'. Let $P(A)=.01$ and $P(\bar{A})=.99$. Assume imperfect diagnostic test, let B be

the event 'test indicates the disease is present'. Through past experience it has been determined that the conditional probability that the test indicates the disease is present given the person has the disease is $P(B|A) = .97$ (likelihood). The corresponding probability is $P(B|\bar{A}) = .05$. Given that the test has been performed to a randomly selected person, what is the probability that this person actually has the disease, i.e. $P(A|B)$?
(16) A sample of 1000 persons known to have a disease (A), and a sample of 5000 known not to have the disease ($\bar{A}$) are tested. Of those with A 99 percent are detected or show a positive response, while only 5 percent with $\bar{A}$ give a positive response. The results of the experiment are shown in the following table:

	A	$\bar{A}$
+	990(.99)	250(.05)
–	10(.01)	4750(.95)
	1000(1.00)	5000(1.00)

Thus the test has a reasonably good reliability.
Suppose the results of the test can be extrapolated to the entire population, then we have:

$$P(+|A) = .99, \quad P(+|\bar{A}) = .05.$$

Let the prior probability be $P(A) = .005$. If the test is used to detect the disease in members of the general public, what proportion of those having a positive reaction to the test should we expect actually to have the disease? In other words, if a person gives a positive reaction to the test, what is the conditional probability that he has the disease $P(A|+)$?

Suggested Readings

Edwards, Ward, Lindeman, Harold, and Leonard J. Savage: Bayesian Statistical Inference for Psychological Research, *Psychological Review* 70, 1963, esp. pp. 201–208.
Raiffa and Schlaifer, Chaps. 2 and 3, Chaps. 7, 9, 10, 11.
Savage, L. J., and other contributors: The Foundations of Statistical Inference, London and New York, 1962, 20–25.
Barnett, V.: Comparative Statistical Inference, London 1973, Chaps. 1, 6, 7.
De Finetti, B.: Probability, Induction and Statistics, London 1972.
Fisher, R. A.: Smoking and Lung Cancer, Edinburgh 1958.
Guenther, W. C.: Concepts of Statistical Inference, New York 1965.
Huntsberger, D. V.: Elements of Statistical Inference, 2nd ed., Boston 1969.
La Valle, I. H.: An Introduction to Probability, Decision and Inference, New York 1970, Chap. 9.

Lindley, D. V.: Making Decisions, London 1971.
Tanaka, K.: On the Estimation of Genetic Risks, Proc. Japan Acad. 43, 1967, 214–218.
Stange, K.: Bayes-Verfahren, Berlin 1977.
Schlaifer, Chap. 21, Appendix. Chaps. 26, 29, 30.
For discussions of prediction, see Hildreth, Clifford: Bayesian Statisticians and Remote Clients, Econometrica 31, 1963, 422–38; and Roberts, Harry V.: Probabilistic Prediction, Journal of the American Statistical Association 60, 1965, 50–62.
Aitchison, J. and J. Dunsmore: Statistical Prediction Analysis, Cambridge 1975.

9. Information, Inference and Decision

9*1 Introduction

In recent years a considerable amount of work has been done on concepts and measures of information within and beyond the fields of engineering and mathematics.

In this chapter an attempt is made to trace the main sources and motivations of various approaches to conceptualize and measure information. The development so far showed that information may explain different things in different contexts, hence it will not make sense to apply a general measure of information to practical situations in which information obtains different meanings.

We will start in Sec. 9*2 by exhibiting the structure of the Shannon-Wiener theory of information, then, in Sec. 8*3, we turn to approaches that give axiomatizations of entropy and information measures without using probability measures. Recently, also A.N. Kolmogorov (1965, 1967) has shown that the basic information-theoretic concepts can be formulated without recourse to probability theory. In Secs. 9*4–9*7 we are concerned with 'information provided by experiments' as used in statistical decision theory. The concept originated in works of D. Blackwell (1953), Blackwell and Girshick (1954) and is now extensively used in the statistical decision literature as well as in the related literature in economics. In Sec. 9*8 some measures of information arising in statistical decisions, based on the notion of a metric as informational distance, are suggested. Secs. 9*9–9*11 cover topics on the *payoff-relevant* character of information in statistical decision rules, as developed and emphasized, among others, by H. Raiffa and R. Schlaifer (1961).

9*2 The Structure of Information Theory

Shannon's Problem. The abstract problem of information theory established by C. E. Shannon (1949) and in a somewhat different form by N. Wiener (1948) is this: Given a probability space $(S, \mathcal{S}, P)$, where S denotes the space of elementary events (basic space), $\mathcal{S}$ a σ-algebra of subsets of S and P a probability measure on $\mathcal{S}$, how much information do we receive about a (randomly selected) point $s \in S$ by being informed that s is in some subset A of S. It is relatively easy to see that the answer depends on the dimension or measure of A, given in terms of the probability measure P attached to A. Hence an information measure is a real-valued set function on $\mathcal{S}$ defined by

$$F[P(A)] = I \circ P(A) = I_P(A) \text{ for any } A \in \mathscr{S},$$

where F denotes some appropriate monotonic transformation. Conceptually, information adopts here the nature of a surprise value or unexpectedness. In this context, note, that I_P is a measurable mapping from $\mathscr{S}$ onto $[0, \infty]$ composed of the measurable mappings $P: \mathscr{S} \to [0, 1]$ and $I: [0, 1] \to [0, +\infty]$, with a commutative property. Hence we have the following commutative diagram:

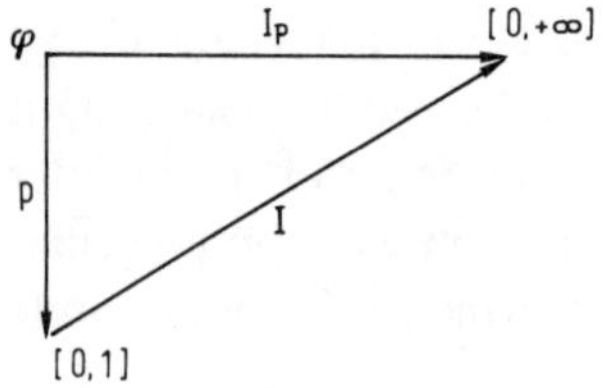

$I \circ P = I_P$ with I being continuous. It is also natural to assume that I_P is nonnegative and continuous.

Moreover, for any two probabilistically independent events A, $B \in \mathscr{S}$, we have $A \perp\!\!\!\perp B \Rightarrow I_P(A \cap B) = I_P(A) + I_P(B)$.

Now it has been shown by Shannon that I_P satisfies the additive representation if it can be represented by $I_P(A) = -c \log_2 P(A)$, where c is any positive real constant (sometimes called Boltzmann's constant in analogy to thermodynamics).

More generally, let $\pi = \{A_i\}_{i=1}^n$ be an n-fold uniform partition into finitely many equiprobable events, sometimes referred to as an experiment. Then the natural question arises what would be the average amount of information, called the entropy H_P with respect to a given partition π. This is computed as

$$(*)\ H_P(\pi) = \sum_{A \in \pi} P(A) \cdot I_P(A), \text{ and } I_P(A) = -\log_2 P(A),$$

if we choose c, by convention, as unit of measurement.

Let Π be the set of all possible partitions of S. The diagram

commutes, that is $H \circ (P, P, \ldots, P) = H_P$, and H is continuous.

Furthermore, for every $A \in \Pi$ we have $H(\{A, \bar{A}\}) = 1$ if $P(A) = P(\bar{A})$, and $H([B|A \cap B, \bar{A} \cap B]\Pi) = H(\Pi) + P(B) \cdot H(\{A, \bar{A}\})$ if $A \perp\!\!\!\perp B$, where A, $B \in \mathscr{S}$ and $[B|A \cap B, \bar{A} \cap B]\Pi$ is the conditional experiment resulting of replacing B in the partition Π by two disjoint events $A \cap B$, $\bar{A} \cap B$. It has been shown by D.K. Fadeev (1958) using P. Erdös' (1946) number-theoretic lemma on additive arithmetic functions that the only function H_P satisfying the above conditions is of the form (*).

The entropy may be interpreted in various ways, either as an average measure of uncertainty removed or as an average measure of information conveyed.

Which interpretation one prefers over the other is irrelevant – as will be clear in the sequel. Thus we see that there is a complete correspondence between uncertainty and information. The definition of information is here naturally tied up to probability, only the existence of the latter enables the measurement of the former.

If we say, roughly, that we have gained information when we know something *now* that we didn't know before, then it actually means that our uncertainty expressed in terms of probability at one instance of time has been removed at a later instance of time – according to whether the event has occurred or has not occurred. Introducing the notion of a random experiment in a statistical context we may talk about uncertainty before an experiment is carried out, at a moment where we have not yet observed anything, and we may talk about information after having performed the experiment. Sometimes Shannon's measure of information has been termed probabilistic information or selective information (Mackay (1969)). There are several approaches (see Renyi (1961), and Kolmogorov (1967)) how to establish the measure H_P, either on pragmatic grounds arising from coding theory or, in an axiomatic way or by starting with the notion of an invariant from ergodic theory. Interestingly, H_P may even result from gambling theory (Kelly (1956)). Shannon's original axioms for the entropy measure have been replaced several times subsequently by weaker conditions. The weakest set of axioms known so far seems to be that given by P.M. Lee (1964). Mathematically, the representation of information involves a study of particular classes of functional equations.

As A.N. Kolmogorov (1965) remarked the probabilistic approach seems appropriate for describing and predicting the transmission of (uniform) mass information over (physically bounded) communication channels $C|H$ as illustrated by the following scheme:

$$\mathbf{x}_1, \mathbf{x}_2, \ldots, \mathbf{x}_n \xrightarrow[\text{encoding}]{} \boxed{\text{channel}} \xrightarrow[\text{decoding}]{}$$

where $\mathbf{x}_1, \mathbf{x}_2, \ldots, \mathbf{x}_n$ is a well-defined sequence of random variables (information source). Such kinds of problems are of fundamental importance in the engineering and physical sciences where probability measures can roughly be identified experimentally as limiting frequencies for a sufficiently long (precisely infinite) sequence of trials forming a collective in the sense of von Mises. But what sense does it make to talk about the entropy of receiving messages from a certain novel of Tolstoi, or about the experiments getting married once, twice or even three times?

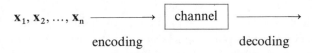

In other words, can we talk about entropy in the sense of Shannon's theory if we do not have a well-established random sequence forming our information source, if events are not repeatable? Philosophers and linguists consider as a basic flaw of Shannon's measure the fact that the probability measure defined is obviously confined to a frequency interpretation. Hence, to the same extent as probability concepts gave rise to extensive discussions up to recent time probabilistic information theory is affected by these discussions concerning the adequate application of the underlying probability concept (see chap. 3*).

The motivation for Carnap and Bar-Hillel (1964) is somewhat different from the theory of transmission of uniform mass information, e.g. the question is how can we evaluate the information provided by a sentence structure which defies representation in a random sequence. In the context of semantic information the concept of an 'ideal receiver' as one with a perfect memory plays a much similar role as that of an ideal 'rational person' assumed in the theory of logical probability due to Carnap.

As a matter of fact it turns out that semantic information theory in the sense of Carnap and Bar-Hillel leads to similar properties as Shannon's entropy measure, however, relative frequences are replaced by logical probabilities (degree of confirmation). If h represents a hypothesis, e evidence, thus c(h, e) the degree of confirmation of a hypothesis h given the evidence e, then by characterizing h as message and e as knowledge, the information received from h given e is the greater the more improbable we consider h given e. This again lends itself to the interpretation of information as a surprise value, i.e. information provided by a logical true sentence is zero, and that of a logically false sentence is infinity.

The question then naturally comes up as to which extent one can base a theory of prediction on a theory of information that uses a rather restrictive probability concept for real-life situations. This concept only applies to carefully prepared situations of well shuffled decks of playing cards, controlled casts of dice and in random sampling.

The problem to achieve rational predictions or making inferences from data has plagued numerous philosophers since D. Hume (see H. Jeffreys (1961)), and this has been reconsidered more recently. It has given rise to a logical theory of probability predominantely based on *inductive inference.* However, this theory incorporated evidence as conditional probability statements, but it did not show the links between information processing (in the human mind) and probability evaluation. Information only comes in by repeatedly revising conditional probability statements as, for instance, propagated by the Bayesian approach in statistical decision theory. But treatment of information processing is essential for any theory of prediction, and it is genuine for any kind of human judgment. Of course, we cannot dispense with probabilities in a general theory of prediction, for if we can, any such theory would be either completely deterministic or arbitrary.

In fact, what we might do is to build a theory of probability on the basis of a completely separate theory of information by generating 'qualitative information', and giving conditions under which numerical probabilities can be established. This procedure would entail a satisfactory theory of prediction (see Appendix).
Of course, probabilitistic information theory, as it stands now, will continue to play a major role in those circumstances in which it makes sense to talk about information in a random sequence which is perfectly legitimate under conditions stated by Kolmogorov.
However, its value for general applications beyond those anticipated by Shannon appears to be rather limited.

9.*3 Information without Probability

In recent years some information theorists were not completely satisfied with probabilistic information theory. The motivation for their dissatisfaction was, of course, different from that of statisticians and philosophers. Although the axiomatics of information theory was considerably refined and weakened, the natural question was raised whether one could develop an information theory without involving the concept of probability (distributions), at least in the basic axiomatic structure. The contribution by R.S. Ingarden and K. Urbanik (1962) answered this question affirmatively. It was the first step to challenge the hitherto accepted view-point that information theory is a branch of probability theory which is also reflected in the organization of textbooks on probability theory. Interestingly enough, the basic motivation evolved from certain experimental situations in physics where it appeared to be meaningful in some situations to talk about information regarding the state of a system (e.g. the entropy of some macroscopic system) although its probability distribution is not known.
Formally, Ingarden and Urbanik achieve to define H (the entropy) directly on a pseudo-metric space of finite Boolean rings (of events) satisfying convenient properties of monotonicity and continuity. A. Renyi (1965) claimed that these results can be achieved by using Shannon's measure in terms of a uniquely defined conditional probability measure which follows from the Ingarden-Urbanik technique so that defining information without probability inevitably leads to introducing probability at a later stage. Renyi's straight-forward conclusion is that the information cannot be separated from probability. However, this misses the real point. First of all, as stated before, in some experimental situations it makes more sense to start with some basic knowledge, experience, evidence of the experimenter on the state or movement of a system (physical, biological or any system which is sub-

ject to experimental control) rather than specifying probabilities in terms of which information should be defined. Second, in a more general context of human decision making or drawing inferences from observations it is often the case that information processing precedes probability evaluations in betting on the future and making predictions on uncertain events. Most reasonable persons would deny that situations of this kind are comparable or even identical with random experiments – as probabilistic information theory does suggest.

Significant work has also been done by J. Kampé de Fériet and B. Forte (see Kampé de Fériet (1970) for a summary and exposition of his results) on constructing information measures without using probabilities. Information is defined as a σ-additive, nonnegative measure (invariant with respect to translations) on a monotone class of events $\mathscr{S}$, retaining its customary nature of 'surprise value' as in probabilistic information theory. The system basically rests on three assumptions:

(1) $$I: \mathscr{S} \to \bar{R}^*, \text{ where } \bar{R}^* \text{ is the extended real line } [0, \infty].$$

The second is a monotonicity assumption in the form:

(2) $$[(A, B) \in \mathscr{S} \times \mathscr{S}, B \subset A] \Rightarrow I(A) \leqq I(B), \ A, B \in \mathscr{S}.$$

Hence, given the zero element o and the unit element S in φ, we have naturally for any $A \in \mathscr{S}$

$$O \leqq I(S) = \operatorname*{Inf}_{A \in \mathscr{S}} I(A) \leqq \operatorname*{Sup}_{A \in \mathscr{S}} I(A) = I(o) \leqq \infty.$$

(2) already suggests the nature of information as a 'surprise value', in particular $I(S) = I(o) = +\infty$, so that information derived from the sure event is zero, the information derived from the impossible event, provided it happens to occur ('surprise'), is infinite.

An additional assumption imposes the condition of monotone continuity, i.e. for a *countable sequence* of events $\{A_n, n = 1, 2, \ldots\}$ we have either

(3) $$A_n \subset A_{n+1} \Rightarrow A = \bigcup_1^\infty A_n \in \mathscr{S} \quad \text{or}$$

$$A_{n+1} \subset A_n \Rightarrow A = \bigcup_1^\infty A_n \in \mathscr{S}$$

which implies, for information defined, as in (1) and (2):

$$[A_n \in \mathscr{S}, A_n \uparrow A] \Rightarrow I(A_n) \downarrow I(A)$$

$$[A_n \in \mathscr{S}, A_n \downarrow A] \Rightarrow I(A_n) \uparrow I(A),$$ known as monotone sequential continuity.

In particular, we have a similar property (as in probabilistic information theory), i.e. for probabilistically independent pairs of events $A_n \in \mathcal{S}$, $n = 1, 2, \ldots$:

$$I(\bigcap_1^\infty A_n) = \sum_1^\infty I(A_n).$$

An immediate consequence of assumption (2) is that information is of Inf-type, e.g. $I(A \cup B) \leqq \text{Inf}[I(A), I(B)]\, A, B \in \mathcal{S}$ so that $I(A \cup B) = F[I(A), I(B)]$ where F is a suitable monotone function. This motivates the introduction of a *partial operation* T of composition $I(A)TI(B) = F[I(A), I(B)]$ which is familiar from the theory of *partially ordered algebras* and its representation by functional equations. Since $\mathcal{S}$ can be completed to a σ-algebra we have $I[\bigcup_1^\infty A_n] = \overset{\infty}{\underset{1}{T}}\ I(A_n)$, $A_n \in \mathcal{S}$, $\bigcap_1^\infty A_n = o$, hence T is σ-composable. T then satisfies well-known algebraic properties for defining an abelian semigroup (see Fuchs (1963), Chap. 10). It is not difficult to show the connection between information measure and the underlying algebraic structure.

Let T be defined here in terms of the union $\cup$, and define a dual operation T* in terms of intersection $\cap$. The presentation of partial operations in terms of the more familiar operations $\cup$ and $\cap$ proves to be convenient in case of forming ordered groups generated by T. We require that the existence of T implies a unique T*, and (T*)* = T, by definition.

The following properties hold for any $A, B \in \mathcal{S}$, T defined, and provided ATB or AT*B exist in $\mathcal{S}$.

P.1: $A \in \mathcal{S} \Rightarrow [AT^*A = A \ \&\ ATA = A]$ for all $A \in \mathcal{S}$.

P.2: ATB = BTA, and dually for T* for all $A, B \in \mathcal{S}$. (commutativity)

P.3: (ATB)TC = AT(BTC), for all $A, B, C \in \mathcal{S}$, and dually for T*. (associativity)

P.4: $ATB \Rightarrow AT^*(ATB) = AT(AT^*B)$ and dually for T* (distributivity)

Define $AT^*B \Leftrightarrow A \leqq\cdot B$ and '$\leqq\cdot$' means 'not more probable than', a relation of qualitative probability.

Then it is relatively easy to see that the properties P.1–P.4 will make $\mathcal{S}$ a lattice-ordered algebra which is also distributive, and hence a Boolean algebra endowed with a binary relation $\leqq\cdot$.

Note that it presents no great difficulties to invoke continuity properties for T* so that $\mathcal{S}$ becomes a topological Boolean algebra (in the order topology). Since T is defined in terms of $\cup$ it is then easy to verify that monotone continuity is equivalent to continuity of the partial operation T and any information measure defined is σ-additive on $\mathcal{S}$.

It is therefore interesting to note here that the introduction of a partial operation suggests certain assumptions about the qualitative ordering in a

partially ordered algebra so that information measures are compatible with this ordering. In terms of this construction it would then appeal to be most natural to present information measures as Boolean homomorphisms on $\mathscr{S}$ (see Sikorski (1964)).
Finally, we remark that due to the nature of information as a 'surprise value' the compatible information measure is order-reversing (antitone) w.r.t. qualitative probability rather than order-preserving (isotone).
The dual properties of T and T* can be shown in the representation of '$\leqq\cdot$' in $\mathscr{S}$ by (information) measures. Since T is commutative it follows that $I(A)TI(B) = I(ATB) = T(I(A), I(B))$, let $I(A)TI(B) \Leftrightarrow I(A) \geqq I(B)$. As defined $AT^*B \Leftrightarrow A \leqq\cdot B \Leftrightarrow A \subseteqq B$ in this case yielding $AT^*B = A$, and conditions for T* are reformulations of axioms for a partial order $\leqq\cdot$. Then $I(ATB) = I(A)TI(B) \Leftrightarrow I(A) \leqq I(B) \Leftrightarrow AT^*B$, by strict compatibility with $A \leqq\cdot B$.

9.*4 Information in Statistical Decision Theory

The structure of a statistical game can be outlined as follows. The statistician plays a game against nature, at his disposal is a class A of possible actions which he can take (or decisions he can make) in view of the unknown state of nature (nature's pure strategy) $s \in S$. (By a change of notation we now consider S as the set of states of nature.)
He may decide to take an action without experimentation (e.g. without 'spying' on nature's strategies) and for doing this may incur a numerical loss $L(s, a)$. The possibility of performing experiments does exist, thus reducing the loss by gaing at least partial information about s. Therefore the concept of information in this context is naturally tied up with payoff-relevance, any bits of information that do not reduce the loss are considered irrelevant.
What prevents the statistician of getting full knowledge of s is the cost of experiments. This cost may assume specific functional forms, but, in general, is considered to be proportional to the number of experiments. Technical definitions are needed in order to look at the general structure of a statistical game. Let Z be the space of outcomes of an experiment, then a function p is defined on $Z \times S$ such that for a fixed $s \in S$ p_s is a probability distribution. The triple $\mathscr{Z} = (Z, S, p)$ is sometimes referred to as the sample space, in general, one does not distinguish between $\mathscr{Z}$ and Z and both may refer to sample spaces. For every subset $A \subset Z$, the probability of the event A is given by

$$P_s(A) = \sum_{z \in A} p_s(z),$$

and P satisfies all properties of a probability measure. A function $d \in D$,

defined on Z mapping $Z \xrightarrow{\text{into}} A$ is called a decision function such that $d(z) = a$.
A risk function is represented by expected loss, i.e. a function R on $S \times D$:

$$R(s, d) = \sum_{z \in Z} L(s, d(z)) p_s(z) = E[L(s, d(z))].$$

Now a *mixed* or *randomized* strategy for nature is the same as a prior probability distribution (for the statistician) on the set of states of nature S, denoted by $\mu \in \mathcal{M}$. The problem of collecting information in a statistical game may be generally posed as follows: Does there exist a partition of Z such that every possible risk attainable with a complete knowledge of $z \in Z$ is also attainable with only the information that z belongs to a set of this partition? Such partitions, if they exist, are as informative as the entire sample space. They are given by the principle of sufficiency.
We are concerned with information provided by an experiment. An experiment **x** is completely described by a random variable associated with the sample space (Z, S, p) giving rise to a set of conditional probability distributions for every possible parameter (state of nature) $s \in S$. **x** might be of fixed sample size or of a sequential type where the experimenter may collect observations finitely many times. To set up the problem assume you (the experimenter, the statistician or generally the decision-maker) are confronted with an uncertain situation where you wish to know about the true value of a parameter (state of nature) $s \in S$. Of course you can make some wild guesses, but you can only gain true knowledge about the true state by experimentation. Let μ be some prior probability distribution of the true state s which indicates the amount of uncertainty or ignorance on your part. (Adopt a Bayesian viewpoint than such μ always exists and is non-null.)
Then the information provided by **x** may be verbally expressed as the difference between the amount of uncertainty you attach to the prior distribution and that amount of your expected uncertainty of the posterior distribution (after having performed **x**), i.e. it reflects the residual value of your uncertainty (reduced).
More technically, let $\mathcal{M}$ be the set of prior probability distributions over S (i.e. the space of randomized strategies for nature), define u as a nonnegative, real-valued measurable function on $\mathcal{M}$ which for obvious reasons should be concave, i.e. decreasing with increasing observations. Then $u(\mu)$ represents the amount of your uncertainty (before experimentation) when your distribution over S is μ. In some cases the uncertainty function u is just equivalent to a risk function in a statistical decision problem, in other cases it can be directly assigned. Under specific circumstances it can be identified with the entropy function or can assume some other form that is compatible with its properties of nonnegativity and concavity. Now performing **x** and observing

values of **x** you may specify a posterior distribution $\phi(\mathbf{x})$, then your measure of information I is determined by

$$I(\mathbf{x}, \mu, u) = u(\mu) - E[u(\phi(\mathbf{x}))|\mu]$$

where $\phi(\mathbf{x})$ is usually obtained by an appropriate application of the well-known Bayes' theorem to get the posterior distribution (see Blackwell & Girshick (1954), de Groot (1970)).
It is usually assumed for reasons of non-triviality that most experiments provide information and that any experiment being more informative than another is also preferable to the other. Therefore, for any given uncertainty function, I is nonnegative, and also for reasons of convervnience, continuous. As we clearly recognize this measure of information provided by an experiment relative to the specification of u and μ naturally evolves from a model of statistical decision. Usually the determination of the uncertainty function hinges upon the loss structure in a statistical game, this becomes clear when we describe comparisons of experiments according to informativeness.

9. *5 Comparison of Information

In the relevant literature of statistical decision theory comparison of experiments are sometimes confined to those which can be represented by Markov matrices (in this context as information matrices). This is very natural in terms of viewing it in the context of a statistical game. Assume the experiment E produces N distinct values $e_1, \ldots, e_N$ (signals, observations) and let be $S = (s_1, \ldots, s_n)$. Then the experiment E can be represented by an $n \times N$ Markov matrix $P = (p_{ij})$ associated to the sample space (Z, S, p) such that $p_{ij} = P_{s_i}(\{s: E(z) = e_j\})$, $p_{ij} \geqq 0$ and $\sum_j p_{ij} = 1$ for each i.
Henceforward, for reasons of simplicity, we adopt an earlier definition of D. Blackwell (1953) in terms of defining experiments as random variables. Incidentally, Blackwell's definition is one of the first better known definitions of 'comparative informativeness' in the context of statistical decision theory. Every experiment E associated to a sample space generates a risk function. Then, according to Blackwell, an experiment E is *more informative* ($>$) than another experiment E′ (the set of experiments being partially ordered) if the risk obtained from E is at least obtainable also from E′, $E > E' \Leftrightarrow R(E) \leqq R(E')$. In other words, the numerical risk for E′ is at least as large as that of E. If the distribution over S is known then comparative informativeness hinges upon the loss structure of the decision problem. This immediately gives rise to an economic view on the evaluation of information. There were further generalizations and improvements of Blackwell's results in recent years, in particular, in connection with the foundations of statistical inference

('informative inference') (see A. Birnbaum (1961)); these results give the main motivations for economic studies on the subject. This view has been originated and consistently pursued by J. Marschak (1971). His 'value of information' $V(\eta)$ (attached to experiment η) w.r.t. any probability distribution μ over S (his space of events uncontrollable to the decision maker) and his benefit function $b: S \times A \to Re$ is just the converse value of Blackwell's risk R(E), this is due to the fact that economists prefer to talk about benefit or utility, whereas statisticians are more pessimistic and talk about losses. Note, again, that the risk function is completely specified by a probability distribution over S and a loss function on $S \times A$.

One can easily see the strong agreement between information provided by an experiment and the value of information by considering an experiment as a Markov matrix. In this case null-information corresponds to identical rows in the Markov matrix, i.e. any observations made through an experiment are independent of any state of nature.

Accordingly, the risk function obtained by the less informative experiment is larger in value than the risk function obtained by the more informative experiment. It is obvious that the dual statement holds if we deal with an economist's benefit function instead of a statistician's loss function.

We have learned of different, but interrelated characterizations of an experiment, either as a partition of Z, as a random variable and in particular as a Markov matrix. Comparative informativeness in terms of partitions of Z given by the principle of sufficiency has also been studied by Blackwell and Girschick (1954).

Let **x** and **y** be two experiments whose values are in the sample spaces, denoted by $Z_{\mathbf{x}}$ and $Z_{\mathbf{y}}$, respectively.

Then experiment **y** is sufficient for experiment **x** if there exists a nonnegative function h on the product space $Z_{\mathbf{x}} \times Z_{\mathbf{y}}$ satisfying the following relations

(i) $$f_{\mathbf{x}}(x \mid s) = \int_{Z_{\mathbf{y}}} h(x, y)\, f_{\mathbf{y}}(y \mid s)\, d\mu(y) \quad \text{for } s \in S \text{ and } x \in Z_{\mathbf{x}},$$

(ii) $$\int_{Z_{\mathbf{x}}} h(x, y)\, d\mu(x) = 1 \quad \text{for } y \in Z_{\mathbf{y}}$$

(iii) $$0 < \int_{Z_{\mathbf{y}}} h(x, y)\, d\mu(y) < \infty \quad \text{for } x \in Z_{\mathbf{y}}.$$

h is a stochastic transformation from **y** to **x**. For each fixed value $y \in Z_{\mathbf{y}}$ the function $h(\cdot, y)$ is a *generalized probability density function* on $Z_{\mathbf{x}}$. Since this function does not involve the parameter s, a point $x \in Z_{\mathbf{x}}$ could be generated according to the generalized probability density function by means of an auxiliary randomization.

Thus, **y** is sufficient for **x**, if regardless of the value of the parameter s, an observation on **y** and an auxiliary randomization make it possible to generate

a random variable which has the same distribution as **x**. The integrability condition on h in (iii) is introduced for technical convenience only.
If **y** is sufficient for **x** then the statistician is strongly advised not to perform the experiment **x** when **y** is available. In fact, one can prove that the sufficient experiment **y** must be at least as informative as the experiment **x**.
Suppose that experiment **y** *is sufficient for the experiment* **x**. *Then, for any uncertainty function* u *and any posterior distribution* ϕ

$$E[u(\phi(\mathbf{x})] \geqq E[u(\phi(\mathbf{y}))]$$

The proof of this result is straight-forward and can be found in M. de Groot (1970).

9.*6 Economizing Information

Despite strong trends in economics and related behavioral science in recent years to use basic results of information theory for their purpose some serious doubts have been expressed concerning the usefulness of H_p for application in economics and for decision-making in general.* Among others, J. Marschak (1971) argues that Shannon's entropy does not tell us anything about the benefit of transmitting information since it assumes equal penalty for all communication errors. What he instead has in mind is a concept of behavioral information processing in an economic system, in particular as related to an economic theory of teams (Marschak and Radner (1972)). From an economic viewpoint information may be regarded as a particular kind of commodity which will be traded at a certain price yielding benefits for consumers and causing costs for producers. Hence, the economic theory of information (still in its infancy) is an appropriate modification of the approach used in statistical decision theory. To put it in other terms, here we are interested in the economic aspect of usefulness of information (based on some kind of utility or loss function) rather than in the (original) engineering viewpoint of transmitting and controlling information flows through a large (noisy or noiseless) communication channel. As a digression, more recently, some information theorists tried to remedy the flaw or restrictiveness of 'equal penalty of all communication errors' by weighing entropy in terms

* R.A. Howard (1966) has put it this way: '... If losing all your assets in the stock market and having whale steak for supper, then the information associated with the occurrence of either event is the same. Attempts to apply Shannon's information theory to problems beyond communications have, in large, come to grief. The failure of these attempts could have been predicted because no theory that involves just the probabilities of outcomes without considering their consequences could possibly be adequate in describing the importance of uncertainty to a decision maker.'

of utility. For any partition π of Z they attach to every $A \in \pi$ a utility such that the entropy is given by $H(\pi) = \sum_{A \in \pi} U(A) \cdot P(A) \cdot I_p(A)$. U(A) satisfies well-known properties of expected utility, i.e. it is for a given preference pattern on π, unique up to positive linear transformations. It is clear that this proposed measure makes sense if the amount of information to be transmitted through a channel exceeds its upper (physical) bound so that a subjective evaluation procedure (via a utility function) reduces irrelevant information. In this approach there is no obvious relationship between the utility of the message and the information derived from the message, and therefore both should be measured separately. Let p_1 be the message 'you will receive five dollars', and let p_2 be 'you will receive five dollars and you will be shot'. Clearly, p_2 is at least as informative as p_1 but p_2 is hardly as desirable as p_1. One could even attach utility to the sources so that the encoder could select only those sources which are useful to the encoder (see Longo (1972)). The approach has been generalized by introducing explicitly a cost function, that is really a tradeoff function being dependent on the length of code words associated to the message (letter) and on the utility of the message. Clearly, the cost is increasing in the first variable but decreasing in the second. The tradeoff function is uniquely fixed as soon as the utility and the cost of coding are determined.

Assessment of the tradeoff and utility function is treated separately. An optimization principle is involved by minimizing the expected tradeoff so determined.

Let us now sketch the basic ingredients of Marschak's approach as discussed in detail by Marschak (1971).

Information processing is defined as $P = \langle X, Y, \eta, \kappa, \tau \rangle$, where X is a set of inputs, Y is a set of outputs, η a transformation from X to Y, κ is a cost function on X, and τ a time-delay function on X. If you consider, as Marschak does, information as an economic good there is sufficient motivation for looking at the economic system as a mechanism (machine), producing and processing information over time which involves costs and delays. In this respect, information processing is indistinguishable from the processing of physical commodities in, say, a transportation network.

On the other hand, Marschak's approach is firmly embedded in the general statistical decision model. We might then conceive η as a stochastic transformation from the random set X (the space of events, non-controllable to the decision-maker) to the random set Y (the space of available and feasible decision acts), $\eta: X \to Y$ then establishes a strategy (action). Up to now we have described the particular case of a one-link processing chain, more generally, we may conceive a (time) sequence of information processing $P^1, \ldots, P^N$ such that for every $n = 1, \ldots, N$ we write $P^n = \langle X^n, X^{n-1}, \eta^n, \ldots \rangle$ and $\eta^1: X^1 \to X^2, \ldots, \eta^{n-1}: X^{N-1} \to X^N$ describe experiments with nature, for example. Hence $X^2, \ldots, X^N$ may be referred to as sets of observations or data, whereas $\eta^n: X^N \to X^{N+1}$ forms a strategy of the decision-maker. A chain of information processing is an information system.

9*7 Decision Theory and Information Algebras

In this section we study the general mathematical background of information structures and link it to the design of decision theory. The content of information is algebraic or qualitative and the approach resembles that taken in Gottinger (1973). At the start, let us consider two variables x and y ranging over two finite sets X and Y. Suppose there exists a many-to-one mapping $\eta: X \to Y$ so that $\eta(x) = y$ and $\eta^{-1}(y)$ exists and constitutes a subset of X. In the context of decision theory η would be called an 'information function' or 'information structure', and X denotes the set of true states of the environment and past history (available to the decision-maker or organization) and Y denotes the set of alternative signals. Such information structures can be generated sequentially so that $(\eta_0, \eta_1, \eta_2, \ldots)$ represents a system of information processing, or processing chain according to Marschak (1971) (In particular, η_0 might denote the information structure generated by observation of nature, and $\eta_1, \eta_2, \ldots$ constitutes a sequence of information generated by group communication.)

Thus the knowledge of x uniquely determines the value of y but this does not hold vice versa.

It is clear that every information structure η induces a partition of X into a class of mutually exclusive subsets each of which is associated with a different y. The knowledge of y enables us to distinguish between those elements of X which belong to different subsets but not between elements within some particular subset.

Accordingly, we could say that y is *less* (or *not more*) *informative* than x depending on whether x does not (or does belong) to some subset $\eta^{-1}(y)$ in X. In other words, the relation of 'being not more informative than' (qualitative information) is induced by the partition on X.

This construction ensures us of the fact that the existence of a state (or states) could only be informative if we get the message about the existence of this state.

Methodologically, we have two ways open to construct an algebra of information sets given the previous considerations. Either we take 'qualitative information' as a primitive concept, satisfying certain order properties, and see what kinds of structural properties could be derived. Such an approach has been pursued by Gottinger (1973).

Or we could ask the question what kinds of algebraic structures are compatible with qualitative information. Certain kinds of algebraic structures are quite straightforward, for example, any partial algebra defined in terms of partial operations can be converted to a partially ordered set and vice versa (see L. Fuchs (1963)). We will consider this problem next.

We consider all subsets of X for which operations of union ($\cup$), interesection ($\cap$) and complementation ($-$) are defined. This class of subsets of X closed under these operations forms an algebra (field) of sets (which need not be restricted to the finite case and could become a σ-algebra), denoted by $\mathscr{X}$. $\mathscr{X}$ contains the empty set $\emptyset$ and the universal set X. Consider those subsets of X determined by $\eta^{-1}(y)$ for all y which form a particular algebra $\mathscr{A}$. A could be derived from (say) $\mathscr{X}$ in such a way that all possible operations of $\cup$, $\cap$ and $-$ are preserved for elements of A. Clearly then $\mathscr{X}$ 'covers' A, written $\mathscr{X} \supset \mathscr{A}$, and $\mathscr{A}$ is a subalgebra of $\mathscr{X}$. Then $\mathscr{A}$ contains all 'relevant' information for the problem at hand.

The relevance of information received is hence provided by the choice of the information structure η, more 'relevant' information can only be received by an appropriate choice of η' inducing a 'finer' partition than the choice of η, hence partitions of X must be η-preserving. Suppose, η' is defined on $\mathscr{X}$ such that $\eta'^{-1}(y_1 = 0) = A$, $\eta'^{-1}(y_2 = 0) = B$, $\eta'^{-1}(y_3 = 1) = C$, then clearly (and intuitively plausible) η' generates a finer partition on X than does η given the information algebra $\mathscr{X}$ and for any fixed message set Y. The last qualification is essential, for suppose a message set Y is isomorphic to an action set A, i.e. there exist, in one-to-one assignment, as many different messages as there are actions. Then Y could be split into as many pieces as we wish, and via η^{-1} we could have an appropriately fine partition of X. Hence, by comparing information structures in terms of their information content it is essential to specify the underlying message set. It should be explicitly mentioned here, in relation to Marschak's and Radner's work (1972) that the degree of fineness of information structures (i.e. those information structures which induce distinguishably fine partitions of X) implies a comparative relation of being 'not more informative than' (i.e. the finer the partition of X the more information is carried by the information structure inducing this partition). A theorem due to Radner and Marschak (1972, p. 54) then says that for a given best decision function the expected payoff for the information structure η' is at least as large as that for η. This theorem relates qualitative information to payoff relevance.

Summarizing, we could say that the function η induces a partition of the set X which is coarser than the original partition. The coarseness is reflected by the fact that X is a richer collection of subsets than $\mathscr{A}$ and $\mathscr{X}$ 'covers' $\mathscr{A}$. In other words, η generates a subalgebra $\mathscr{A}$ in $\mathscr{X}$ and $\mathscr{X}$ is finer than $\mathscr{A}$, or $\mathscr{A}$ is nested in $\mathscr{X}$. Two pieces of information are *equivalent* if their underlying algebras are the same or if they are nested in each other (mutually nested).

The situation becomes more complicated when we are dealing with the situation where more than one agent (e.g. nature) could choose actions and therefore generate information.

Consider a simple example where $x = (x_1, x_2, x_3)$, not necessarily ordered this way, with subscripts referring to the decision-makers. Each variable x_i can assume values 1 or 0, i.e.. only binary information is provided. Suppose it happens that x_1 will appear first and depending on whether $x_1 = 0$ or 1, x_2 or x_3 will become the second or third state variable. The set of possible x, X, then consists of the set $\{[000], [001], \ldots, [110], [111]\}$, where $[\cdots]$ denotes the state sets over all possible permutations of the variables.

$$\mathscr{X} = \{\emptyset, [000], [001], \ldots, [111], [000] + [001], \ldots, [000] + \\ + [111], \ldots, [000] + [001] + [010], \ldots, X\}$$

where '+' here denotes algebraic addition.

Complexity of measages in this algebra could be increased almost indefinitely, by increasing the number of variables, respectively. In this way we could establish a nested sequence of subalgebras differing in terms of coarseness and fineness among each other. The information content in the state sets is preserved under η in Y, where for proper representation X and Y should have the same dimension.

The subalgebras in the previous example are easy to establish. Define

$$\begin{aligned} \mathscr{A}^{(1)} &= \{\emptyset, A^1, \bar{A}^1, X\}, \quad A^1 \equiv [000], \bar{A}^1 = X - A^1 \\ \mathscr{A}^{(2)} &= \{\emptyset, A^2, \bar{A}^2, X\}, \quad A^2 \equiv [00X_3] + [1X_20], \bar{A}^2 = X - A^2 \\ X_3 &= \{x_3 \colon x_3 \in [0,1]\}, \quad X_2 = \{x_2 \colon x_2 \in [0,1]\}. \end{aligned}$$

The equivalent function specification is given by

$$y^{(1)} = \eta^{(1)}(x) = \begin{cases} 1, & \text{if } x_1 = 0,\ x_2 = 0,\ x_3 = 0 \\ 0, & \text{otherwise.} \end{cases}$$

$$y^{(2)} = \eta^{(2)}(x) = \begin{cases} 1, & \text{if } x_1 = 0,\ x_2 = 0,\ x_3 \in [0,1] \text{ or} \\ & \quad x_1 = 1,\ x_3 = 0,\ x_2 \in [0,1] \\ 0, & \text{otherwise.} \end{cases}$$

The information provided by $\mathscr{A}^{(1)}$ tells us whether or not the sequence $x_1 = 0$, $x_2 = 0$, $x_3 = 0$ happened, $\mathscr{A}^{(2)}$ reveals the information whether or not the sequence $x_1 = 0$, $x_2 = 0$, $x_3 \in [0,1]$ or $x_1 = 1$, $x_3 = 0$, $x_2 \in [0,1]$ occurred. We have $\mathscr{A}^{(2)} \not\supset \mathscr{A}^{(1)}$ and $\mathscr{A}^{(1)} \supset \mathscr{A}^{(2)}$. Now, if all messages (signals, propositions) encoded in $\mathscr{A}^{(1)}$ and $\mathscr{A}^{(2)}$ respectively are correct, $\mathscr{A}^{(1)}$ is considered to be more informative than $\mathscr{A}^{(2)}$ and vice versa when the data are negative.

This is intuitively plausible. The previous examples demonstrate the economy of notation that can be achieved by adopting an algebraic point of view in dealing with 'qualitative information'. Principally, no problems are involved in treating continuous variables, $\mathscr{A}$ and $\mathscr{X}$ simply become σ-algebras which is an immediate extension of finite algebras discussed so far. Then the function η will be measurable on $\mathscr{X}$.

9.*8 Measures of Information in Statistical Decisions (Games)

We consider a game in which the statistician is able to select a decision strategy on the basis of information available to him.

Hence, let us consider a game (S, Y, φ) between nature and the statistician with payoff function φ. Let S and Y be compact metric spaces so that φ satisfies some mild continuity condition, e.g. a Lipschitzian condition in $S \times Y$. It is well-known that subsets of metric spaces form a class of Borel sets, hence in defining a probability distribution on a compact metric space it is obvious that this distribution is defined on Borel sets of this space. Since every random variable **x** associated to a sample space (Z, S) induces a probability distribution μ on $Z \times S$, it will be more convenient for our purpose to refer to μ as an experiment whose outcomes $z \in Z$ for any $s \in S$ are governed by the conditional distribution μ_s with values $\mu_s(z)$. In order to reveal the structure of information in this game we will assume that the person must take a decision $y \in Y$ prior to the experiment μ, and by adopting a Bayesian view, μ should be known to him in choosing a Bayesian strategy which takes into account prior information in a systematic fashion.

This means that a decision $y \in Y$ is taken that minimizes the average of the payoff value,

(1) $$E\{\varphi(s, y)\} = \int_S \varphi(s, y)\, d\mu_s(z).$$

Now let us consider the possibility that the statistician can obtain additional information on his decision problem by performing an *auxiliary* experiment. Hence, given a modified space of outcomes (compact metric space) Z′, consider a corresponding experiment μ' with (conditional) pdf μ'_s on Z′ together with $\mu_s(z|z') \equiv \mu_{sz'}(z)$ which is the conditional pdf relative to z′ on Z. It is in the spirit of the Bayesian approach to assume that a person can perform an auxiliary experiment μ' prior to taking a decision. In this case the average payoff value will be

(2) $$\int_{Z'} \{\min_y \int_S \varphi(s, y)\, d\mu_{sz'}(z)\}\, d\mu'_s(z')$$

We may call the difference

(3) $$v(\mu, \mu') = \min_y \int_S \varphi(s, y)\, d\mu_s(z) - \int_{Z'} \{\min_y \int_S \varphi(s, y)\, d\mu_{sz'}(z)\}\, d\mu'_s(z')$$

the value of information in experiment μ generated by experiment μ'. This value does not change if we add or subtract some positive amount. By adopting a Bayesian strategy, the statistician would attempt to choose a decision which minimizes his expected loss in terms of the payoff value, i.e.

$$\varphi(s) = \min_{y} \varphi(s, y),$$

so that the value is given by

$$w(\mu) = \min_{y} \int_S \varphi(s, y)\, d\mu_s(z)$$

which represents his expected loss resulting from the uncertainty of the outcome of experiment μ.

For the next considerations assume that the loss is normalized by the condition $\max_{s,y} |\varphi(s, y)| = 1$.

Put everything into discrete terms and assume the sets Z, Y and Z′ to be finite, let

$$S = \{s_i\}, Y = \{y_j\}, Z' = \{z'_k\}, \mu = \{\mu_i\}, \varphi = \{\varphi_{ij}\}, \mu' = \{\mu'_k\}.$$
$$(i = 1, \ldots, m;\ j = 1, \ldots, n;\ k = 1, \ldots, l)$$

Replace $\mu_s(z, z')$ by μ_i^k omitting s since no ambiguity will arise. For simplicity, let $w = w(\mu)$, $v = v(\mu', \mu)$, define $h = h(\mu)$ *as the entropy of the experiment* μ corresponding to (1), and let $I = I(\mu', \mu)$ be the amount of information μ generated by experiment μ', corresponding to (3). (log denotes natural logarithm.)

Thus,

$$h = \sum_i \mu_i \log(1/\mu_i) \quad \text{and}$$

$$I = \sum_i \mu_i \log(1/\mu_i) - \sum_k \mu'_k \sum_i \mu_i^k \log(1/\mu_i^k).$$

It seems natural in view of the approach adopted here to use the metric in a compact metric space for constructing some notion of informational distance in a subjective sense.

From the Bayesian point of view we may assume that a person – before performing an experiment – knows about a particular presentation of nature's pure strategy, given by a point $s \in S$.

Now, after having performed the experiment, this person observes the actual state to be $s_o \in S$. Let δ: $S \times S \to Re$ be the ordinary metric such that δ associates a real number $\delta(s, s_o)$ with every pair (s, s_o) of elements of S. Then $\delta(s, s_o)$ represents a change of the *informational state* of a person (change of belief) in terms of a distance, satisfying wellknown conditions of a numerical metric. Given a set of experiments $\mathbf{x}_1, \ldots, \mathbf{x}_n$, sequentially designed, the search problem of a person would consist in observing a sequence of points

$s_1, \ldots, s_n$ approaching the true state $s_o \in S$. Now in the context of a statistical game (S, Y, φ) there is an interesting way to reformulate an informational metric in terms of an economic value of information. Let us assume a person, by observing s, takes a decision y out of his decision set

$$\mathscr{D}(s) = \{y: \varphi(s, y) = \psi(s)\}$$

with $\psi(s) = \min_{y \in Y} \varphi(s, y)$.
Hence, the value of information of a person selecting a decision y on the basis of observation s compared to a true state s_o can be given as a number

$$m(s_o, s) = \max_{y \in \mathscr{D}(s)} \varphi(s_o, y) = \min_{y} (s_o, y)$$

Let δ be an ordinary metric such that

$$\delta(s_1, s_2) = \max_{y} |\varphi(x_1, y) - \varphi(x_2, y)|.$$

Now, if $\delta(s_0, s_n)$ converges to zero for n sufficiently large, by implication $m(s_0, s_n)$ converges to zero for n sufficiently large. Hence, the inequality

$$m(s_0, s) \leqq 2\delta(s_0, s) \text{ holds }.$$

Let $\mathscr{M}$ denote the space of all probability distributions μ over S, characterizing randomized strategies for nature. Then the payoff value in the game $(\mathscr{M}, Y, \lambda)$ is given by $\lambda(\mu, y) = \int_S \varphi(s, y) d\mu$. Accodingly, we may introduce in $\mathscr{M}$ a metric δ in $\mathscr{M}$ which associates with every pair (μ_1, μ_2) a number $\delta(\mu_1, \mu_2)$.
In order to obtain a value of information in this case we may assume accordingly that the a priori probability distribution known to the player is not the true distribution μ_0 but some distribution close to it. Suppose he knows the conditional distribution $\eta(z|\mu, z')$, if the prior distribution is μ and the outcome of the experiment ν is z'. Assume that the player starts with some distribution μ which is close to the true distribution μ_0. Then by taking a decision a priori the decision-maker minimizes

$$\int_S \varphi(s, y) d\mu(z) \quad \text{w.r.t.} \quad y \in Y.$$

If the decision is taken after the experiment ν has been performed then he minimizes (setting $\eta(z|\mu, z') \equiv \eta_{\mu, z'}(z)$)

$$\int_S (s, y) d\eta_{\mu, z'}(z) \quad \text{w.r.t.} \quad y \in Y.$$

Taking into account that the true distribution is μ_0 we may compute the value of information in the game $(\mathscr{M}, Y, \lambda)$ by

$$\bar{v} = \bar{v}(\mu, \nu) = \int_S \varphi(s, y) d\mu(z) - \int_{Z'} \int_S \varphi(s, y_{z'})$$

$$d\eta_{\mu_0, z'}(z)\, d\nu(z');\ \bar{y} \in \mathscr{D}(\mu);\ \bar{y}_{z'} \in \mathscr{D}(\eta_{\mu_0, z'}).$$

Note that the existence of the metric is presupposed. Since we consider the metric as some mesure of informational distance in a subjective sense it would be interesting to pursue properties of the underlying qualitative structure. Various structures of this sort have recently been examined in terms of proximity structures and extensive measurement [Krantz et al. (1973)]. By choosing a metric as a measure of informational distance in a statistical game one can fully exploit the generality of metric spaces. If necessary one can generalize the metric to a probabilistic metric constituting uncertainty about the true distance.

9.*9 Expected Value of Information

Let us first recall a brief but formal description of decision theory. Start with the payoff table, which gives acts that might be taken, events that might obtain, and utilities for each act-event combination. For simplicity, consider events that can be described by the possible values θ of a *discrete*-valued parameter $\boldsymbol{\theta}$. Denote any possible act by a. The utility of taking act a if event θ obtains is denoted by $U(a, \theta)$.
Besides the payoff table we require a (prior) probability distribution of $\boldsymbol{\theta}$, $P(\theta)$. Assume first that an immediate terminal decision is to be made. For any act a compute its expected utility $\sum_\theta P(\theta)\, U(a, \theta)$.
Finally, choose that act for which expected utility is maximized. The maximum expected utility is written

(1) $$\max_a \sum_\theta P(\theta)\, U(a, \theta).$$

(For simplicity, assume in this section that a unique maximum exists in all cases). Suppose now that sample evidence, represented by the symbol x, is obtained before a terminal decision is made. By application of Bayes' theorem, the prior distribution $P(\theta)$ of $\boldsymbol{\theta}$ becomes the posterior distribution $P(\theta|x)$. Then any act a is evaluated by its expected utility $\sum_\theta P(\theta|x)\, U(a, \theta, x)$. Choose the act for which this is maximized, and call the maximum expected utility

(2) $$\max_a \sum_\theta P(\theta|x)\, U(a, \theta, x).$$

We write $U(a, \theta, x)$ instead of $U(a, \theta)$ to emphasize that it may cost something, directly or indirectly, to obtain x. This cost of sampling is a sunk cost when the final decision is made; that is, it is the same for all a and θ, and so can be either included or ignored without affecting the decision. For the next problem, however, the cost is not yet sunk.

Next in order of complexity, consider a specific sampling plan that promises an observation of the random variable **x**. What is the expected utility of carrying out this sample and then making a terminal decision in the light of $P(\theta|x)$? Work backwards from the solution to the previous problem. The prior distribution $P(\theta)$ in conjunction with the proposed sampling plan implies a predictive distribution $P(x)$ for **x** in the usual way; that is $P(x) = \sum_\theta P(\theta)\,P(x|\theta)$, where $P(x|\theta)$ is the conditional distribution of **x** given θ for the sampling plan. *For any* x the maximum utility is given by (2), that is $\max_a \sum_\theta P(\theta|x)\,U(a, \theta, x)$.

Now take the expectation of (2) with respect to $P(x)$:

$$(3) \qquad \sum_x P(x) \max \sum_\theta P(\theta|x)\,U(a, \theta, x).$$

This is the expected utility, as seen in advance, of executing the sampling plan in question and then taking the best act after the sample evidence x is available. Now recognize explicity that $U(a, \theta, x)$ has two components: $U(a, \theta)$, as originally defined (ignoring sampling costs), and an expected cost of sampling (not necessarily measured in monetary units), denoted $C(x)$, where $C(0) = 0$ and $x = 0$ represents the dummy outcome of a sample of size 0, that is, no sample at all. If, as is often reasonable, $U(a, \theta, x) = U(a, \theta) - C(x)$, we can decompose (3) as

$$(3a) \qquad \sum_x P(x) \max_a \sum_\theta P(\theta|x)\,U(a, \theta) - \sum_x P(x) \sum_\theta P(\theta|x)\,C(x).$$

The first term of (3a) is the expected utility, ignoring sampling costs, of carrying out the sample plan. The second term which simplifies to $\sum_x P(x)\,C(x)$ is the expected cost of sampling. The expected value of sample information, EVSI, is defined as (1) subtracted from the first term of (3a):

$$(4) \qquad \sum_x P(x) \max_a \sum_\theta P(\theta|x)\,U(a, \theta) - \max_a \sum_\theta P(\theta)\,U(a, \theta).$$

The summation of the second term can be written $\sum_\theta P(\theta)\,U(a, \theta) = \sum_x P(x) \sum_\theta P(\theta|x)\,U(a, \theta)$; by substitution in (4) the EVSI can be expressed as

$$(4a) \qquad \sum_x P(x) \max_a \sum_\theta P(\theta|x)\,U(a, \theta) - \max_a \sum_x P(x) \sum_\theta P(\theta|x)\,U(a, \theta).$$

From (4a) it is apparent that the EVSI can never be negative. That is, by tailoring the act a to the sample outcome x, we cannot lose expected utility: a *posteriori* we would always be free to take the act that was best *a priori*, in which case (4a) would be 0. If in the light of an observed x we choose a different act from the one preferred *a priori*, we do so only because the expected utility is larger. Moreover, we can gain in expected utility only if *some* sample outcome x will change the choice of acts. If no sample outcome could change the best *a priori* decision, the EVSI is 0. In words, the EVSI is the weighted average posterior expected utility, the weights being given by P(x), minus the prior expected utility. The fact that the EVSI can never be negative can be expressed by saying that the weighted average posterior expected utility cannot be less than the prior expected utility. But this does not rule out the possibility that the *actual* posterior expected utility can be less than the prior. Suppose, for example, that no sample outcome could change the best act, that ist, the EVSI is zero. Then unless sampling is completely uniformative, $P(\theta|x) = P(\theta)$ for all x, there will typically be some outcomes for which posterior expected utility $\sum_\theta P(\theta|x)\, U(a, \theta)$ is lower than prior expected utility $\max_a \sum_\theta P(\theta)\, U(a, \theta)$, and others for which it is higher.

9.* 10 Sampling Information

In general, suppose that there are two acts 1 and 2 with conditional utilities given by (1) $U(a_1, \theta) = c_1 + b_1 \theta$, and (2) $U(a_2, \theta) = c_2 + b_2 \theta$, where the c's and b's are real numbers, $b_1 > b_2$, and θ is a symbol for a value taken by an uncertain parameter $\boldsymbol{\theta}$. We want to choose a_1 if $E[U(a_1, \theta)] > E[U(a_2, \boldsymbol{\theta})]$; otherwise, unless the two expectations are equal and either act is optimal, we want to choose a_2. Since both utility functions are linear functions of θ, making use of the expectation we obtain (3) $E[U(a_1, \boldsymbol{\theta})] = c_1 + b_1 E(\boldsymbol{\theta})$ and (4) $E[U(a_2, \boldsymbol{\theta})] = c_2 + b_2 E(\boldsymbol{\theta})$.
Therefore choose a_1 if $c_1 + b_1 E(\boldsymbol{\theta}) > c_2 + b_2 E(\boldsymbol{\theta})$, that is, if

$$(5) \qquad E(\boldsymbol{\theta}) > \frac{c_2 - c_1}{b_1 - b_2} = \theta_b.$$

We use θ_b to denote the *breakeven point*; we prefer a_1 to a_2, are indifferent to, or prefer, a_2 to a_1, according as $E(\boldsymbol{\theta}) > \theta_b$, $E(\boldsymbol{\theta}) = \theta_b$, or $E(\boldsymbol{\theta}) < \theta_b$. (it must be assumed that θ_b lies within the interval of values of θ that $\boldsymbol{\theta}$ can exhibit; otherwise one act is dominated by the other and can be deleted from consideration without regard for the probability distribution. If $b_1 < b_2$, the direction of the inequality (5) is reversed).
We now turn to the more complicated problem of evaluating the expected value of sample information, the EVSI. Repeating eqs. (4) and (4a) of Sec. 9, for convenience, for the discrete case the EVSI is

$$(6) \qquad \sum_x P(x) \max_a \sum_\theta P(\theta|x)\, U(a, \theta) - \max_a \sum_\theta P(\theta)\, U(a, \theta),$$

or

$$(7) \qquad \sum_x P(x) \max_a \sum_\theta P(\theta|x)\, U(a, \theta) - \max_a \sum_x P(x) \sum_\theta P(\theta|x)\, U(a, \theta).$$

In the application of this section, two special features facilitate evaluation of

(6) of (7). First, there are just two acts, a_1 and a_2. Supposing for concreteness that a_1 is optimal *a priori*, then for all x such that a_1 is still optimal *a posteriori*, the corresponding terms of (7) are zero.
We may therefore rewrite (7) as

(8) $$\sum_{\{x: a_2 \text{ opt}\}} P(x) \sum_{\theta} P(\theta|x)\, U(a_2, \theta) - \sum_{\{x: a_2 \text{ opt}\}} P(x) \sum_{\theta} P(\theta|x)\, U(a_1, \theta)$$
$$= \sum_{\{x: a_2 \text{ opt}\}} P(x) \sum P(\theta|x)\, [U(a_2, \theta) - U(a_1, \theta)].$$

The second special feature is the linearity of the utility functions $U(a_1, \theta)$ and $U(a_2, \theta)$, which implies

(9) $$U(a_2, \theta) - U(a_1, \theta) = (c_2 - c_1) + (b_2 - b_1)\theta$$
$$= \frac{c_2 - c_1}{b_1 - b_2}(b_1 - b_2) + (b_2 - b_1)\theta$$
$$= (b_1 - b_2)(\theta_b - \theta).$$

Substituting (9) in (8) we obtain the EVSI

(10) $$\sum_{\{x: a_2 \text{ opt}\}} P(x) \sum_{\theta} P(\theta|x)(b_1 - b_2)(\theta_b - \theta) = (b_1 - b_2)$$
$$\cdot \sum_{\{x: a_2 \text{ opt}\}} P(x)\, (\theta_b - E(\boldsymbol{\theta}|x)),$$

where $E(\boldsymbol{\theta}|x) = \sum_{\theta} \theta P(\theta|x)$.

We can express (10) in a convenient computational form. Each possible x defines a posterior distribution of $\boldsymbol{\theta}$, $P(\theta|x)$, by Bayes' theorem. Denote the mean of this distribution by θ''. Before **x** is observed $\boldsymbol{\theta}''$ is a random variable, with distribution $P(\theta'')$ induced by $P(x)$. The prior distribution of $\boldsymbol{\theta}$ and conditional distribution of **x** given θ serve to determine $P(x)$, also $P(\theta|x)$ for each x, and therefore $P(\theta'')$. From the work on posterior terminal analysis, we know that for $b_1 > b_2$, a_2 is optimal if and only if $\theta'' < \theta_b$.
Hence we can rewrite (10) as

(11) $$(b_1 - b_2) \sum_{\theta'' < \theta_b} P(\theta'')\, (\theta_b - \theta'') =$$
$$= (b_1 - b_2)\, [\theta_b P(\boldsymbol{\theta}'' < \theta_b) - \sum_{\theta'' < \theta_b} \theta'' P(\theta'')].$$

We have derived (11) on the assumption that a_1 was best *a priori*. Had we assumed a_2 best, the same reasoning would have led to

(11a) $$(b_1 - b_2)\, [\sum_{\theta'' > \theta_b} \theta'' P(\theta'') - \theta_b P(\boldsymbol{\theta}'' > \theta_b)].$$

To evaluate (11) numerically, we need to deduce the distribution of $\boldsymbol{\theta}''$, and evaluate $(P(\boldsymbol{\theta}'' < \theta_b)$ and $\sum_{\theta'' < \theta_b} \theta'' P(\theta'')$. To illustrate how this is done we consider a two-action problem on the mean μ of a normal process of known variance σ^2, with a normal prior distribution for μ, $f_N(\mu|\bar{x}', \sigma/\sqrt{n'})$. Using $\bar{x}''$ to denote the posterior mean, the counterpart of the left-hand side of (11) is

$$(12) \qquad (b_1 - b_2) \int_{-\infty}^{\mu_b} (\mu_b - \bar{x}'')\, D(\bar{x}'')d\bar{x}''.$$

Here μ_b is assuming the same role as θ_b to be a *certainty equivalent*. We wish to deduce $D(\bar{x}'')$. A sample of size n is considered. The predictive density for $\bar{x}$ is therefore $f_N\left(\bar{x}|\bar{x}', \sigma\sqrt{\frac{1}{n'}+\frac{1}{n}}\right)$. For any value $\bar{x}$ that $\bar{\mathbf{x}}$ can exhibit, we would be led by the usual formula to a normal posterior density $f_N(\mu|\bar{x}'', \sigma/\sqrt{n''})$. *In advance of sampling* the only uncertainty about $f_N(\mu|\bar{x}'', \sigma/\sqrt{n''})$ is the uncertainty about $\bar{\mathbf{x}}''$. The uncertainty about $\bar{\mathbf{x}}''$, in turn, stems from the prior uncertainty about $\bar{\mathbf{x}}$; that is, $\bar{\mathbf{x}}'' = (n'\bar{x}' + n\bar{x})/n''$. We see that $\bar{\mathbf{x}}''$ is a linear function of the normally-distributed random variable $\bar{\mathbf{x}}$, which has predictive density $f_N\left(\bar{x}|\bar{x}', \sigma\sqrt{\frac{1}{n'}+\frac{1}{n}}\right)$. Therefore the prior distribution of $\bar{\mathbf{x}}''$ is normal with mean

$$(13) \qquad E(\bar{\mathbf{x}}'') = \frac{n'\bar{x}' + n\bar{x}'}{n''} = \bar{x}'$$

and variance

$$(14) \qquad \sigma^2(\bar{\mathbf{x}}'') = \left(\frac{n}{n''}\right)^2 \sigma^2 \left(\frac{1}{n'} + \frac{1}{n}\right)$$
$$= \frac{n}{n''} \cdot \frac{\sigma^2}{n'}.$$

Summarizing, the prior distribution of $\bar{\mathbf{x}}''$ is given by the density $f_N(\bar{x}''|\bar{x}', \sigma(\bar{\mathbf{x}}''))$, where $\sigma(\bar{\mathbf{x}}'') = \sqrt{\frac{n}{n''}}\frac{\sigma}{\sqrt{n'}}$. Substituting in (12), we have

$$(15) \qquad (b_1 - b_2) \int_{-\infty}^{\mu_b} (\mu_b - \bar{x}'')\, f_N(\bar{x}''|\bar{x}', \sigma(\bar{\mathbf{x}}''))\, d\bar{x}''.$$

By standardization $u = (\bar{x}'' - \bar{x}')/\sigma(\bar{\mathbf{x}}'')$, $d\bar{x}'' = \sigma(\bar{\mathbf{x}}'')du$, and writing

$$\mu_b - \bar{x}'' = (\bar{\mathbf{x}}'')\left[\frac{\mu_b - \bar{x}'}{\sigma(\bar{\mathbf{x}}'')} - \frac{\bar{x}'' - \bar{x}'}{\sigma(\bar{\mathbf{x}}'')}\right] = \sigma(\bar{\mathbf{x}}'')\,(u_b - u),$$

we can express (15) as

$$(16) \qquad (b_1 - b_2)\, \sigma(\bar{\mathbf{x}}'') \int_{-\infty}^{\mu_b} (u_b - u)\, f_N(u|0,1)du,$$

where $u_b = (\mu_b - \bar{x}')/\sigma(\bar{\mathbf{x}}'')$. The integral of (16) is easily evaluated as $u_b F_N(u_b|0,1) + f_N(u_b|0,1)$. In conclusion, the EVSI for the normal case, assuming a_1 best *a priori*, is

(17) $$(b_1 - b_2)\,\sigma(\bar{\mathbf{x}}'')\,[u_b F_n(u_b|0,1) + f_N(u_b|0,1)].$$

Had a_2 been best *a priori*, the same argument would have led to

(17a) $$|b_1 - b_2|\,\sigma(\bar{\mathbf{x}}'')\,[f_N(u_b|0,1) - u_b G_N(u_b|0,1)].$$

Both cases, and the corresponding result when it is assumed that $b_2 > b_1$, can be subsumed under

(17b) $$|b_1 - b_2|\,\sigma(\bar{\mathbf{x}}'')\,[f_N(u_b|0,1) - |u_b|\,G_N(|u_b||0,1)].$$

It is interesting to examine what happens to the EVSI as $n \to \infty$.
Since $\sigma^2(\bar{\mathbf{x}}'') = \frac{n}{n''}\frac{\sigma^2}{n'}$, the limiting standard deviation is $\frac{\sigma^2}{n'}$ since $\frac{n}{n''} \to 1$ as $n \to \infty$. The limiting distribution of $\bar{\mathbf{x}}''$ is thus normal with mean $\bar{x}'$ and standard deviation $\sigma/\sqrt{n}$. It is, in fact, the prior distribution of $\boldsymbol{\mu}$. Equating $n \to \infty$ with perfect information, we can call this limiting EVSI the *expected value of perfect information*, or EVPI.

In general, the EVPI gives the maximum EVSI, and so sets an upper bound on the amount we would be willing to pay for sample information. If the EVPI is smaller than the cost of even a small sample, this upper bound gives the useful information that sampling is unlikely to be worthwhile. If the EVPI is large compared to the cost of a small sample, detailed investigation of the EVSI may be warranted.

9.*11 Diagnostic Testing

Another type of decision problem is a special case of the two-action problem of Sec. 10. We illustrate this by a cancer diagnosis example.

Suppose that for some reason it is possible to make only one test; perhaps the test always gives the same answer, right or wrong, when repeated on the same individual. The present problem is this: given the result of the test, + or −, should we diagnose that the person has cancer? By "diagnose that the person has cancer", a_C, we mean "pursue a further course of diagnosis or treatment". By "diagnose not cancer," $a_{\bar{C}}$, we mean simply to take no further action.

In this problem there are just two, incompatible events: "has cancer," (C) "does not have cancer" ($\bar{C}$). We define the losses as follows:

Event	*Act* a_C	*Act* $a_{\bar{C}}$
C	0	$L(a_{\bar{C}}, C)$
$\bar{C}$	$L(a_C, \bar{C})$	0

$L(a_C, \bar{C})$ is the loss of a false positive diagnosis; $L(a_{\bar{C}}, C)$ is the loss of a false negative. Suppose now that the test says +. By application of Bayes' theorem, the expected loss of a_C is

$$(1) \qquad \frac{P(C)\,P(+|C)}{P(+)} \cdot 0 + \frac{P(\bar{C})\,P(+|\bar{C})}{P(+)}\, L(a_C, \bar{C}) = $$

$$= \frac{P(\bar{C})\,P(+|\bar{C})}{P(+)}\, L(a_{\bar{C}}, \bar{C}).$$

The expected loss of $a_{\bar{C}}$ is

$$(2) \qquad \frac{P(C)\,P(+|C)}{P(+)} \cdot L(a_{\bar{C}}, C) + \frac{P(\bar{C})\,P(+|\bar{C})}{P(+)} \cdot 0 = $$

$$= \frac{P(C)\,P(+|C)}{P(+)}\, L(a_{\bar{C}}, C).$$

To diagnose cancer, take a_C, if (1) < (2), that is, if

$$(3) \qquad \frac{L(a_{\bar{C}}, C)}{L(a_C, \bar{C})} > \frac{P(\bar{C})\,P(+|\bar{C})}{P(C)\,P(+|C)} = \frac{P(\bar{C}|+)}{P(C|+)}.$$

In a numerical example let $P(\bar{C}) = .995$, $P(C) = .005$ and $P(+|\bar{C}) = .05$, $P+|C) = .95$. Therefore the right hand side of (3) is

$$\frac{(.995)\,(.05)}{(.005)\,(.95)} = 10.47.$$

This means that $L(a_{\bar{C}}, C)$ must be at least 10.47 times $L(a_C, \bar{C})$ to warrant the diagnosis a_C; that is, the consequences of ignoring cancer when it is present must be at least 10.47 times as serious as the consequences of further diagnostic testing or treatment if cancer is not present.
The inequality (3) can also be written, diagnose a_C if

$$(4) \qquad \frac{P(+|C)}{P(+|\bar{C})} > \frac{P(\bar{C})}{P(C)} \cdot \frac{L(a_C, \bar{C})}{L(a_{\bar{C}}, C)}.$$

The factor $P(\bar{C})/P(C)$ is the prior odds ratio against cancer. The factor $L(a_C, \bar{C})/L(a_{\bar{C}}, C)$ is the ratio of the loss of false positive diagnosis to that of false negative. The ratio $P(+|C)/P(+|\bar{C})$ is the *likelihood* ratio, the ratio of the data given C to the probability of the data given $\bar{C}$. In order to diagnose

a_C, the likelihood ratio in *favour of* C must exceed the product of the prior odds ratio against C and the loss ratio of false positive diagnosis to that of false negative: (4) provides the criterion for terminal analysis.
In general, there are two incompatible events E_1 and E_2, and acts a_1 and a_2 such that $L(a_1, E_2), L(a_2, E_1) > 0$, $L(a_1, E_1) = L(a_2, E_2) = 0$.
Given any amount of data x bearing on the problem, choose a_1 if

(5) $$\frac{P(x|E_1)}{P(x|E_2)} > \frac{P(E_2)}{P(E_1)} \cdot \frac{L(a_1, E_2)}{L(a_2, E_1)}.$$

or

$$\frac{P(E_1|x)}{P(E_2|x)} > \frac{L(a_1, E_2)}{L(a_2, E_1)}.$$

The EVPI is simple; for a_1, it is

(6) $$P(E_2|x)\, L(a_1, E_2).$$

for a_2, the EVPI is

(7) $$P(E_1|x)\, L(a_2, E_1).$$

In (6) and (7), $P(E_1|x)$ and $P(E_2|x)$ are the posterior probabilities computed by Bayes' theorem. For example,

(8) $$P(E_1|x) = \frac{P(E_1)\, P(x|E_1)}{P(x)}.$$

9.*12 Problems

(1) A certain psychiatric disorder is known to cure itself without treatment with probability $p = .50$. A treatment is tried out on 100 patients and 56 cures are obtained. Assume a diffuse prior for **p**, where p is the probability of cure for the treatment.

(a) Suppose that the cost of treatment is zero, and that the utility to the patient equals his probability of cure. If you were a physician, would you recommend the treatment for a patient? What would be the EVPI? What is the risk that you have made the wrong decision?

(b) Same as (a), except that the cost of treatment, measured in utility units, is .03.

(2) Discuss the following statements taken from Ledley and Lusted (1961) for medical decision-making: 'When alternative diagnoses still remain after all possible tests have been made, the value of different treatments must be weighed with regard to the alternative diagnoses. Similarly, when a decision is to be made on whether to continue with further, and more

difficult testing or to accept the diagnosis as accurate enough, then the values of the treatments associated with the alternative diagnoses clearly enter into consideration. The determination of the appropriate value for a particular treatment-diagnosis combination ... can involve intangible factors. Many such value judgments involve social, economic, ethical and moral considerations concerning the patient, his family, and the society in which he lives.'

(3) Calculate the EVPI in the following two situations where the entries are monetary units or utilities (linear in money).

(a)

	θ_1	θ_2
a_1	90	60
a_2	80	110
$P(\theta)$	.25	.75

(b)

	θ_1	θ_2	θ_3
a_1	300	200	100
a_2	200	100	200
$P(\theta)$	.2	.5	.3

(4) A contractor decides to enter a bid on a construction project for which there are many bidders. His conditional utility function is $-K + \hat{x}$, where K is his expected cost if he gets the job and $\hat{x}$ is the amount he bids. He assesses a probability density $D(x)$ for the low bid $\mathbf{x}$ of all the other bidders.

(a) Show that if $u = \dfrac{x - E(\mathbf{x})}{\sigma(\mathbf{x})}$, his bid $\hat{x}$ can be computed from

$$\hat{u} = \frac{K - E(\mathbf{x})}{\sigma(\mathbf{x})} + \frac{P(\mathbf{u} > \hat{u})}{D(u)}.$$

(b) If $K = \$50{,}000$, $\mathbf{x}$ is normal with $E(\mathbf{x}) = \$47{,}000$ and $\sigma(\mathbf{x}) = \$3{,}000$, what should be the bid?

(c) Should he bid at all? Explain.

(5) A university is required by law to admit all high school graduates in the state. From extensive past experience, it finds that students who successfully complete the first year had obtained scores on an achievement test prior to matriculation that are normal with mean 110 and standard deviation 10; for students who fail, the scores are normal with mean 90 and standard deviation 10. Of all students who enter 30 per cent fail to complete the first year.

(a) If a prospective student scores 98 on the test, what are the odds he will fail?

(b) If he were to make a formal analysis of the problem, what loss ratio would be relevant and what would it have to be to justify attempting the first year?

(6) If the error of wrongly convicting an innocent person is 10 times as serious as the error of wrongly acquitting a guilty one, what should be the minimum probability of guilt for the decision to convict?

Appendix A – Chapter 9*

Interaction between Information and Probability

With a few notable exceptions there have been no attempts so far to axiomatize subjective information comparable to axiomatizations of subjective probability.

L. J. Savage (1954) among others introduced subjective probability as a primitive notion expressed mathematically as a binary relation '$\leqq\cdot$' (qualitative probability) in a Boolean algebra of events $\mathscr{S}$ satisfying certain order-properties. You may question the so-called primitive concept of a qualitative subjective probability '$\leqq\cdot$' and suggest that there exists a more primitive notion on which all subjective probability evaluations of events are virtually based. This could be the concept of 'qualitative subjective information'.

Thus we assume that $\leqq\cdot$ is a *derived* concept and that the basic concept will be a relation $\leqq$: ('not more informative than'), defined in a family of information sets, say $\mathscr{T}_0$, generating ($\rightarrow$) a respective family of events. Let information sets $\mathscr{A}$, $\mathscr{B} \in \mathscr{T}_0$ be undefined terms as events are undefined terms in the Kolmogorov probability algebra: we may represent them generically by a sequence of observables such as data, messages, symbols, statements, or even outcomes of previous random experiments, for example, we might have observations represented by a sequence $\langle$H, T, H, H, H, T, H, H$\rangle$. Then the information that on the next throw either H or T occurs is completely specified by the sequences of binary digits $\langle 1, 0, 1, 1, 1, 1, 0, 1, 1\rangle_H$ or $\langle 0, 1, 0, 0, 0, 1, 0, 0\rangle_T$, respectively.

The process of generating a family of events by a family of information sets can be properly defined by constructing a Boolean homomorphic map. This is well motivated since it is reasonable to assume that both $\mathscr{S}$ and $\mathscr{T}_0$ form Boolean algebras with an appropriate structure.

Definition 1: A map $\mathrm{H}: \mathscr{T}_0 \in \mathscr{A} \rightarrow \mathrm{H}(\mathscr{A}) \in \mathscr{S}$ is a Boolean homomorphic map, mapping the zero element $\mathrm{O} \in \mathscr{T}_0$ and the unit element $\mathscr{E} \in \mathscr{T}_0$ into $\mathscr{S}$ and being order and structure preserving, i.e. preserving all three Boolean operations $\wedge$, $\vee$, ^{c} (finite meet, join and complementation, henceforth we use $\cap$ and $\cup$ with the understanding of set-theoretic product and union) such that for $\mathscr{A}$, $\mathscr{B} \in \mathscr{T}_0$:

$$\mathrm{H}(\mathscr{A} \cap \mathscr{B}) = \mathrm{H}(\mathscr{A}) \cap \mathrm{H}(\mathscr{B}),$$
$$\mathrm{H}(\mathscr{A} \cup \mathscr{B}) = \mathrm{H}(\mathscr{A}) \cup \mathrm{H}(\mathscr{B}),$$
$$[\mathrm{H}(\mathscr{A})]^c = \mathrm{H}(\mathscr{A}^c).$$

Now let $\mathscr{A}' = \mathscr{A} \cup \mathscr{B}$ and $\mathscr{A} \subseteq \mathscr{A}'$ so that $\mathrm{H}(\mathscr{A}') = \mathrm{A}' = \mathrm{A} \cup \mathrm{B}$ and

$H(\mathscr{A}) = A$. Then no problem is involved by ordering $\mathscr{T}_0$ (and also $\mathscr{S}$ via H) according to the statements

$$(*)\qquad \mathscr{A} \leqq : \mathscr{A}' \Rightarrow \mathscr{A} \subseteq \mathscr{A}' \quad \text{and}$$
$$\mathscr{A} \leqq : \mathscr{A}' \Rightarrow A \leqq \cdot A', A, A' \in \mathscr{S}.$$

However, we run into difficulties by imposing the ordering on any two different elements $\mathscr{A}, \mathscr{B} \in \mathscr{T}_0$, for then it can no longer be reasonably postulated that a condition similar to (*) holds, viz.

$$(**)\qquad \mathscr{A} \leqq : \mathscr{B} \Rightarrow \mathscr{A} \subseteq \mathscr{B} \quad \text{and}$$
$$\mathscr{A} \leqq : \mathscr{B} \Rightarrow A \leqq \cdot B \Leftrightarrow A \subseteq B.$$

This can be made intuitively clear by a simple example.

Example: Suppose A means "there will be a thermonuclear war within the next five years" and B means "there will be rain in Los Angeles on January 31". We argue that probability beliefs on which event is considered as qualitatively more probable shall be based exclusively on the information available with respect to these events. Let $\mathscr{A}$ generating A be equivalent to saying "there will be a thermonuclear war within the next five years, *some independent experts on thermonuclear war predict*" and $\mathscr{B}$ generating B may be equivalent to saying "*all weather bureaus in California predict on January* 30 that there will be rain in Los Angeles on January 31". Obviously, in this case it is meaningless to require that (**) holds. Subsets of $\mathscr{A}$ or $\mathscr{B}$ may exist and their elements need not yield direct information on the occurrence of events A or B. For example, let it be the case, verified by observation, that the event "rain in L. A. on January 31" (A) has always been preceded by the event "barometric pressure low in Alaska on January 25–30" (A′). Thus $\mathscr{A}'$ generating A′, by implication also generates A. (This interpretation has been motivated by a question of J. Marschak.)
To avoid the above-mentioned difficulty we are going to suggest a *standardization procedure* of information sets by forming a new structure $\mathscr{T}$ order-isomorphic to $\mathscr{T}_0$, consisting of a zero $\bigwedge$ and a unit element $\bigvee$, such that $\mathscr{A}$ is a directed set ordered increasingly with respect to $\leqq:$, i.e. $\bigwedge \leqq : \bigvee \Rightarrow \bigwedge \subseteq \bigvee$. The elements $\bigwedge$ and $\bigvee$ constitute minimal and maximal elements of the structure $\mathscr{T}$, respectively and, in terms of interpretation, they correspond to J. Marschak's (1970) null and perfect information matrices partially ordered by the relation 'not more informative than', although Marschak's approach differs from this one in several respects. The rationale for obtaining a suitable zero and unit element in $\mathscr{T}$ is suggested by two further definitions which quite naturally fit into Definition 1.
Definition 2: A neg-information set (say with respect to any event X)

$O_X \in \mathscr{T}_0$ is defined as follows: If all information available to the person suggests (or, more intuitively, if all information sources agree with each other) that "event X does *not* happen" then we say that the occurrence of X is virtually impossible, i.e. the neg-information set generates the quasi-null event: $H: O_X \rightarrow X \doteq 0 \in \mathscr{S}$ ('$\doteq$' means 'qualitatively equally probable'). Example: $H: \{\langle 0,0,0,0,0,0,\ldots\rangle_{X_n=\text{Heads}}\} \rightarrow X_{n+1} \doteq 0$. (X n times, n very large). The concept of a neg-information set is justified because there is no information whatsoever available indicating that event X is going to happen. Dually we define a *universal information set:*

Definition 3: If all information available suggests that "event Y does happen", then we agree to say that event Y is virtually certain; i.e. the universal information set $\mathscr{E}_Y \in \mathscr{T}_0$ generates the quasei-sure event: $H: \mathscr{E}_Y \rightarrow Y \doteq E \in \mathscr{S}$. Example: $H: \{\langle 1,1,1,1,1,1,\ldots\rangle_{Y_n=\text{Tails}}\} \rightarrow Y_{n+1} \doteq E$ (Y n times, n very large). As it follows by definition, the quasi-null event should not be understood as an impossible event in a strictly logical sense but as an event the individual conceives (based on his information available) as not being possible to occur although the occurrence of this event might still be possible from a logical point of view. This convention identifies all negligible events as quasi-null events which seems to agree with Savage's view (1954). A similar qualification and distinction as valid for the quasi-null event also holds for the quasi-sure event by a dual argument. Fortunately, as D.A. Kappos (1969) has shown, it turns out that the formal structure of a Boolean algebra can be maintained in case of quasi-null and quasi-sure events so that a corresponding "quasiprobability algebra" can be established.

Two different but related types of duality, essentially due to the linking-up of information and event structure (via a Boolean homomorphism) arise from the definition of neg-information and universal information.

First, it is clear that neg-information of any event A yields automatically universal information on the complementary event A^c and vice versa. This observation results from the Boolean structure of events.

Second, neg-information and universal information are themselves dually defined, i.e. the complement of neg-information on any event A is universal information on the same event and vice versa. This also implies that the complement $\mathscr{A}^c$ of any information set $\mathscr{A}$ consists of neginformation about the occurrence of event A.

Thus in the first case duality in the Boolean algebra of events induces equivalence in the Boolean algebra of information sets; in the second case duality in the Boolean algebra of information sets pertains to the same event in the Boolean algebra of events.

If the above-stated definitions hold, the process of generating the quasi-null event as well as the quasi-sure event yield the zero element $\bigwedge$ and the unit element $\bigvee$ in the new structure $\mathscr{T}$. From this it is only a small and natural step toward the assumption that we can define in a similar way standardized information sets (s.i. sets) $\alpha, \beta, \gamma \ldots$ in $\mathscr{T}$ derived from $\mathscr{A}$, $\mathscr{B}, \mathscr{C}, \ldots$ in $\mathscr{S}_0$ and ordered in between the lower and upper bounds $\bigwedge$ and $\bigvee$ respectively. Thus, for some $\alpha, \beta \in \mathscr{T}$ the following statement should be true:

$$(*) \qquad \bigwedge \leqq : \alpha \leqq : \beta \leqq : \bigvee \Rightarrow \bigwedge \subseteq \alpha \subseteq \beta \subseteq \bigvee.$$

Observe that $\mathscr{T}$ is to be considered as a field of subsets of some space, being identical with the unit element $\bigvee$. We may then have the dual sequences of pairs $(\bigwedge, \bigwedge^c)$, $(\alpha, \alpha^c), \ldots, (\beta, \beta^c)$, $(\bigvee, \bigvee^c)$ and $(\bigvee^c, \bigvee)$, $(\beta^c, \beta), \ldots, (\alpha^c, \alpha)$, $(\bigwedge^c, \bigwedge)$.

The first sequence is order-increasing with respect to the first element in each pair but decreasing with respect to the complementary element. By duality, the same is true for the second sequence. The process of standardizing information sets bears some resemblance to psychophysical experiments insofar as those assume that an individual is given two arbitrarily fixed weights and is asked to order other weights between these fixed bounds. However, from a philosophical point of view, the ordering of s.i. sets is much in the spirit of ordering 'attributes' by inclusion according to Boole's First Law. It is justified by the lattice ordered structure to which we refer later.

The underlying idea from a behavioristic point of view is that an individual knows about neg-information and universal information of arbitrary events and that he is capable of ordering all other information according to some rule. (It is implicitly assumed that a person at a given timepoint will evaluate only the maximal amount of information which he receives on a given event.)

The justification for this is further demonstrated by introducing a refinement process. In this context it is worth noting that the so-called principle of insufficient reason (or principle of indifference) can be adequately restated within our framework in an explicit form:

If we have as much information about the occurrence of an event as about the occurrence of the complementary event, then we have no reason to believe this event to be more likely than the complementary event. Therefore, we might say that the standardized information set corresponding to the principle of insufficient reason forms a midpoint between $\bigwedge$ and $\bigvee$.

Let us give two simple kinds of interpretation how the relation 'not more informative than' is connected between the structures $\mathscr{T}_0$ and $\mathscr{T}$. One should bear in mind that the relation of being 'not more informative than' is specified on the assumption that the respective events occur. The order is of course reversed if we relate comparative informativeness to the statement that the respective events do not occur (i.e. that the complementary events occur). The reversibility of order follows from the symmetry property of the relation $\leqq:$. It is then obvious that via the process of generating events by information sets, a compatible ordering according to 'not more probable than' applies to events. In this context, for example, see B. O. Koopman (1940).

One may say that $\mathscr{A}$ is evaluated as not more informative than $\mathscr{B}$ if and only if the standardized information sets α and β (derived from $\mathscr{A}$ and $\mathscr{B}$) satisfy the condition $\alpha \leqq : \beta \Rightarrow \mathrm{a} \subseteq \beta$.

First, if $\mathscr{A}$ is regarded as not more informative than $\mathscr{B}$, then the standardized information α concerning "event A occurs" is almost as large as the standardized information β concerning "event B occurs" (i.e. β contains at least as much information as α), provided both sources of information are considered as equally *reliable*.

Second, if $\mathscr{A}$ is evaluated as not more informative than $\mathscr{B}$, then the s.i. β is regarded as at least as reliable as the s.i. α.

Examples: For the first case let α consist of the sequence of an equally large number of observables $\langle 0,0,0,0,0,1 \rangle$ or (say) $\langle 0,0,1,0,0,0 \rangle$ and let β consist of the sequence $\langle 0,0,0,0,1,1 \rangle$ or (say) $\langle 0,0,1,0,0,1 \rangle$, then clearly β carries at least as much information as α.

For the second case, consider α to consist of $\langle 0,0,0,0,1,1 \rangle$, let β consist of $\langle 0,0,1,0,0,1 \rangle$ and assume β is regarded as at least as reliable as α, then $\mathscr{A}$ is considered to be not more informative than $\mathscr{B}$.

After all, we realize that information (or subjective knowledge) in this context is broadly conceptualized: it covers facts, experience, evidence and agrees with the intuitive meaning of information used in ordinary language.

We here retain the concept of information despite its specific technical meaning in information theory. Information theory suggests the entropy of a random experiment as a measure of the (expected) amount of information (before it is known which random event will occur, for example, which outcome will actually occur by throwing a coin or a dice).

At least in inference processes with non-repeatable events or with a small number of repeatable events, this measure is of limited value. For it is based on the assumptions:

(1) that all restrictive conditions for setting up a random experiment are fulfilled, and

(2) that the probabilities of which event actually occurs are known to the experimenter so that probabilities generate information in the sense that the more likely an event is, the less information is transmitted to the experimenter by the knowledge of its actual occurrence (probabilistic information). (Critical remarks concerning the use of the entropy as a suitable measure of the value of information have been made by J. Marschak (1970)).

We suggest a quite different approach by assuming a somewhat inverse relationship between information and uncertainty (in terms of probabilities) in the sense that the more information we receive about an event, the less uncertain we feel about its occurrence. So evaluation of information sets should precede probability evaluations of events based on relations $\leqq$: and $\leqq\cdot$, respectively.
Consequently, the basic suggestion is to define information first, and then (subjective) probability, rather than the other way around. Hence this suggests reversing Koopman's (1940) intuitive thesis in probability which holds the view that "it is for experience to be interpreted in terms of probability and not for probability to be interpreted in terms of experience". Experience (also objective experience) in my view seems to be prior to probability whatever interpretation you may attach to it.
In connection with our information concept, we have to assume that misinformation, biased information or simply lies will be evaluated as no information at all. This requirement is necessary to avoid pathological evaluations of information with respect to the postulational basis of an information structure. How to decide on misinformation? This is a matter of individual concern regarding its judgement on the reliability of transmitted information from some information source. Hence, although two sequences of observables might yield the same information on two different events, they may be discriminated against each other if one of them proves to be less reliable than the other. However, it should be pointed out that it is irrelevant for a decision-maker (at the time when facing the decision) that some information turns out to be false a posteriori, but it only matters that he believes in the information obtained by him to be honest information. We also disregard a noisy channel in which the received message is not a faithful copy of the one transmitted.
To simplify the main argument I do omit considerations on the cost of information which proves to be negligibe in many practical decision situations but which may be significant for more complex situations involving serious consequences. (The evaluation of information costs is dealt within statistical decision theory, where it is usually assumed that the cost function is a monotonic increasing function of the number of observations.)
According to the arguments above, probability beliefs on events will be based exclusively on the information content a person possesses of each event. This rules out other subjectivistic considerations based on arbitrary feelings, intuition or even metaphysical imagination. It is much more pertinent to sound scientific inference when scientists try to rationalize inference from scientific hypotheses; yet this suggestion does not exclude subjective evaluation reflecting the scientists' state of information, for it is generally acknowledged that some scientists may have different degrees

of information and therefore may infer different conclusions. Conclusions are used here in a technical sense, defined by J.W. Tukey (1960), as "a statement which is to be accepted as applicable to the conditions of an experiment or observation unless and until unusually strong evidence to the contrary arises". They "are established with careful regard to evidence, but without regard to consequences of specific actions in specific circumstances".

Although we start out motivated by Savage's work, the approach used here is perhaps more related to the inference problem of the Keynes-Carnap-Jeffreys type of scientific inference without necessarily having decision acts in mind. For example, according to H. Jeffreys (1961), inferences from past observational data to future ones can only be made by a generalized (inductive) logic, not a deductive one. He is interested in inferences given observational data (a data structure $\mathscr{D}$) such that for two propositions H, H':

$$H \mathrel{\cdot\gtreqless\cdot} H' \qquad \text{given } \mathscr{D}.$$

In contrast to this, we are interested in the ordering of $\mathscr{D}$ according to "not more informative than", so that for two elements $\delta, \delta' \in \mathscr{D}$ (corresponding to our s.i. sets) we may infer

$$\delta \leqq : \delta' \Rightarrow H \leqq \cdot H'.$$

This is a somewhat further elaboration of Jeffrey's ideas, who explicitly points out on several occasions that statements on information are prior to those of probability.

Also this is much in the spirit of inductive inference underlying Bayesian decision theory; however, instead of incorporating information in conditional probability statements, we separate statements on information from those on probability and treat them analytically in a different but related context.

We should emphasize that recent work by Z. Domotor (1970) is similar in motivation to this work; however, it pursues a different method in terms of the theory of relational structure and measurement. The structure studied by Domotor involves an (infinite) Boolean algebra of events endowed with qualitative binary relations $\perp\!\!\!\perp$ and $\precsim$ such that for any two events A, B $\in \mathscr{S}$ the following statements hold:

(1) $A \perp\!\!\!\perp B \langle = \rangle$ Event A is independent of event B

(2) $A \precsim B \langle = \rangle$ Event A does not have more information than event B.

Then Domotor gives conditions which ensure the existence of an information measure in a similar way as the existence of a probability measure can be shown. He assumes that the events themselves convey information, whereas we assume that events are only known by information. This issue can only be settled empirically. We would have to devise experiments which first have to show whether individuals look on events via information and whether they order s.i. sets as suggested by the axioms and theorems. I conjecture that this is the case.

Domotor also provides a useful survey on various approaches to axiomatize information without probability with the exception of the qualitative approach by D. Blackwell (1953). Blackwell and D.V. Lindley (1956) assume that we get information from experiments which involves the comparison of knowledge before and after the experiment. This is one way how we can specify elements of our information sets, i.e. as outcomes of previous random experiments and comparing those with outcomes of other experiments according to informativeness, but here the similarity to these qualitative approaches ends.

We are dealing here with binary relations of qualitative information ($\leqq$:) generated by information structures. These structures themselves form an abstract tool in the study of general topological spaces and it is worth pointing out some formal aspects underlying this approach. The development of general topology was based on several seemingly different concepts of a topological structure including uniform structures (N. Bourbaki) or neighbourhood structures (first studied by F. Hausdorff), defined as relations between subsets of a topological space. These different structures have inspired several authors to seek for a common and basic notion which unifies all these structures and includes them as special cases. An appropriate notion is the order relation '$<$' between open or closed subsets of a space, being at least transitive. On the other hand, if this order relation is known, then the corresponding (order) topology is uniquely determined on some space. There are other examples of topological structures where order relations can be introduced in such a way as to redefine these structures in terms of order. As it turns out, this is possible for a general class of topological structures.

A. Csaszar (1963) has suggested such a general theory of topological structure based on orderings between subsets of a space. He calls these structures *topogeneous structures*. Moreover, and quite interestingly in this context, it turns out that topogeneous structures include Boolean structures which prove to be significant in defining measures on these structures compatible with probability measures defined on Boolean algebras (or equivalently, by Stone's representation theorem, on fields of sets wihch may be understood as algebras of events).

Thus, these kinds of structure provide interesting algebraic and topological properties and furthermore are simple enough to attract serious attention, – for further details see Gottinger (1974).

For reasons of convenience, the essential features of this approach can be summarized as follows:

(i) The concept of an information set is dealt with as an element of an abstract algebraic structure, as an event is treated to be an 'undefined term' in a Kolmogorov probability algebra.

(ii) 'Information' is conceptually confined to 'information pertaining to the occurrence of an event' since we are interested in the inductive problem of making predictions on (future) events. Hence this problem may also be considered as covering a particular aspect of qualitative semantic information by substituting statements on logical truth of a sentence by statements on the occurrence of an event. This implies that any measure-theoretic representation will be that of a normed Boolean measure, not having the nature of a 'surprise value' as in conventional information theory.

(iii) Qualitative information '$\leqq$:' is introduced as a binary relation (ordering) in an information structure, and according to (ii) is interpreted as 'not more informative than' w.r.t. the occurrence of the respective event. It is natural (but not necessary) to view qualitative information as a subjective ordering in the information structure. By the nature of this ordering, the information structure forms a topogeneous structure.

(iv) A qualitative (subjective) information structure generates a qualitative (subjective) probability structure by a Boolean homomorphism. This is to make precise the idea that a person will only evaluate qualitative probability on the basis of qualitative information.

Appendix B – Chapter 9*

An Illustrative Application of the 'Value of Information' to Medical Screening

In the extensive literature on screening and prevention programs it is always implicitly assumed that selective screening on high risk patient groups, for those with coronary disease or breast cancer, leads to a significantly higher detection of true positives, and, therefore, entails a corresponding increase of the number of expected lives saved. Consequently, it is argued that this justifies increased costs of screening programs and related medical care. In this note the value of a screening program is derived on the basis of decision analysis using as a single criterion mortality costs. The conclusion

drawn suggests that increased screening costs could only be justified up to a certain qualified limit, but are not justified beyond this limit.
Suppose you consider two disease complexes A and B, A is a very serious disease, requiring careful monitoring and possibly elective surgery. B is far less serious that needs no further treatment but reveals similar symptoms as A. A screening program is defined as a set of tests conducted on the patient or class of patients that serves in finding unique identifications for patients having disease A.
The physician is considered to be a decision-maker or problem-solver who, to the best of his knowledge and to the availability of given medical technology, structures the decision situation in such a way that the best option is the one which minimizes expected mortality or morbidity considered as expected costs in the overall problem. Additional criteria could be meaningfully taken into account, and they would involve a weighting of multicriteria, but, for the sake of simplicity, we concentrate only on the unique criterion of mortality.
The screening program, consisting of a set of diagnostic tests, often applied sequentially, is considered to be a detection device for finding out whether the patient has disease A or B. We use 'tests' here in a general sense. They might consist of patient history, physical findings or laboratory results. They may be presented in a form suitable for computational purposes, see Ledley and Lusted (1961). In general, this detection device is imperfect, i.e. *error-bound*, so that we are left with asking questions about the reliability of the test(s). For this purpose we could set up a *Test-Reliability Matrix* for our simple problem

Table 1.

	Disease in Patient	
Test results	A	B
A	True positive	False positive
B	False negative	True negative

Here the entries in this table, read along the first or second row, respectively, could be interpreted as:

First row: 'Test results indicate disease A and the patient has disease A'
'Test results indicate disease A and the patient has disease B'
Second row: 'Test results indicate disease B and the patient has disease A'
'Test results indicate disease B and the patient has disease B'

Since by nature of the problem A is far more serious than B, ensuing a sub-

stantial higher cost in terms of mortality or morbidity therefore requiring immediate action on the physician's side, the Test-Reliability Matrix reflects this view in the naming of the entries. (In the case A has been ruled out, one could set up another table comparing B with C, etc. so that the disease with highest priority, requiring most medical attention, is taken proper care of.) Of particular concern here are those patients who on the basis of the test results will be treated on the false disease (false positives) and those for whom the results missed the true disease (false negatives). Suppose then on the basis of these tests, for diseases A and B, completely different therapies, T_1 and T_2, are suggested, for instance T_1 may involve surgery for constraining stomach cancer, T_2 is a mild drug treatment for treating a nonmalignant tumor. Suppose further we have sufficient statistical evidence on therapies T_1 and T_2 with regard to mortality costs, we could set up an outcome table on the decisions (costs) of treatment T_1 and T_2.
The numbers in the entries, used here only for illustrative purposes, are collected statistically for a sufficiently long period of time. But for more

Table 2. Outcomes of decisions (costs) measured by mortality per 1000 patients

	Disease	
Treatment	A	B
T_1	1.50	.70
T_2	30	0

differential costs

practical reasons it might be advisable to decompose the data according to patient groupings pertaining to age or specific environmetntal conditions. Different groups such as old vs.young, or men vs. women may have quite distinct mortality costs, and the overall aggregate average cost matrix may not be applicable to group specific circumstances. For collecting enough group specific, disaggregate data we may run into difficulties of sufficient data aquisition. In that case we may apply advanced statistical techniques (i.e. multiple regression analysis) for overcoming these difficulties.
For any action, T_1 or T_2, the average mortality cost, given as the expected value of mortality, can be computed after specifying the probability of each disease state, A or B. Unless one has a sufficient data base one often finds it difficult to calculate the probability of the disease state. In this case the physician is required to make an introspective judgment or *reasonable* guess and to come with a subjective probability reflecting his professional judgment. Various methods to attain a subjective probability can be applied, see De Finetti (1972) or Savage (1971), in terms of betting quotients, or comparing disease states with events for which well-known (objective) probabilities exist.

Suppose the physician's prior probability of disease state A is $P(A) = .05$, and for B it is $P(B) = .95$. Then, on the basis of Table 2, we compute the expected value of decision:

$$EV(T_1) = .05 \times 1.5 + .95 \times .70 = .075 + .665 = .74$$

$$EV(T_2) = .05 \times 30 + .95 \times 0 = 1.5$$

Clearly, the action with lowest average mortality cost is best.
The computations show that if you want to make a *terminal* decision or equivalently, if the costs of gaining information about specifying P exceed the benefit of this information, for patients with .05 probability of having disease A it is better to apply T_1 than T_2.
In fact, looking at the average mortality costs, T_1 costs .74/1000 in mortality, but T_2 costs 1.5/1000 in mortality. This is so because the consequence of applying T_2 if A is true is severe enough to outweigh its small probability. (The underlying assumption is that 'waiting three months' or 'adopting a mild drug treatment plan' substantially decreases those patients' survival chances with disease state A).
As we can summarize, at this point, the best decision depends on the probabilities of the various disease states and on the costs of mortality associated to the given diseases. By fixing the mortality rates, one can easily determine the *threshold probability* at which point it becomes advisable to switch from strategy T_2 to strategy T_1. The threshold probability can be calculated as follows:

$$EV(T_1) = P \times 1.5 + (1 - P) \times .70 + .80\,P$$

$$EV(T_2) = P \times 30 + (1 - P) \times 0 = 30\,P$$

Equalizing, $EV(T_1) = .70 + .80\,P = EV(T_2) = 30\,P$, yields $P = .024$
Costs of mortality depending on threshold probabilities

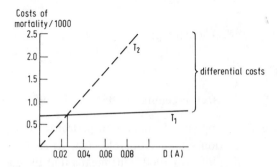

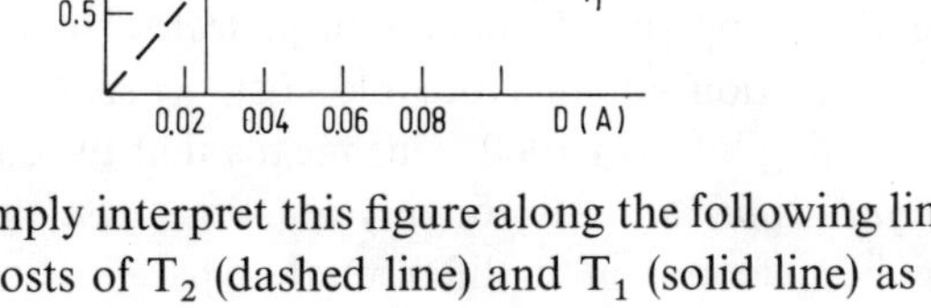

One can simply interpret this figure along the following lines. We graph the mortality costs of T_2 (dashed line) and T_1 (solid line) as a function of the probability of A. If there is no chance of A occurring, there is no cost to

T_2, but there is always a cost to the more severe treatment T_1. (If T is not considered as a treatment, but as yet another test it could be understood that applying the test itself affects the mortality rate. Suppose that in the case of breast cancer, screening for women mammography is generally applied. Then the additional risk for applying mammography for a particular patient group is reflected in its impact by increased mortality costs and therefore could be fit into this framework).

But to the extent that A becomes more likely, the 'T_2-strategy' quickly be-becomes more dangerous. Up to the threshold level one should adopt a 'wait strategy', above this level one should switch to a more radical therapy. Costs and probabilities obviously are interdependent. If you vary the costs in terms of probability, you correspondingly shift the threshold probabilities. Recalling that a screening program consists of a sequence of tests to be performed, it appears as common sense reasoning, that under ideal circumstances a diagnostic test should show those persons or population groups to have the disease who actually have the disease. In other words, the best that any screening program can do is to *correctly* classify all patients. Since this requirement can be fulfilled only under exceptional, ideal circumstances, we could consider this state as our reference system and set out to enquire about the costs that obtain in such a system. It is clear that the costs in such a system cannot be decreased, given the present level of medical technology and medical knowledge. Since the value of a *perfect* screening program is the one that diagnoses a high risk factor group correctly and consequently leads to an adequate therapy, one would be interested in the value of information that minimizes diagnostic mistakes emanating from any screening program, coming close to a perfect screening program.

In other words, by improving the diagnostic-treatment situation one asks how much is more information worth?

By referring to Table 2 a perfect screening program yields mortality costs by computing

$$\begin{aligned} EV(T_1 \mid (\text{perfect screening})) &= P \times 1.50 + (1 - P) \times 0 = \\ &= .05 \times 1.50 + .95 \times 0 = .075 \end{aligned}$$

as compared to

$$EV(T_1 \mid (\text{imperfect screening})) = .05 \times 1.50 + .95 \times .70 = .74$$

In verbal interpretation, applying T_1 in case of perfect screening kills only .075/1000 of the population, an unavoidable cost, whereas applying T_1 given imperfect screening kills .74/1000. This means that the cost of action in the light of *perfect information* is roughly ten times less than the cost associated to the best action on undifferentiated patients (apply T_1 to everyone). The *expected valve of perfect information*, therefore, is equal to the difference of these two, since the mortality cost of .075/1000 appears unavoidable unless better methods of treatment are available.

To emphasize the point of optional treatment with or without screening on patient groups, we shall rewrite costs for each disease state in terms of regrets caused by mistakes. (To set up a regret matrix is a familiar procedure in statistical decision theory.)

The number 28.50 in the lower left entry of the matrix comes from 30/1000, the costs of a 'wait strategy', minus 1.50/1000, the costs of the only correct

Table 3. Outcome expressed as differential mortality cost per 1000 (regret) due to improper treatment

	Disease in patient	
Treatment	A	B
T_1	0	.70
T_2	28.50	0

treatment, T_1. The upper left hand entry gets zero, since the action is correct. The upper right entry remains as it is, since the cost of the correct action, T_2, (to be deducted) is zero.

Up to now we considered only the value of perfect screening as compared to no screening at all, taking the unavoidable mortality costs of a correct treatment as a basic reference point. The situation where perfect information can be acquired is rare, whereas partial information is often obtainable. Nevertheless, the expected value of perfect information is useful because it provides an upper bound to that for partial information. Therefore, more generally, we could exhaust the whole spectrum on evaluating different screening programs and figuring out the value of information in terms of mortality costs. It should be obvious that a crucial point in comparing these programs is the validity of their test results, that is the degree of accuracy according to which these tests identify and classify the correct disease-state patients.

Consider only a possible result of test validation for illustrative purposes.

Table 4. Test validation

	Disease in patient	
Test results	A	B
A	.8	.1
B	.2	.9

Such numbers might be obtained by collecting data on a series of patients who are all given the test, and then later investigated to see whether they

really had the disease or not. Unless a representative sample of them can be autopsied, there may be problems with this test verification.
(The above table suggests that sensitivity of the test is .8, and specificity of the test is .9.)
Now, how do test results affect estimates of the probability of disease? Bayesian statistics provide techniques for revising initial or prior probabilities in the light of new information. The information must be new to have any effect. In statistical analysis, the events are said to be independent if information about the occurrence of one event does not change our estimate of the probability that the other event occurred.
Independence of medical evidence is hard to judge, to estimate whether two tests are really independent in their predictions, one may have to collect substantially more cases. Sometimes there may be theoretical reasons to believe tests are independent – one may be biochemical, and another anatomical. Bayes'theorem weights prior probabilities by their likelihood, it follows from the definition of conditional probability. The conditional probability of A given that the test indicates A is defined by

$$P(A|\text{Test} = A) = \frac{P(A \text{ and Test} = A)}{P(\text{Test} = A)},$$

i.e. is defined to be the probability of both A and a true A-test result divided by the total probability of a positive A test result. In the numerator, we see the effects of our hypothetical test on patients .05 of whom are assumed (apriori) to have A. The test identifies 80% of them correctly, so $.05 \times .8 = .04$ are identified correctly as having A by the test. Also in the denominator are the 10% of B falsely called A by the test. The test will say that $.05 \times .8 + .95 \times .1 = .135$ have A, and $.04/.135 = .296$ of those so identified really will have it. A similar calculation shows, namely

$$P(A|\text{Test} = B) = \frac{P(A \text{ and Test} = B)}{P(\text{Test} = B)} = \frac{.05 \times .2}{.05 \times .2 + .95 \times .9} = .012$$

that only .012 of those the test says have B will have A. The test has split the formerly homogeneous group of patients, each of whom pretended to have a 5% chance of A, into two distinct groups. One group has an almost 30% chance of A, and the other about a 1% chance of A.
Let us see how we could assemble the various bits of information contained in Bayes' theorem: the differential cost (regret) matrix and the test validity data, forming the *likelihood*, to construct *the value of a test* represented only by a single criterion, the mortality rate. In general, *the value of the test is simply computed by subtracting the average costs of the best action before the information of the test is available, from the best action afterwards.*

Table 5. Flow-chart

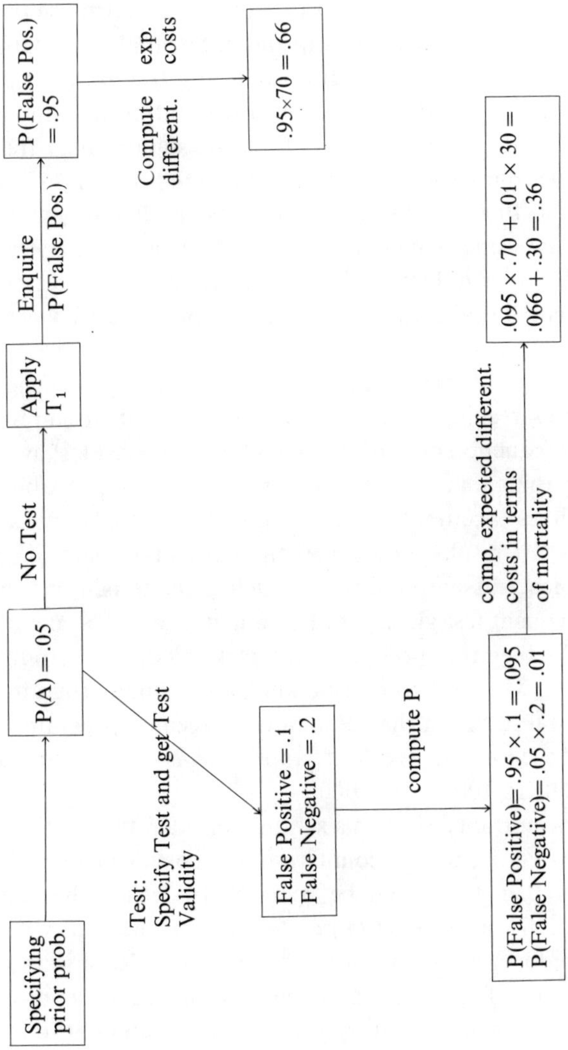

These computations presented in a flow-chart form use the added costs of mistakes over correct actions in the differential cost matrix. Applying T_1 immediately kills .70/1000 of those having B. Given the prior probability on B the *expected additional mortality* without the test amounts to $.095 \times .70 = .66$. After the test only 10% of these are subject to T_1-treatment, whereas 20% of the true A cases wait, for a differential cost of .36. The test has saved exactly .30/1000 deaths. Unless the test itself kills more than that, it is justified by using reduction of mortality as a single criterion. (It may not be justified by a different criterion, e.g. resource costs associated to the test but this could be determined only by an appropriate benefit cost calculation of the test.)

In principle, the same computations go through in a sequence of tests making the entire screening program. Suppose one wants to improve the results in a further reduction of mortality by taking the latest test as a reference point. The only thing that changes is to replace the prior probabilities by posterior probabilities – computed according to Bayes' theorem on the basis of the previous test results. Of course, one has to take care of a strict statistical independence assumption by conducting the tests. If it turns out, say, that the subsequent test yields a differential cost of .20, as compared to the first test of .36, then the subsequent test is worth at most .16 in mortality. Suppose, then, without loss of generality, a screening program consists only of these two tests. Then the value of the screening program is the sum of the value of each of the two tests, applied *independently* and *sequentially*, e.g. $.30/1000 + .16/1000 = .46/1000$.

If besides mortality, there is a serious consideration by the medical decision maker of taking into account resource costs generated by the screening program, then this could be achieved by letting the consumer (patient) determine his *willingness to pay* for the unit monetary cost of the test in exchange for a reduction of mortality. From decision theoretic principles we know that if someone has a 1 in 1000 chance of having a life-threatening problem, he might be willing to pay a certain amount to find out.

In fact, J. P. Acton (1973), by using this methodology as originally proposed by T. C. Schelling (1968), worked out a refined catalogue of questionnaires that inquired about people's preferences with regard to various public programs including a screening-monitor-pretreatment program for heart diseases.

However, it appears as an immediate problem that consumers of medical care may not adopt this obviously rational approach, anxiety may prevent them to find out whether there is a medical problem that can be detected by screening.

In the sequel we deal with some important extensions and complications of the previous analysis.

(1) Test results out of screening programs may not be split into two categories, but instead may discretely range over several levels. Readings of biochemical levels might give rise to several, non-unique interpretations. The picture interpreted by a radiologist may present convincing, weak, confusing or no evidence of the disease in question. Suppose that the information in the patient's history and physical findings have been grouped into five categories, as shown in the next table.
For instance, the category 'A likely' contains 30% of A cases and 10% of B cases.

Table 6.

Test results	Disease A	B
A	.2	.1
A likely	.3	.1
Non-conclusive	.3	.3
B likely	.1	.2
B	0	.3

If a test could provide that much of more detailed, refined information it should not be arbitrarily calibrated to two categories, calling the top two categories A and the bottom three B. It is important to report test information as precisely and completely as possible.
(2) As indicated previously, costs in health programs have a multicriteria representation, the investigation of single components may be only of limited value. For some diseases health costs are fairly easy to evaluate, long-range aftereffects are not too important. For cancer and many other diseases, other health costs must be considered. Suppose a breast cancer screening program screens women at 50, and saves 10 people who otherwise would have died at 55, extending their lives to 70. On the other hand, suppose the radiation of testing causes 10 additional cases of cancer so that 10 people who would otherwise have died at 70, die instead at 65. The net change in mortality of the program is zero, but the net gain in years of life is 100. In such case you feel that years-of-life is a better measure of health costs than simple mortality. For cancer, in particular, quality-of-life is important. Healthy years are rated higher than low-quality years.
We can minimize either average immediate mortality costs, or average years-of-life costs or average resource costs. The best cost-minimizing action is different for different types of costs. Not all costs can be minimized at the same time. Thus, even the best treatment plan involves tradeoffs of one type of cost for another. This seems to be in accord with pursuing 'compromising strategies' by implementing screening programs, and, in fact, this is proposed by some researchers in the field (see L. E. Blumenson, 1977).

(3) If various categories of costs such as resource costs, disability days (a surrogate measure of years-of-life costs) and mortality are plotted against threshold probabilities of disease state A, on a continous scale between 0 and 1, the medical resource costs of a *delayed* T_1-treatment could amount to being only twice as high as a timely T_1-treatment, but according to Table 2 the mortality costs are 30 times as high. This is reflected by the fact that the probability of A for the minimum mortality costs is considerably lower than the probability point for the minimum resource costs. In other words, *aggressive treatment costs money but saves lives.*

In general, all the marginal cost curves rise sharply as the probability of A increases. A T_1-strategy is definitely indicated for high probabilities. All the cost curves decrease starting from probability zero. Excessive T_1-treatment at low probability of a serious disease is expensive and dangerous. (In fact, this seems to support empirical findings that excessive surgery at low probability of serious diseases is likely to cost lives besides eating up a substantial portion of resource costs.)

Suppose the physician chooses to reduce the threshold probability slightly (e.g. applying a T_1-strategy on patients with slightly lower probabilities of A), he could save (say) 100 more lives a year at a cost of 10,000,000 monetary units and 50,000 disability days. Each life thus costs 100,000 monetary units and 500 days. Is this an acceptable price for a life saved? Now, if you think life is worth more, you should choose a threshold probability point closer to the minimum mortality point. If you think the costs are too high, you should use a somewhat higher probability point.

J. P. Acton, *Evaluation Public Programs to Save Lives: The Case of Heart Attacks*, Rand Corporation, R-50-RC, Santa Monica, Ca. (1973).

L. E. Blumenson, "Compromise Screening Strategies for Chronic Disease", *Mathematical Biosciences* 34, (1977), 79–94.

B. de Finetti, *Probability, Induction and Statistics*, Wiley: London, New York (1972).

R. S. Ledley and L. B. Lusted, "Medical Diagnosis and Modern Decision Making", *Proc. of Symp. Appl. Math.*, Vol. XIV, Am. Math. Soc., Providence (1961).

L. J. Savage, Elicitation of Personal Probabilities and Expectations', *Jour. Amer. Statist. Assoc.* 66, 1971, 783–801 (1971).

T. C. Schelling, "The Life you Save may be your Own", in *Problems in Public Expenditure Analysis* (S. B. Chase, ed.), Brooking: Washington, D. C. (1968).

Suggested Readings

Aitchison, J.: Choice against Chance. An Introduction to Statistical Decision Theory, Reading (Mass.) 1970.

Bar-Hillel, Y. and R. Carnap: 'An Outline of a Theory of Semantic Information', Tech. Rep. No. 247, Research Lab. of Electronics, M.I.T. 1952, in *Language and Information*, Bar-Hillel, Y. ed., Reading, Mass. 1964, 221.

Birnbaum, A.: 'On the Foundations of Statistical Inference', Ann. Math. Statist. 32, 1961, 414.
Blackwell, D.: 'Comparison of Experiments', Proc. 2nd Berkeley Symp. Math. Statist. and Probability, 1953, 93.
Blackwell, D. and M.A. Girshick: Theory of Games and Statistical Decisions, New York 1954.
Blackwell, D., 'Comparison of Experiments', *Proc. 2nd Berkeley Symp. Math. Stat. Prob.*, 1953, 93–102.
Csaszar, A., *Grundlagen der allgemeinen Topologie*, Budapest, 1963.
Domotor, Z., '*Qualitative Information and Entropy Structures*', in *Information and Inference* (ed. by J. Hintikka and P. Suppes) , Dordrecht, Holland, 1970, 148–194.
Groot de, M.: Optimal Statistical Decisions, New York 1970.
Erdös, P.: 'On the Distribution Function of Additive Functions', Ann. of Math. 47, 1946, 1.
Fadeev, D.K.: 'On the Concept of the Entropy for a Finite Probability Model', Uspehi Mat. Nauk 11, 1958, 227 (in Russian).
Fuchs, L.: Partially Ordered Algebraic Systems, London 1963.
Gottinger, H.W.: 'Qualitative Information and Comparative Informativeness', Kybernetik 13, 1973, 81.
Gottinger, H.W., 'Subjective Qualitative Information Structure', *Theory and Decision* 5, 1974 , 69–97.
Hartmanis, J., Generalized Partitions and Lattice Embedding Theorems', *Proc. Symp. Pure Math. II*, Am. Math. Soc., Providence, 1961.
Hartmanis, J. and Stearns, R.E., *Algebraic Structure Theory of Sequential Machines*, Englewood-Cliffs, 1966.
Howard, R.A.: 'Information Value Theory', IEEE Trans. Syst. Science and Cyber. SSC-2, 1966, 22.
Ingarden, R.S. and K. Urbanik: 'Information without Probability', Colloq. Math. 9, 1962, 131.
Jeffreys, H., *Theory of Probability*, 3rd ed., Oxford, 1961 .
Kappos, D.A., *Probability Algebras and Stochastic Spaces*, New York , 1969.
Kampé de Fériet, J.: 'Mésure de l'information fournie par un évènement', Les Probabilités sur les Structures Algébriques, Paris 1970, 191.
Kelly, J.L.: 'A new Interpretation of Information Rate', Bell System Technical Jour. 35, 1956, 917.
Kolmogorov, A.N.: 'Three Approaches to the Definition of the Concept "Quantitiy of Information"', Problemy Peredaci Informacii 1, 1965, 3 (in Russian).
Kolmogorov, A.N.: 'Logical Basis for Information Theory and Probability Theory', IEEE Trans. Information Theory IT-14, 1967, 662.
Koopman, B.O., 'The Axioms and Algebra of Intuitive Probability', *Ann. Math.* 41, 1940, 269–292.
Lindley, D.V., 'On a Measure of the Information provided by an Experiment', *Ann. Math. Stat.* 27, 19 56, 986–1005.
Krantz, D.: Foundations of Measurement II, New York 1973.
Lee, P.M.: 'On the Axioms of Information Theory', Ann. Math. Statist. 35, 1964, 415.
Longo, G.: Quantitative-Qualitative Mesure of Information, CISM Courses and Lectures No. 138, Wien 1972.
Lusted, Introduction to Medical Decision-Making, Springfield, Ill. 1968.
Ledley, R.S. and L.B. Lusted: 'Medical Diagnosis and Modern Decision Making, Proc. Symp. Appl. Math. 14, 1961.
MacKay, D.M.: Information, Mechanism and Meaning, Cambridge 1969.

Marschak, J.: 'Economics of Information Systems', in Frontiers of Quantitative Economics, Amsterdam 1971.

Marschak, J. and R. Radner: Economic Theory of Teams, New Haven 1972.

Marschak, J., 'Economics of Information Systems', in *Frontiers of Quantitative Economics* (ed. by M.D. Intriligator), Amsterdam, 1970, 32–107.

McGuire, C.B., 'Comparisons of Information Structures', Working Paper No. 262, Center for Research in Management Science, University of California, Berkeley, published in *Decision and Organization* (ed. R. Radner and C.B. McGuire), Amsterdam, 1972, 101–130.

Renyi, A., *Foundations of Probability*, San Francisco, 1970.

Raiffa and Schlaifer, Chapt. 1, Sec. 3.4, Part II.

Schlaifer, Chapt. 22, Sec. 30.4, Part IV.

Rényi, A.: 'On Measures of Entropy and Information', Proc. 4th Berkeley Symp. Math. Statist. and Probability, 1961, 547.

Rényi, A.: 'On the Foundations of Information Theory', Bull. International Statistical Institute 33, 1965.

Savage, L.J., *The Foundations of Statistics*, New York, 1954.

Shannon, C.E. and E. Weaver: The Mathematical Theory of Communication, Urbana, Ill. 1949.

Sikorski, R.: Boolean Algebras (2nd ed.), Göttingen–Berlin 1964.

Tukey, J.W., 'Conclusions vs. Decisions', *Technometrics* 2 (1960), 423–433.

Wiener, N.: Cybernetics, Cambridge, Mass. 1949.

10. Sequential Analysis and Optimal Stopping

10.1 General Considerations

We are here going to analyze and discuss a very important class of decision problems which involve time explicitly as an irreversible resource. These problems are known as dynamic or sequential decision problems. They have a most natural formulation since every real-life decision has to take care of 'time-induced' changes to which the decision maker has to adjust or to adapt. These types of problems may be extremely complex: they may involve changes in preferences, technology and resources: the environment. Complexities may be added by uncertainty or lack of information and multidimensionality. A general, very useful technique of resolving dynamic decision problems has been introduced by R. Bellman's programming (1957). The original class of decision problems treated by dynamic programming was restricted to deterministic problems. Later dynamic programming in conjunction with the theory of Markov chains and general stochastic processes have covered uncertainty, and the case of conflict among many decision-makers acting sequentially in time has been treated by differential game theory. In statistics, sequential analysis was developed by A. Wald (1947) in the forties as a consequent extension of statistical decision theory.

All these problems, although originating in various subjects, have common elements and also involve similar methods.

We first describe some of the problems and methods and then turn toward statistical problems in which Bayesian methods play a crucial role. Bayes' theorem obtains new importance in view of obtaining new information by sequential experimentation.

10.2 Sequential Decision Problems

In every conventional decision problem one is faced with the situation to act in one or another way. Then if the decision is taken and a particular event occurs, a certain result will be obtained. In a sequential decision problem one has another option which could be summarized as 'wait and see', or 'go on and take another observation'. This choice problem constitutes one stage, if the choice problem is carried over several stages then the obvious question arises when should the decision maker stop collecting further information. This depends upon his expected utility of taking one more observation. But it is difficult to compute the expected utility of taking one more observation. In order to find the best decision now, i.e. whether to stop and make a decision or to go on and take another observation, it is necessary to know the best decision in the future. Consequently, the search for an optimal decision should not proceed according to chronological time but in reverse order to work backwards in time since the present optimum involves the future optimum. This fundamental fact is incorporated in the principle of *dynamic programming.*

Let U(w, t) be the expected utility of the best sequential scheme when starting from a situation in which the parameters describing the distribution of θ are w and t, w changes randomly and t deterministically. (w could be the mean of the distribution of θ, and t the inverse of the variance, i.e. the precision.) Let $\bar{U}(w, t)$ be the expected utility of taking the best decision now, without further observations. Then U(w, t) is either $\bar{U}(w, t)$ (and it is not worth taking further observations) or it is worth taking further observations. In the latter case we start with U(w, t) and look at the change of the situation, i.e. w and t change to w′ (randomly) and t + h (deterministically). Let then $P(w'|w, t)$ be the distribution of w′ given w and t, let c(t, h) be the cost of 'taking one more observation' from t to t + h.

Then in general, by taking further observations the expected utility functional is

$$U(w, t) = \int U(w', t+h)\, P(w'|w, t)\, dw' - c(t, h).$$

The optimality principle, according to dynamic programming, requires that

$$U(w, t) = \max\{\bar{U}(w, t) : \int U(w', t-h)\, P(w'|w, t)\, dw' - c(t, h)\}$$

This optimality principle yields a unique criterion on optimal stopping depending on wheter or not

$$U(w, t) = \max\{\bar{U}(w, t)\}$$

10.3 The Marriage Problem

This type of sequential decision problem is representative for a very general class of decision problems that can be solved via dynamic programming, or with other tools (Chow (1964)].

A known number of ladies, n, are going to be inspected in a random order. You are able to rank them according to some fixed criterion catalogue as to which lady will best meet your standards. Let r, an integer, be that number indicating the rank among n ladies, $1 \leqq r \leqq n$. At any stage of this procedure you may either propose to one lady (by which the procedure stops) or continue inspecting. Whenever you inspected a girl and you didn't propose she will never come back, i.e. she will never get inspected again.

If you propose to a lady she will always accept. What is the optimal stopping rule? The desirability of every lady to be inspected is represented by a utility index U_i, the utility of being married to the i−th lady with the i−th rank with

$$U_{i-1} \geqq U_i \geqq U_{i+1}$$

We denote by r the number of n ladies, and by s the apparent rank after some ladies have been inspected, hence r changes deterministically and s changes randomly.

Correspondingly, we denote the expected utility by U(s, r) and $\bar{U}(s, r)$, respectively. Now, the probability that the r−th lady of apparent rank s will have true rank S is easily calculated by the binomial equation

$$\text{(1)} \qquad \binom{S-1}{s-1}\binom{n-S}{r-s}\bigg/\binom{n}{r} = P_{S:\,s,\,r}$$

Hence we have

$$\text{(2)} \qquad \bar{U}(w, t) = \bar{U}(s, r) = \sum_{i=s}^{s+n-r} P_{S:\,s,\,r}$$

as the expected utility, and $\bar{U}(s, r)$ is considered to be a known function. Given the situation to have chosen the s−th rank out of r inspections, the probability that the next lady will have apparent rank s′ is clearly 1/(r+1) for all s′ so that P(s′|s, r) equals 1/(r+1).

Hence, the expected utility functional becomes

$$\text{(3)} \qquad U(s, r) = \max\{\bar{U}(s, r): \sum_{i=1}^{r+1} U(i, r+1)/r+1)\}$$

Consider two cases.

1) Set $U_1 = 1$ and $U_i = 0$ for $i > 1$, i.e. follow the instruction 'always take the best'. Then the optimality criterion – to search for – is according to (3).

$$\text{(4)} \qquad U(1, r) = \max\{r/n: \sum_{i=1}^{r+1} U(i, r+1)/(r+1)\}$$

and

$$\text{(5)} \qquad U(s, r) = \sum_{i=1}^{r+1} U(i, r+1)/(r+1) \quad \text{for} \quad s > 1$$

U(s, r) must be a function only of r since with increasing r it is more likely to find the true top rank S which coincides with s. (4) and (5) may be written in terms of recursive functions.

$$\text{(6)} \qquad U(1, r) = \max\{r/n, n_r\}$$

$$\text{(7)} \qquad n_r = \frac{1}{r+1}\{U(1, r+1) + r n_{r+1}\}.$$

2) Suppose $U(1, r) > \bar{U}(1, r) = r/n$, i.e. the utility of continuing exceeds that of proposing. It follows from (6) that $U(1, r) = n_r$ and from (7), by reducing the value of r by one, $u_{r-1} = u_r$.
Therefore, $u_r > r/n$, $u_{r-1} > (r-1)/n$ and from (6) $U(1,r) > \bar{U}(1,r) > U(1,r-1) > (r-1)/n$. If it is not worth proposing to a lady who is best out of r it is not worth proposing to a lady who is best out of (r−1). The best strategy must be to propose to a lady who is best out of r, provided r is large enough. How large should r be?
Suppose that $U(1, r) = \bar{U}(1, r) = r/n$ and $U(1, r') = r'/n$ for all $r' \geqq r$. From (7) we derive

$$(8) \qquad u_r = \frac{1}{r+1}\left\{\frac{r+1}{n} + r u_{r+1}\right\} \quad \text{of if} \quad v_r = u_r/r : v_r = \frac{1}{nr} + v_{r+1},$$

for all r. Adding together the r.h.s. of these equations we get

$$(9) \qquad v_r = \frac{1}{n}\left\{\frac{1}{r} + \frac{1}{r+1} + \ldots + \frac{1}{n-1}\right\} \quad \text{and}$$

$$(10) \qquad \frac{1}{r} + \frac{1}{r+1} + \ldots + \frac{1}{n-1} < 1 \qquad \text{(bounded by 1).}$$

As long as (10) exists it is worth proposing to the best lady out of r.
Let r = R be the least such value, that is

$$(11) \qquad \frac{1}{R} + \frac{1}{R+1} + \ldots + \frac{1}{n-1} < 1 < \frac{1}{R-1} + \frac{1}{R} + \frac{1}{R+1} + \ldots + \frac{1}{n-1}$$

Then from (7) with $r = R - 1$:

$$(12) \qquad u_{R-1} = \frac{1}{R}\left\{\frac{R}{n} + (R-1)u_R\right\} = \frac{R-1}{n}\left\{\frac{1}{R-1} + \frac{1}{R} + \ldots + \frac{1}{n-1}\right\}$$

from (9).
If n is large the value of R is given by $\int_R^n dx/x = 1$ where the series (10) is approximated by an integral and hence $n/R = e$ is the base of natural logarithm. Hence for large n the optimum rule is to inspect until a proportion e^{-1} (0.368) has been inspected and then to propose to any subsequent lady of apparent rank one. The expected utility, given by (12), is calculated by e^{-1}. If someone looks for a marriage partner at 18 through 40 (i.e. 22 years) one should never propose until age $18 + .368 \cdot 22 = 26$.

10.4 Stopping Rule Problems

The essential features of a stopping rule problem can be split into two parts, consisting of:

(1) A probabilistic mechanism, that is, a random device that moves from state to state under a known, partially known, or unknown probability law.
(2) A payoff and decision structure such that, after observing the current state, we have a choice of at most two decisions.
(a) Take your accumulated payoff to date and quit.
(b) Pay an entrance fee for the privilege of watching one more observation.
This procedure is very natural for casino or gambling problems.
Some of the following examples have been lucidly described by L. Breiman. Unrestricted coin-tossing, restricted coin-tossing, house-hunting problem, purchasing a used car, parking place problem, the stock market problem, the job searching problem, the dynamic inventory problem.
Other classes of problems contain the product design problem, medical diagnosis and sequential control processes.
The gambling problem often involves the following scheme:
An urn contains N red balls and M blue balls. You are allowed to draw with or without replacement as long as there are any balls in the urn. Each time you draw a red ball you receive one dollar and each time you draw a blue ball you lose one dollar. This situation can be formulated as follows.
Let $\{\mathbf{x}_k, k = 1, 2, \dots\}$ be a sequence of random variables, and let $\mathbf{x}_k = +1$ provided the k − th toss results in heads and −1 provided it results in tails. Then $\mathbf{s}_n = \sum_1^n \mathbf{x}_k$ is the accumulated profit at the n − th toss. If you and your opponent are infinitely wealthy you could adopt two decision rules: Stop and collect your profits (or pay your losses) or continue for at least one more toss. (In case of a restricted coin-tossing situation, where your initial fortune $\mathbf{s}_0$ is finite, there may be at some stage a forced stopping rule, e.g. $\mathbf{s}_n = -\mathbf{s}_0$, you have lost all your money and must quit.)
An attractive strategy would be 'to stop when you are ahead'. Such coin-tossing game can be treated fully by Markov devices. Examples of this type will be encountered in a subsequent section on gambling problems. As a probabilistic device we can understand a Markov chain with a countable number of states and specified stationary transition probabilities. Under the conditions specified, Markov devices work well far gambling problems. Other devices are possible, those which require more or less restrictions such as simple random walks, Brownian motion, martingales, or other stochastic processes (see L. Breiman (1968), L. Doob (1965), Dubins and Savage (1965), Griffeath and J.L. Snell (1974)). For practical applications and computational work they rely in most cases on the functional equation approach of dynamic programming. The initial state $\mathbf{s}_0$ covers all relevant information of the past. The Markov property is defined by the assumption that if $\mathbf{s}_n$ (e.g. accumulated winnings) is the state at time n, then P ($\mathbf{s}_{n+1} = s_j$ given $\mathbf{s}_n = s_j$ and all past history up time n) = $P(s_j | s_i)$ is the specified transition probability of moving to state s_j from state s_i, satisfying

$$P(s_j \mid s_i) \geqq 0, \sum_{s_j} P(s_j \mid s_i) = 1.$$

One immediate empirical outcome of the Markov property is to be seen in the fact that the past is incorporated in the present so that the transition probabilities are only conditioned on the present state.

10.5 Payoff and decision structure

Any stopping rule problem may involve a specification of the initial conditions and a payment of the entrance fee (as a compensation for taking part in a game). After some duration of the play you may either collect your winnings or losses to date or continue playing. The collection of your winnings or losses may be referred to as your (sequential) payoff. The terminal payoff $F(s_i)$ is the integral payoff over time. Payoff and entrance fees are virtually dual notions in this context. To the decision rule 'stop and collect the payoff $F(s_i)$' we will associate a stopping set T_s containing all forced stopping states at which we must stop and collect $F(s_i)$. For example, you may end in a state s_i where the game is forced to stop, for whatever reason. Likewise, consider a set T_c, disjoint from T_s, containing all forced continuation states associated to the decision rule 'continue and pay the fee $f(s_j)$', i.e. being in a state s_j we may be forced to continue playing, the set of these states is the set of forced continuation states. So payoffs and costs (of observation) are dually related. Consider a simple coin-tossing game. The probabilistic device has the Markov property with transition probabilities:

$$\begin{aligned} P(s_j \mid s_i) &= \tfrac{1}{2} \quad \text{for} \quad s_j = s_{i+1}, \\ &= \tfrac{1}{2} \quad \text{for} \quad s_j = s_{i-1}, \\ &= 0 \quad \text{for other values of } j. \end{aligned}$$

A well defined stopping rule must tell us when to stop along each possible sequence of states, since otherwise it would be possible for the device to produce a sequence of states along which our rule would not hold. Therefore, a stopping rule involves a matching process between a criterion catalogue represented by expected utility and computational costs in terms of 'costs of observation'. The best stopping rule, the solution we are seeking, makes the expected utility or expected monetary value as large as possible. In general, expected total payoff (rather than utility) is defined by

$$EZ = \sum Z(s_0, s_1, \ldots, s_n)\, P(s_0, s_1, \ldots, s_n)$$

where the sum is taken over all stopping sequences on the list weighted by the probability of the sequence. $Z(s_0, s_1, \ldots, s_n)$ is the payoff function.

A stopping rule then involves a binary choice 'either stop or continue observing, sampling etc.'. Let T be the set of these rules, then a stopping rule T* is *optimal* with respect to the total expected payoff if $E_{T*} Z \geqq E_T Z$ for all other stopping rules T.
Stability of a stopping rule means that it can be approximated, in terms of payoff, by rules in which we decide to quit after a large but fixed number of plays. This corresponds to a forced stopping rule.

10.6 Decision Trees

A heuristic device for representing sequential decisions is given by decision trees. Also it presents an intuitive meaning to the idea of structuring and organizing complex decisions in a time context, where a decision problem can be broken down into a sequence of problems which follow one another in a natural time order. Standard examples of that sort are the product decision problem or other R & D decision problems, the medical diagnosis and treatment problem and the investment decision problem, but the list can be extended almost indefinitely. Example of a product decision problem can be traced as follows: The decision grows from the left to the right, and it reflects the structure of decisions (decision nodes) and uncertainty (random nodes) in a sequential framework. Although it proceeds in a chronological order, it has been demonstrated by the optimality principle of dynamic programming that to obtain an optimal decision in terms of maximizing expected utility (or minimizing expected loss) it is necessary to proceed in the reverse direction since an optimal sequential decision can only be maintained if each of the next steps of the decision have shown to be optimal. A decision tree consists of a series of branches (corresponding to the complexity of the problem). Summarizing, the decision tree method proceeds in the following stages:
(1) the tree is written out in chronological order, the decisions and events being described by branches in the order in which they occur,
(2) probabilities are attached to branches emerging from random nodes in any coherent way,
(3) utilities are attached to the terminal branches,
(4) proceeding back from the terminals to the base, by taking expectations at random nodes and maximizing at decision nodes, the best decisions and their expected utilities are determined.
This procedure is well adapted to computational work and to the structure of dynamic programming, see D.V. Lindley (1970), Chapt. 8.

10.7 Adaptive Processes and Optimal Stopping

Another type of application of optimal stopping rule is motivated by adaptive processes occuring in sequential sampling. Suppose that there are two drugs available for treatment of a certain disease. It is not known which one is more efficient. How are the drugs to be used to save as many patients as possible? If two large samples are used initially we can determine which is better with high confidence. But this implies that a high proportion of patients would have been treated with the inferior drug. A more successful procedure would consist in trying the drugs initially on small sample groups, observing the outcomes, weighting the next test in favor of which seems to be the better drug on the basis of current knowledge, and continuing in this fashion. This procedure involves optimal stopping at a stage when sufficient information is collected allowing to choose the superior drug. Learning and acting simultaneously are already involved. For adaptive control processes a decision-making device (or controller) is called upon to perform under various conditions of uncertainty, conditions which may range from complete knowledge to total ignorance. In fact, optimal stopping rules can be viewed as control devices governing a deterministic or stochastic dynamic system. The evolution of the system will be the result of the interaction between the laws of motion of the system and the sequence of actions taken over time.
To show the connection between adaptive system theory and optimal stopping rules we exhibit the simple transformation of a deterministic process.
We assume that when a system is in the current state s and a decision a is made, the new state of the system s_1 is $s_1 = T(s, a)$. Then if the system is observed to be in state s_1 and the decision a_1 is made, the system is transformed into $s_2 = T(s_1, a_1)$.
Next with the system observed to be in state s_2 and the decision a_2 to be chosen, the new state is $s_3 = T(s_2, a_2)$, etc.
Then after N stages the system will be transformed into state $s_N = T(s_{N-1}, a_{N-1})$. Therefore the pair (s, a) generates a semigroup of transformations over the state space S. The optimality of process is to obtain a final state at which the (expected) net gain or loss is maximal or minimal. The expected gain or loss consists of the difference of the gain or loss associated to the final state and the costs involved to obtain that state, hence it is a function of the final state $\phi(s_N)$.
Bellman's principle of optimality is very natural in pursuing this goal, and the functional equation technique is very appropriate in reaching it. It states:
An optimal sequence of decisions has the property that whatever the initial state and decision are, i.e. given the pair (s_0, a_0) *the remaining decisions must be optimal with regard to the state resulting from the initial decision.*
A more interesting and less restrictive case is that of partially known trans-

formations. Those involve processes in which the outcome of a decision is not precisely known. This means instead of considering deterministically known states we are concerned with random states. Let it be assumed that the controller or decisionmaker does not know the exact distribution of possible resulting random states, rather he has an initial estimate of this distribution that may be justified by adopting the Bayesian philosophy, and in the process of decision-making he is able to modify this estimate in the light of the actually observed history of the process which can be transformed via Bayes formula to obtain new information. This idea is basic to learning system theory in a random environment (K. S. Fu (1968)). An interesting application of this procedure for the treatment of patients has been given by J. Cornfield (1969).

We first give a general treatment of this situation before we turn to specific sequential estimation techniques in this frame work.

Let the decision maker's knowledge be specified by an information pattern I. This information pattern contains all the information about the past on which the future actions are to be based. It may be represented by an a priori probability density function. The overall state of the system plus the decision maker's knowledge is specified by a point in a new state (s, I). Then, if the state of the system is (s, I) and the decision a is made, the new state is s_1: $I_1 = T(s, I, a, r)$, where r is a random variable having an a priori probability distribution function $G(s, I, a, r)$, knowledge of which in itself is part of the information pattern. The new information pattern I_2 is specified by a transformation

$$I_2 = T_2(s, I_1, a, r).$$

The goal is to determine a sequence of decision $\{a_1, a_2, \ldots, a_N\}$ that will minimize the expected value of a preassigned function of the final state $\phi(s_N, I_N)$. Since the exact distribution functions are not known, the expected value is taken regarding the a priori distribution functions as the true ones. Introduce a sequence of functions $\{f_k(s, I)\}$

$$f_k(s, I) = \operatorname*{Min}_{\{a_1, \ldots, a_k\}} E[\phi(s_k, I_k)].$$

Then the principle of optimality yields the relationships

$$\text{(1)} \qquad f_{N+1}(s, I) = \operatorname*{Min}_{a} \int_{r} f_N(T_1(s, I; a, r), T_2(s, I_1, a, r))\, dG(s, T; a, r), \quad N = 1, 2, \ldots$$

and for N = 1 we have

$$\text{(2)} \qquad f_1(s, I) = \operatorname*{Min}_{a} \int_{r} \phi(T_1(s, I; a, r), T_2(s, I_1; a, r))\, dG(s, I; a, r).$$

The relationships (1) and (2) can be used for establishing the existence of optimal policies.

10.8 Sequential Estimation

Sequential estimation and related sequential detection processes of this type to be discussed occur in radar and communication technology where the receiver uses variable rather than fixed sample sizes. In such cases the principle of optimality provides a natural mathematical formulation and a numerical solution. Let us assume that the task of a controller is to estimate the value of an unknown probability p. Take a binary sequential experiment where p is the unknown probability that a certain random variable takes the value unity, and $1-p$ is the probability that it takes the value zero. The controller is to conduct a series of experiments, record the outcomes, and make an estimate of p on the basis of this experience plus any a priori information available. There are also costs associated with performing each experiment and possibly making wrong estimates of p. The problem is to determine when the experiment should be stopped and what estimate should be made by the controller. Let us specify the situation in detail. Suppose that at the beginning of the process the controller is in possession of the prior information that n ones out of s trials have been observed. Regarding the observation of the outcome of the process itself, we assume that n of r trials have resulted in a one, but here we disregard information concerning the order in which the events occurred. Since p is unknown we regard it as a random variable, its distribution function changes during the course of the process. First consider only the prior information, the change of the distribution function is given by

$$(1) \qquad dG(p) = \frac{p^{n-1}(1-p)^{s-n-1}}{B(n, s-n)}\, dp,$$

where B is a beta function.

Second after m one have been observed in r addition trials, we consider it to be

$$(2) \qquad dG_{r,m} = \frac{p^m(1-p)^{r-m}\, dG(p)}{\int_0^1 p^m(1-p)^{r-m}\, dG(p)},$$

a Bayes' approach.

Let $c_{r,m}$ denote the expected cost of incorrect estimation after r additional trials have resulted in ones and set

$$(3) \qquad c_{r,m} = \alpha \int_0^1 (p_{r,m} - p)^2\, dG_{r,m}(p),$$

where $p_{r,m}$ is the estimate which minimizes $c_{r,m}$. The value of $p_{r,m}$ is given by the formula

$$p_{r,m} = \int_0^1 p\,dG_{r,m}(p) = \frac{m+n}{r+s} \tag{4}$$

which yields an intuitively reasonable estimate for p. A calculation then shows that

$$c_{r,m} = \alpha \frac{m+n}{r+s}\left[\frac{m+n+1}{r+s+1} - \frac{m+n}{r+s}\right]. \tag{5}$$

Now suppose that if m experiments have been performed the cost of the next experiment is k(m), allowing for the cost of the experiment to vary during the process, a feature that entails interesting possibilities. We shall assume that in the absence of additional information estimated probabilities are to be regarded as true probabilities. Also we wish to require that no more than R experiments be performed, thus we introduce a *forced termination rule* of the sequential process. This forced termination rule makes sense in many practical situations, particular those which are alike the marriage problem. If the termination rule comes into effect the process must be truncated at this point. By dynamic programming one can determine the optimal control policy. In doing this the cost function $f_r(m)$ is defined by

$$f_r(m) = \text{expected cost of a process beginning} \tag{6}$$

with m ones in r experiments having been observed, and using an optimal sequence of decisions.

Then the principle of optimality yields the functional equation

$$f_r(m) = \text{Min}\begin{cases} T_c\colon k(r) + p_{r,m} f_{r+1}(m+1) + (1-p_{r,m}) f_{r+1}(m) \\ T_s\colon \alpha \dfrac{m+n}{r+s}\left[\dfrac{m+n+1}{r+s+1} - \dfrac{m+n}{r+s}\right] \end{cases} \tag{7}$$

which holds for $m = 0, 1, 2, \ldots, r$ and $r = R-1, R-2, \ldots, O$. The sets T_c and T_s denote the continuation and stopping rule sets respectively. In view of the termination rule we also have

$$f_R(m) = \alpha \frac{m+n}{R+s}\left[\frac{m+n+1}{R+s+1} - \frac{m+n}{R+s}\right]. \tag{8}$$

These relations quickly enable us to calculate the sequence of functions $f_R(m), f_{R-1}(m), \ldots, f_0(m)$.

At the same time we can determine whether to stop or continue and what estimate to make of p in the event the process is terminated.

The functional equations have been investigated computationally by R. Bellman and others (1959, 1961) for a wide range of values for the parameters α

and R, and for several cost functions k(m). When the cost of experimentation was constant from experiment to experiment, or when it increased and when one out of two ones had been observed a priori it was found that the optimal policy essentially consisted of:

1) Continuing the experiments if r was small (not enough information present on which to base an estimate).
2) Stopping the experiments if r was sufficiently large.
3) Continuing the experiments for intermediate values of r, unless extreme runs of either zeros or ones occurred and stopping otherwise.

On the other hand, in the case of a decreasing cost of experiment the optimal control policy is more complex. This is intuitively plausible since the cost of experimentation may have dropped to such a low level that it might be profitable to do at least one more experiment before making the estimate.

10.9 Gambling Problems

Consider the classical ruin problems as formulated by Feller (1950). Suppose a gambler with an initial capital $\mathbf{s}_0$ plays against an infinitely rich adversary but the gambler always has the option to stop playing whenever he likes to. The gambler then adopts the strategy (policy) of playing until he loses his capital or obtains a net gain $\mathbf{s}_n - \mathbf{s}_0$ at the $n-$th play. Then p is his probability of losing and $1-p$ the probability of winning. In other words, the gambler's net gain $\mathbf{g}$ is a random variable with the values $s_n - s_0$ at probability $1-p$ and $-s_0$ at probability p. The expected gain is $E(\mathbf{g}) = s_n(1-p) + p \cdot -s_0$. The treatment of this problem can be facilitated by interpreting the gambler's process as a random walk with absorption barrier $(\mathbf{o}, \mathbf{s}_n)$. Such kind of problem immediately leads to a problem of sequential sampling. Let a particle start from a position $\mathbf{s}_0$ such that $\mathbf{o} < \mathbf{s}_0 < \mathbf{s}_n$, we seek the probability p_{s0} that the particle will attain some position $\leqq 0$ before reaching any position $\geqq \mathbf{s}_n$. Then the position of the particle at time n is the point $\mathbf{s}_0 + \mathbf{x}_1 + \mathbf{x}_2 + \ldots + \mathbf{x}_n$ where the $\{\mathbf{x}_k\}$ are mutually independent random variables with the common distribution $\{p_r\}$. The process stops when for the first time either $\mathbf{x}_1 + \ldots + \mathbf{x}_n \leqq -\mathbf{s}_0$ or $\mathbf{x}_1 + \ldots + \mathbf{x}_n \geqq \mathbf{s}_n - \mathbf{s}_0$. In sequential sampling the $\mathbf{x}_k$ represent certain characteristics of samples or observations. Measurements are taken until a sum $\mathbf{x}_1 + \ldots + \mathbf{x}_k$ falls outside or inside the preassigned limits. In the first case it leads to rejection, in the second case to acceptance. The main ideas of sequential sampling are due to A. Wald (1947). The whole problem can be formulated in terms of a Markov chain. The idea of finding optimal gambling strategies for favorable and unfavorable games has been pursued rigorously in the literature on stochastic processes. In particular, martingales have been found very useful for studying optimal stopping times and stopping rules. However, their investigation requirec more advanced methods than developed here. The more advanced reader is advised to consult L. Breiman (1968) Ch. 5, Doob (1963), Ch. II, VII and Dubins and Savage (1965); the standard reader is referred to Feller (1950).

10.10 Sequential Statistical Problems

Consider a statistical problem where the statistician can take observations $\mathbf{x}_1, \mathbf{x}_2, \ldots, \mathbf{x}_n$ at different time from some population involving a parameter w whose value is unknown.
After each observation he can evaluate the information having accumulated up to that time and then make a decision whether to terminate the sampling process or to take another observation (to continue) sampling. This is called sequential sampling. In general, there are some costs of observation (the costs of an experiment), at some stage of sampling the incremental benefits of taking one more observation are offset by the incremental costs of observation. The criterion for the statistician is to minimize the total risk, therefore, in many situations he will compare fixed sample size sampling with sequential sampling with respect to this criterion. Although the benefits of sequential sampling may be determined in advance, the costs of sampling may assume different forms, one particular reasonable form is that costs of sampling may be sharply increasing in the process of taking more and more observations. The risk of the sequential decision rule d in which at least one observation is to be taken is

$$\begin{aligned}\varrho(\xi, \delta) &= E\{L[w, \delta_N(\mathbf{x}_1, \ldots, \mathbf{x}_n)] + c_1 + \ldots + c_N\} \\ &= \sum_{n=1}^{\infty} \int_{\{N=n\}} \int_{\Omega} L(w, \delta_n(x_1, \ldots, x_n)) \cdot \\ &\qquad\qquad \xi(w | x_1, \ldots, x_n) d\nu(w) dF_n(\mathbf{x}_1, \ldots, \mathbf{x}_n | \xi) \\ &\qquad + \sum_{n=1}^{\infty} (c_1 + \ldots + c_n) \varrho\{N = n\}\end{aligned}$$

with $\xi(\cdot | \mathbf{x}_1, \ldots, \mathbf{x}_n)$ being the posterior generalized probability density function of w after the values $\mathbf{x}_1 = x_1, \ldots, \mathbf{x}_n = x_n$ have been observed. A Bayes sequential decision procedure is a procedure δ for which the risk $\varrho(\xi, \delta)$ is minimized, hence it is optimal.
It is said a sequential decision process δ is bounded if there is a positive integer n such that $P_r(N \leqq n) = 1$. The existence of bounded sequential procedures reflects the existence of a termination rule of the game. For practical applications there are many reasons for introducing a forced

termination rule since there are situations which force ourselves to make a decision not to continue.

10.11 Existence of Optimal Stopping Rules

Define a generalized probability density function φ.
For a g.p.d.f. φ of w let $\varrho_0(\varphi)$ be defined as follows:

$$\varrho_0(\varphi) = \inf_{d \in D} \int_{\Omega} L(w, d)\varphi(w) d\nu(w)$$

Then $\varrho_0(\varphi)$ is the minimum risk from an immediate decision without any further observation when the p.d.f. of w is φ.
Let $\mathbf{x}_1, \mathbf{x}_2, \ldots,$ be a sequence of observations which have a specified joint distribution, and for $n = 1, 2, \ldots,$ let $\mathbf{y}_n = \mathbf{y}_n(\mathbf{x}_1, \ldots, \mathbf{x}_n)$ be a random variable whose value depends on the first n-observations $\mathbf{x}_1, \ldots, \mathbf{x}_n$. Suppose that the statistician terminates the sampling process after having observed the values of $\mathbf{x}_1, \ldots, \mathbf{x}_n$, his gain is $\mathbf{y}_n$. The question is does there exist a stopping rule which maximizes the expected gain $E(\mathbf{y}_n)$. For a given stopping rule the expection $E(\mathbf{y}_n)$ exists iff the following relation is satisfied.

$$E(|\mathbf{y}_N|) = \sum_{n=1}^{\infty} E(|\mathbf{y}|N = n) P \quad (N = n) < \infty.$$

We are interested in determining whether there exists a stopping rule which maximizes the expected gain $E(\mathbf{y}_N)$.

10.12 Sequential Statistical Analysis

After having shown that the idea of sequential decision making pertains to many real-life decision processes we are going to demonstrate now that they are also particularly useful for the theory of statistical decision.
Suppose that there is a stream of potential observations $\mathbf{x}_1, \mathbf{x}_2, \ldots,$ generally infinite, but sometimes finite, as in the case of sampling from a finite population. In the simplest case the variables $\mathbf{x}_1, \ldots, \mathbf{x}_k$, could be considered as independent observations from a fixed population with probability function

$$f_k(x_1, \ldots, x_k | \theta) = f(x_1 | \theta) f(x_2 | \theta) \ldots f(x_k | \theta),$$

where $f(x|\theta)$ is the probability function of the population, if we restrict ourselves to the discrete case only.
An optimum decision procedure is one that would minimize the overall expected loss (or, equivalently, maximize expected utility). One special

problem that one encounters in the loss structure, and which is not considered in samples of fixed size, is the cost of obtaining observations or *cost of sampling*: In the sequential case the cost of sampling must be added to the loss ordinarily associated with the consequences of taking a certain action. In general, it is reasonable to let depend the cost of sampling on the state of nature, the number of observations and sometimes even upon the values of the observations. Hence, define $C(\theta, k, \mathbf{x}_1, \ldots, \mathbf{x}_k)$ as the cost of observations.
A very simple special kind of assumption is that all costs being proportional and independent of the state of nature that obtains, e.g.

$$C(\mathbf{x}_1, \ldots, \mathbf{x}_k) = kC.$$

For simplicity we will work with the latter function in what follows. The sequential nature of sampling is generally exhibited in two ways. First, the sequential nature of the experiment has to be defined, and second a termination rule has to provide a criterion at which step of the sequential process one has to stop taking further observations. Therefore, the experimental design involves two key notions: a stopping rule and a terminal decision rule. A sequential decision rule is specified for each number of observations $\mathbf{x}_1, \ldots, \mathbf{x}_k$ by a function d_k, so that $d_k(\mathbf{x}_1, \ldots, \mathbf{x}_k)$ represents a certain action after $\mathbf{x}_1, \ldots, \mathbf{x}_k$ observations are at hand. A class of such sequential decision functions $d_0, d_1, d_2, \ldots$, defined by $d = \{d_0, d_1(\mathbf{x}_1), d_2(\mathbf{x}_1, \mathbf{x}_2), \ldots\}$ is called a *terminal decision rule* for a given sequential process under consideration, where d_0 is one of the action when no data are at hand.
A stopping rule is associated to a terminal decision, characterized by a family of functions.

$$s = \{s_0, s_1(\mathbf{x}_1), s_2(\mathbf{x}_1, \mathbf{x}_2), \ldots\}, \quad \text{where}$$

$$s_k(\mathbf{x}_1, \ldots, \mathbf{x}_k) = \begin{cases} 0, & \text{if at least one further observation should be taken, given } \mathbf{x}_1, \ldots, \mathbf{x}_k \text{ have been observed.} \\ 1, & \text{if no more observations should be taken given that } \mathbf{x}_1, \ldots, \mathbf{x}_k \text{ are at hand.} \end{cases}$$

Now given a sequence of observations $\mathbf{x}_1, \mathbf{x}_2, \ldots$ the function s_k should be uniquely determined by the conditional probability that precisely k observations will be taken, i.e.

$$P(N = k \mid \mathbf{x}_1, \mathbf{x}_2, \ldots) = s_k(\mathbf{x}_1, \ldots, \mathbf{x}_k).$$

Then the probability of stopping, to be computed before the observations will be known, and given a particular stopping rule is

$$P_s(N = k) = E[s_N(\mathbf{x}_1, \ldots, \mathbf{x}_N)].$$

An interesting example is provided by a hypothesis testing problem to be discussed later more extensively.
Let $a < m < b$ and let $L_n = L_n(\mathbf{x}_1, \dots, \mathbf{x}_n)$ denote the likelihood ratio

$$L_n = \frac{f_0(\mathbf{x}_1)\, f_0(\mathbf{x}_2) \dots f_0(\mathbf{x}_n)}{f_1(\mathbf{x}_1)\, f_1(\mathbf{x}_2) \dots f_1(\mathbf{x}_n)}$$

where f_0 and f_1 are probability (or density) functions that characterize two states of nature (the hypothesis H_0 and H_1, respectively). The define the sequential decision rule

$$d_n(\mathbf{x}_1, \dots, \mathbf{x}_n) = \begin{cases} \text{reject } H_0 \text{ if } L_n < m \\ \text{accept } H_0 \text{ if } L_n \geqq m. \end{cases}$$

The stopping rule will be defined as follows: let $s_0 = 0$, and for $n > 0$,

$$s_n(\mathbf{x}_1, \dots, \mathbf{x}_n) = \begin{cases} 0, \text{ if } a < L_n < b \\ 1, \text{ if } L_n \leqq a \text{ or } L_n \geqq b. \end{cases}$$

Then the pair (s, d) defines a sequential decision procedure for the problem of testing a simple hypothesis against a simple alternative.

10.13 Bayesian Procedures

Suppose a sequence of observations $\mathbf{x}_1, \mathbf{x}_2, \dots$ is available at cost kC for k observations. For a given sequential procedure (s, d) the total loss, including the costs of observation will be

$$l(\theta, d_N(\mathbf{x}_1, \dots, \mathbf{x}_N)) + NC$$

with N being a random variable (its distribution determined by θ and the stopping rule s), whose value is given by the number of observations actually used in reaching a decision.
The expected loss or risk is then

$$R(\theta, (s, d)) = E[l(\theta, d_N(\mathbf{x}_1, \dots, \mathbf{x}_N)) + NC]$$

and the Bayes risk for a prior $P(\theta)$ is obtained by further averaging with respect to that prior

$$B(s, d) = E[R(\theta, (s, d))].$$

The problem then is to find a pair (s, d) which minimizes the Bayes risk. This involves a two-stage procedure: first determine the minimizing d for each stopping rule, and then choose the stopping rule that produces the overall minimum. We can state the following result whose various technicalities do not permit a proof here for which the reader is referred to Blackwell & Girschick (1954), Chap. 9.

For a given stopping rule s and a given prior $P(\theta)$ the Bayes risk $B(s, d)$ is minimized by the decision rule $d^* = (d_0^*, d_1^*, \ldots, d_i^*, \ldots)$ where d_i^* is the Bayes rule applied to any fixed-sample size problem with i observations $\mathbf{x}_1, \mathbf{x}_2, \ldots, \mathbf{x}_i, \ldots$

Sometimes a sequential statistical problem has only a finite number of stages, this demonstrates the similarity to problems such as restricted coin tossing games, the marriage problem and other problems discussed in the previous section where, in general, termination is enforced. In view of statistical sequential analysis the introduction of forced termination is motivated by the consideration that one may run out of data, for instance, if one takes samples without replacement from a finite population.

When the number of stages is finite, the above result can be obtained in a process of backward induction, on the basis of computational procedures as developed by dynamic programming, to determine the optimal stopping rule s* such that the Bayes procedure (s*, d*) is 'best' for a given prior distribution. In order to outline the approach suppose that the stages of observation are restricted to n (and not more), corresponding to observations $\mathbf{x}_1, \ldots, \mathbf{x}_n$. If it happens that the Bayes procedure requires taking all n observations, the terminal decision is made according to the Bayes criterion, i.e. the posterior distribution obtained on the basis of n observed values is applied to the given loss function to obtain averages in terms of which the available actions are ordered and the optimal one is chosen. If the stopping rule s*, on the other hand, requires at least $n-k$ observations, the problems of whether to stop (and use the Bayes terminal rule for those observations) or to obtain more sampling data is resolved by comparing two conditional expected losses;

(i) the expected loss conditional on the previous $n-k$ observations, and
(ii) the expected conditional loss if one takes more observations (including costs for future observations).

Having determined the optimum procedure for $k=0$, the computations and comparisons can be made for $k = 1, 2, \ldots$ revealing the optimum among rules calling for at least $n-1, n-2, \ldots$ observations. Proceeding recursively this way the Bayes rule is completely determined via backward induction.

10.14 Hypothesis Testing

This section exhibits an example of testing a statistical hypothesis with two states of nature and two actions, e.g. testing a simple null against a simple alternative hypothesis. Consider the problem of testing the hypothesis that a population is normal with mean $\mu_1 = 0$ against the alternative that it is normal with mean $\mu_2 = 2$ the variance being the same in both cases: $\sigma_1^2 = \sigma_2^2 = 1$. The actions available are a_1, to accept H_0, and a_2, to reject H_0 with losses as given in the following table (in which c_1 and c_2 are positive constants).

	H_0	H_1
a_1	0	c_1
a_2	c_2	0

Furthermore $P(\theta_1) = p$, $P(\theta_2) = 1 - p$ be the prior distributions for states of nature θ_1 and θ_2, respectively.
If there are no observations available (no data case) the Bayes action is chosen on the basis of Bayes risks which yields in this particular case:

$$B_p(a_1) = c_1(1-p)$$

$$B_p(a_2) = c_2 p.$$

The minimum of this determines the proper action. Now suppose that at least one observation from the population is being taken, at a certain cost. The cost of observation being fixed at each observation, the Bayes decision rule for a given observation is the one that minimizes the Bayes risk, e.g. the likelihood ratio rule:

$$\text{Reject} \quad H_0 \text{ if } \frac{f_0}{f_1} < \frac{c_1(1-p)}{c_2 p}$$

$$\text{Accept} \quad H_0 \text{ otherwise}$$

where f_i denotes the density of the observation under H_i.

$$\text{Since} \qquad \frac{f_0}{f_1} = \frac{e^{-x^2/2}}{e^{-(x-2)^2/2}} = e^{2-2x}$$

the inequality for rejecting H_0 can be expressed in terms of x as

$$x > 1 - \tfrac{1}{2}\log\frac{c_1}{c_2} + \tfrac{1}{2}\log\frac{p}{1-p} = F(p).$$

For example, if $c_1(1-p) = c_2 p$, then do act as if the mean is 0 if the observation is closer to 0 than to 2, otherwise act as if the mean is 2. The minimum Bayes risk for given $p = H(H_0)$ implying the rejection limit $F(p)$ is then

$$\varrho(p) = c_2 p\alpha + c_1\beta(1-p) = c_2 p[1 - \Phi(F)] + c_1(1-p)\Phi F - 2)$$

where $\Phi(\cdot)$ is the probability distribution function of the standard normal distribution. The total cost of taking an observation and using the Bayes rule for that observation is the value of $\varrho(p)$ plus the cost of the observation. The minimum Bayes risk, over all rules that use either no observations or

one observation, can be found graphically (see Fig. 10–1). The figure shows $\varrho(p)$ with zero cost of observation, and also with two other constant costs of observation (moderate and high) and the rejection limit $F(p)$ is shown for the two hypotheses.
The Bayes rule for the situation pictured in the figure is as follows

(i) if $p \leqq c$, reject H_0 with no observation,
(ii) if $c \leqq p \leqq d$ take the observation and use the approriate Bayes rule,
(iii) if $p \geqq d$, accept H_0 with no observation.

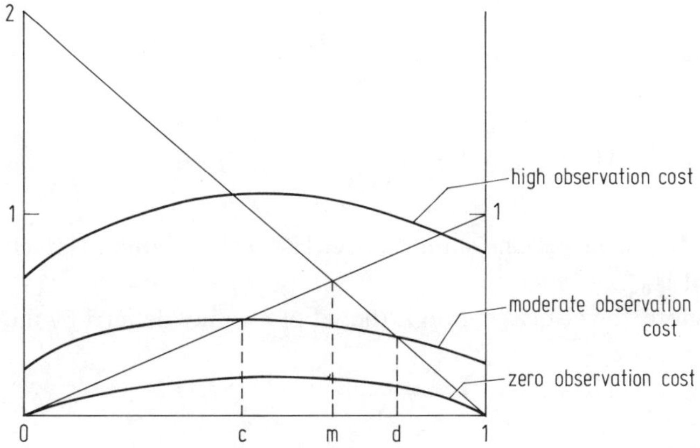

The argument above can also be used for the study of a sequential problem in which at most $n+1$ steps are permitted in order to determine the Bayes procedures in the class of procedures requiring either n or $n+1$ steps.
Thus suppose one considers only stopping rules that require at least n observations. If such a stopping rule is to be a part of a Bayes procedure, the associated terminal decision rule, whereever the sampling stops, is an ordinary fixed sample size Bayes decision rule. For stopping rules calling for exactly n observations, with a terminal decision at that point, a Bayesian decision rule is obtained by applying the posterior probabilities for H_0 and H_1 directly to the original loss structure.
Thus if at least n and at most $n+1$ observations are assumed you are in almost the same position as in the example above – with the notable difference that in place of the prior p in this example one now uses the posterior probabilities based on the first n observations. Given the random vector $\mathbf{z} = (\mathbf{x}_1, \ldots, \mathbf{x}_n)$ of the first n observations and the original prior probabilities $p = P(H_0)$ and $1-p = P(H_1)$ the posterior probability can be calculated as follows:

$$\hat{p}_0 = P(H_0 | \mathbf{z} = z) = \frac{p f_0(z)}{w(z)}$$

$$\hat{p}_1 = P(H_1 | \mathbf{z} = z) = \frac{(1-p)\, f_1(z)}{w(z)}$$

where

$$f_0(z) = f(z|H_0) = P(\mathbf{z} = z | H_0)$$
$$f_1(z) = f(z|H_1) = P(\mathbf{z} = z | H_1)$$

denote the probability (or density) functions of the data **z**, and

$$w(z) = pf_0(z) + (1-p)\, f_1(z).$$

The expected posterior loss is computed for each action.

Accept $\quad H_0\colon 0 + c_1 \hat{p}_1 = \dfrac{c_1(1-p)\, f_1(z)}{w(z)}$

Reject $\quad H_0\colon c_2 \hat{p}_0 + 0 = \dfrac{c_2 p f_0(z)}{w(z)}.$

If the first is larger one should reject H_0, if the second is larger one should accept H_0.
Therefore, the critical region is the set of **z**-values defined by the rule

Reject $\quad H_0$ if $\dfrac{f_0(\mathbf{z})}{f_1(\mathbf{z})} < \dfrac{c_1(1-p)}{c_2 p}.$

The constant $c_1(1-p)/c_2 p$ cannot be calculated without knowing the losses c_1 and c_2 and the prior probabilities, however, it can be shown that the family of tests satisfying this rule includes all Bayes tests and only Bayes tests. The ratio $L = f_0/f_1$ is called the likelihood ratio and tests with critical region are called likelihood ratio tests. Analogously, we can deal with the case of sequential tests.
The inequality that determines whether or not the observation is to be taken, e.g. $c < \hat{p}_0 < d$ where c and d are determined as in the example above. They can be expressed in terms of the likelihood ratio, by substitution for the posterior probability $\hat{p}_0$;

$$c < \frac{wf_0(z)}{wf_0(z) + (1-w)\, f_1(z)} < d.$$

By rearranging this formula

$$c < 1 + \frac{1 - wf_1(z)}{wf_0(z)} < \frac{1}{d}$$

or in terms of

$$L_n = f_0(z)/f_1(z)$$

with $$a = \frac{1-w}{w}\,\frac{c}{1-c}, \quad b = \frac{1-w}{w}\,\frac{d}{1-d}.$$

Then the Bayes procedure is as follows:

Calculate the likelihood ratio based an n *observations, if it falls in the interval from* a *to* b, *take one more observation and use the Bayes test for* $n+1$ *observations. If the likelihood ratio for the* n *observations is less than* a, *reject* H_0, *if it exceeds* b *accept* H_0 *without taking the* $(n+1)$ – st *observation.*

10.15 The Sequential Likelihood (Probability) Ratio Test

This test has been first developed by A. Wald (1947) and is designed for testing a simple hypothesis H_0 against a simple alternative H_1. For a test to achieve error sizes α and β, define constants $a = \alpha/(1-\beta)$ and $b = (1-\alpha)/\beta$ and use these as limits for the likelihood ratio L_n computed after each observation is taken. If $L_n \leqq a$, the sampling stops and the null hypothesis is rejected, if $L_n \geqq b$ the sampling stops and the null hypothesis is accepted. If $a < L_n < b$, another observation is taken. The test assumes the availability of observations $\mathbf{x}_1, \mathbf{x}_2, \ldots$ and that at least one observation is taken. It can be shown that although the error sizes actually achieved with the test are not exactly those specified, they are close enough for practical purposes. It can be shown that the sequential likelihood ratio test terminates with probability 1 both under H_0 and H_1. Wald and Wolfowitz (1948) have shown that for assigned error sizes the sequential likelihood ratio test minimizes the expected number of observations n. Define the expected number by

$$E(n) = \frac{E(\log L_n)}{E\mathbf{z}}$$

where $\mathbf{z}$ is the logarithm of the likelihood for a single observation, and the numerator is approximately given by

$$E(\log L_n) = (\log a)\, P(\text{rej.}\, H_0) + (\log b)\, P(\text{acc.}\, H_0)$$

For the case of Bernoulli population, given the observation z,

$$\log \frac{l(\theta_0|z)}{l(\theta_1|z)} = \log \left(\frac{\theta_0}{\theta_1}\right)^z \left(\frac{1-\theta_0}{1-\theta_1}\right)^{1-z}$$
$$= z \log \frac{\theta_0(1-\theta_1)}{\theta_1(1-\theta_0)} + \log \frac{1-\theta_0}{1-\theta_1}$$

where $l(\cdot|z)$ denotes the likelihood function of the Bernoulli parameter to be tested for $z = 0, 1$.

Thus we have

$$\mathrm{E}\mathbf{z} = \mathrm{z}\log\frac{\theta_0(1-\theta_1)}{\theta_1(1-\theta_0)} + \log\frac{1-\theta_0}{1-\theta_1}.$$

The sequential likelihood ratio test looks very much like the Bayes sequential procedure defined in the preceeding section. The essential difference is that there is no zero stage in the sequential likelihood ratio test, with the probability of making a decision with no data at all because a specific loss structure is not assumed. It can be shown, however, that given any sequential likelihood ratio test there exist losses c_1 and c_2 and a sampling cost per observation such that the Bayes sequential test for some prior distribution is exactly the given sequential likelihood ratio test.

10.16 Problems

(1) Let $\mathbf{x}_1, \mathbf{x}_2, \ldots$ be a sequential random sample from a Bernoulli distribution with unknown parameter w. Suppose also that the value of w has to be estimated and that for $0 \leqq d \leqq 1$ and $0 < w < 1$, the loss function l is specified as follows:

$$l(w, d) = \frac{(w-d)^2}{w(1-w)}$$

Suppose that the prior distribution of w is a uniform distribution on the interval (0, 1), and the cost per observation is c.
Show that the optimal sequential decision procedure requires a fixed number of observations.

(2) Consider a decision problem in which a sequential sample can be taken from a Bernoulli distribution with unknown parameter w at a cost of c units per observation. Suppose that w must be estimated when the loss function is $l(w, d) = (w-d)^2$ if $d \in (0, 1)$ and if the prior distribution of w is uniform on the interval (0, 1),
(a) determine the optimal procedure,
(b) show that the optimal decision procedure requires that not more than three observations are taken.

(3) Consider a sequential decision problem in which $\Omega = \{w_1, w_2\}$, $D = \{d_1, d_2\}$ and the loss function l is as given in the table:

	d_1	d_2
w_1	0	50
w_2	50	0

Assume that each observation **x** can have only the value 1, 2 or 3 and that the probability function of **x** when $w = w_i$ $(i = 1, 2)$ is

$$f_1(1) = \tfrac{1}{4} \qquad f_1(2) = \tfrac{1}{2} \qquad f_1(3) = \tfrac{1}{4}$$
$$f_2(1) = \tfrac{1}{4} \qquad f_2(2) = \tfrac{1}{4} \qquad f_2(3) = \tfrac{1}{2}$$

Compute the risks p_0, p_1 and p_2 as functions of the prior probability $p = P(w = w_i)$.

(4) If f denotes the distribution of w at any stage show that an optimal procedure is to continue sampling if and only if $p_1(f) < p_0(f)$.
(5) Whenever a gambler makes a bet, he either wins $1 with probability 1/2 or loses $1 with probability 1/2. He makes a sequence of independent bets of this type and continues until he has either realized a gain of r dollars or a loss of s dollars, where r and s are fixed positive integers. Show that the probability that he will stop betting because he has gained r dollars is $s/(r+s)$ (according to D.V. Lindley (1965)).
(6) A traffic light has a constant probability $\lambda\,dt$ of changing to green after being red or to red after being green in any infinitesimal time interval dt, so that a car arriving at a random instant has a probability of $\frac{1}{2}$ of passing through without waiting and a probability element $\frac{1}{2}\lambda\exp(-\lambda w)dw$ of waiting a time w, where $w > o$. Two cars approach the traffic light, the second one arriving at a time interval a after the first. Find the jint distribution of their waiting times, w_1 and w_2, and hence the distribution of $w_2 - w_1$.
If the two cars travel always with the same speed between traffic lights and are following the same route, can you say anything about the distribution of the time by which the second car is behind the first, after they have passed a large number of traffic lights operating independently with the same coefficient λ?

Suggested Readings

Bellman, R.: Dynamic Programming, Princeton, N.Y., 1957.
Bellman, R.: Adaptive Control Processes: A Guided Tour, Princeton, N.Y., 1961.
Bellman, R., and R. Kalaba: A Mathematical Theory of Adaptive Control Processes, Proc. Nat. Acad. Science, U.S.A. 45, 1959, 1288–1290.
Bellman, R., Kalaba, R., and D. Middleton: Dynamic Programming, Sequential Estimation and Sequential Detection Processes, Proc. Nat. Acad. Sci., U.S.A. 47, 1961, 338–341.
Blackwell, D., and M.A. Girshick: Theory of Games and Statistical Decisions, New York 1954.
Breiman, L.: Stopping Rule Problems. In: Applied Combinatorial Mathematics, New York 1964, 284–319.
Breiman, L.: Probability, Reading, Mass. 1968.
Chow, Y.S., et al.: Optimal Selection based on Relative Rank (The Secretary Problem), Israel Jour. of Math. 2, 1964, 81–90.

Doob, L.: Stochastic Processes, New York 1963.
Dubins, L. E., and L. J. Savage: How to gamble if you must: Inequalities for Stochastic Processes, New York 1965.
Feller, W.: An Introduction to Probability Theory and its Applications, Vol. 1, New York 1950.
Fu, K. S.: Sequential Methods in Pattern Recognition and Machine Learning, New York 1968.
Griffeath, D., and J. L. Snell: Optimal Stopping in the Stock Market, Annals of Probability 2, 1974, 1–13.
Lindley, D. V.: Dynmic Programming and Decision Theory, Applied Statistics 10, 1961, 39–51.
Lindley, D. V.: Introduction to Probability and Statistics, Part 1, Cambridge 1965.
Lindley, D. V.: Making Decisions, London 1970.
Wald, A.: Sequential Analysis, New York 1947.
Wald, A., and J. Wolfowitz: Optimum Character of the Sequential Probability Ratio Test, Ann. Math. Statist. 19, 1948, 326–339.
Cornfield, J., et al.: An Adaptive Procedure for Sequential Clinical Trials, Jour. American Statist. Assoc. 64, 1969, 795–770.

Appendix A – Chapter 10

Markovian Decision Process

Consider the situation in which a decisionmaker periodically observes a process, at times $t = 0, 1, 2, \ldots$, and at each observation classifies the process as being in one of a possible number of states. After each observation, the decisionmaker chooses an action from a set of possible actions. At this point a cost, which depends on the current state of the process and on the particular action chosen, is incurred and the next state of the process is chosen according to transition probabilities which depend on the current state and the particular action chosen. The objective of the decisionmaker is to choose actions in a manner such that some particular cost criterion is minimized. The cost criterion used will be the total expected discounted cost of operating over the infinite future. The above basically describes a *Markovian Decision Process* with the particular cost criterion as defined.

We review some of the concepts and definitions associated with the finite-state Markovian Decision Process, for general references see C. Derman (1970) or D. P. Bertsekas (1976). We define the concept of a *policy* for taking actions for the decisionmaker and we develop the expressions for the *expected discounted costs* associated with the use of certain types of policies. Consider the Markovian Decision Process (MDP) defined by the following objects:

State space $S = \{1, 2, 3, \ldots, N\}$, for finite N,
Action space $A = \{a_1, a_2, \ldots, a_M\}$, for finite M,
Cost set $C = \{C(i, a_j)\colon i \in S, a_j \in A\}$, where all costs are taken to be finite,
Transition probabilities $= \{q_{ij}(a_K)\colon i, j \in S, a_K \in A\}$,
Discount factor α, such that $0 < \alpha < 1$.

At times, $t = 0, 1, 2, \ldots$, a decisionmaker (DM) observes the current state $X_t \in S$, of the process. After observing the current state, the decisionmaker then chooses an action $a_t \in A$ and incurs a cost $C(X_t, a_t) \in C$. The next state of the process is then chosen according to the transition probabilities $q_{X_t^j}(a_t)$. A policy for the DM will be defined as any rule for taking actions at each observation point $t = 0, 1, 2, \ldots$. A particular policy may be such that at each observation point, t, the action taken, a_t, may depend on the entire observed sequence of states and actions from time $t = 0$ up to and including the current observation X_t. A policy will be called *Markovian* if at each point $t = 0, 1, 2, \ldots$, the action taken, a_t, depends on the current state, X_t, of the process but does not depend on the observed sequence of states and actions from time $t = 0$ up to and including time $t - 1$. A particular policy may be randomized in the sense that at each observation time $t = 1, 2, \ldots$, the action a_t is chosen according to some random procedure. A particular policy, W, will be called deterministic if at each observation point $t = 0, 1, 2, \ldots$, there exists a map f_t: $S \rightarrow A$ such that the policy W chooses the current action a_t according to the rule $a_t = f_t(X_t)$. In other words, a deterministic policy may be defined in terms of a sequence of maps from S into A by

$$W = (f_0, f_1, f_2, \ldots).$$

A particular policy, W, will be called *stationary* if there exists a single map f: $S \rightarrow A$ such that at each observation point $t = 0, 1, 2, \ldots$, the policy W chooses the current action a_t according to the rule $a_t = f(X_t)$. A stationary policy W therefore may be defined as $W = (f, f, f, f, \ldots)$. We simply consider a stationary policy W and its associated map f as being the same. Therefore, we say that a stationary policy for MDP is a map f: $S \rightarrow A$.
For any policy W, we define the total expected discounted cost of starting in state i at $t = 0$, and using the policy W over the infinite future, i.e.

$$V_W(i) = E_W\left[\sum_{t=0}^{\infty} \alpha^t C(X_t, a_t) | X_0 = i\right],$$

where E_W is used to indicate the dependence of the conditional expectation on the policy W. If W is the stationary policy defined in terms of the map f, then we note that

$$V_f(i) = C(i, f[i]) + \alpha \sum_{j=1}^{N} q_{ij}(f[i]) V_f(j)$$

Other criteria for minimization may be defined for the MDP. However, here we only consider the case where the decisionmaker attempts to minimize the total expected discounted cost. Howard (1960) analyzed MDP's having finite-state and finite-action spaces and proved that an optimal stationary policy (i.e. a stationary policy which minimizes the total expected discounted cost) always exists. The Howard Policy Improvement Routine is a method by which an optimal stationary policy for MDP may be found.

Suggested Readings

Bertsekas, D. P.: Dynamic Programming and Stochastic Control, New York 1976.
Derman, C. D.: Finite State Markovian Decision Processes, New York 1970.
Howard, R. A.: Dynamic Programming and Markov Processes, Cambridge, Mass., 1960.

Appendix B – Chapter 10

Optimal Search Process

Suppose that an object moves around within a finite number of regions (cells) at each time instant according to known probabilistic laws.
A *searcher* adopting a *search rule* checks sequentially one region at a time, until the object is found. At his disposal is an *effort budget* which tells him when to stop searching, i.e. when the costs of searching exceed the prospective gains of searching. Various optimality conditions for search rules may be invoked: they may vary between those that maximize the probability of detecting the target with a given effort and those that minimize the expected search costs needed to find the target. Alternatively, one may consider minimizing the expected number of periods to find the object or, if appropriate, minimizing total expected losses until the object is found.
Such optimization problems are of eminent interest in operations research, see J. M. Dobbie (1968), or S. M. Pollock (1971), most of the models studied so far have been Markovian-type search models.
In economic decision problems one is interested in comparing various decision rules with regard to the costs involved by implementing such rules. Here rather than facing the impossibility of choosing an optimal strategy 'rules of thumb' may constitute satisfactory strategies constituting a reaction to the complexity of decision rules (see H.A. Simon (1972)).
Search and complexity appear to be intimately related – as we encounter choice problems invoking a combinatorial structure (such as chess). If we are in a very large market the optimal search consists of finding the minimal price offered by one agent for one unit of commodity, however, with every search costs are involved and finding the minimal price after many searches need not be optimal since search costs may be prohibitive. Here the proper optimal search procedure would consists of minimizing the expected cost of search for a minimal price (among all alternative searches), or, alternatively, of maximizing the probability of finding the agent with a given minimal price and within a fixed number of searches (constituting the cost budget). Both optimization procedures are also genuine for statistical search problems (see de Groot (1970)). The standard search problem, treated statistically, is as follows: Suppose that an object is hidden in one of r possible locations ($r \geqq 2$) and let p_i be the prior probability that the object is in location i. The statistician must find the object but he can search in one location at a time. Hence he must devise a *sequential search procedure* which specifies at each stage that a certain one of the r locations is to be searched.
Consider an information system (a file) consisting of N cells, with information

stored in tabular form. That is, the record r(i) stored in cell i is in the form of a pair $[x_i, \varphi(x_i)]$, the file being arranged in ascending order of the argument x_i. An example of such an arrangement is a dictionary.
Given a particular argument x, we find $\varphi(x)$ by searching for the cell containing $[x, \varphi(x)]$. The search proceeds by comparing x against the arguments in a sequence of cells $i_1, i_2, \ldots$. This sequence is to be chosen so as to minimize the average number of comparisons required for locating the correct cell, in other words, for a given search cost associated to each comparison we want to minimize the expected cost of search over the sequence under consideration.
Take the following assumptions.
(i) In a comparison of x against x_i, only three possible outocomes exist, namely, $x > x_i$; $x < x_i$; $x = x_i$.
(ii) Let **x** be an integer-valued random variable denoting the location of x. We assume that the *prior* probabilities $p_k = P\{\mathbf{x} = k\}$ are given, with

$$(1) \qquad \sum_{k=1}^{N} p_k = 1$$

(iii) Let S be the set of integers 1 through N, and let S′ be a non-empty subset of S. We assume that the *posterior* probability distribution of **x** is unchanged except for renormalization; i.e.

$$(2) \qquad P\{\mathbf{x} = k \mid \mathbf{x} \in S'\} = \frac{p_k}{P(S')}, \quad k \in S'$$
$$= 0, \qquad k \notin S'$$

where $\quad P(S') = \sum_{i \in S'} p_i.$

Let $T[(p_k), N]$ formally denote the *minimum* average number of comparisons per successful search, given N cells and *prior* distribution (p_k). It is clear that the search procedure starts with the selection of a cell for the first comparison. Suppose cell n is selected and x is compared with x_n. The following situation then results:
(a) With probability p_n, $x = x_n$ and the search terminates.
(b) With probability $P_{n-1} = \sum_{i=1}^{n-1} p_i$, $x < x_n$ and x must be contained in the first n − 1 cells. If we renumber the first n − 1 cells backwards starting with cell n − 1, the new distribution becomes

$$(3) \quad p'_k = \frac{p_{n-k}}{P_{n-1}}, \quad k = 1, \ldots, n-1.$$

(c) With probability $1 - P_n = \sum_{i=n+1}^{n} p_i$, $x > x_n$. Upon renumbering the last

N − n cells, we find the new distribution to be

$$p_k'' = \frac{p_{n+k}}{1 - P_n}, \quad k = 1, \dots, N - n. \tag{4}$$

It is clear that whichever cell is optimal for the first choice, succeeding choices must remain optimal for the overall sequence to be optimal. Therefore, $T[., N]$ must satisfy the following functional equation:

$$T[(p_k), N] = \frac{\min}{1 \leqq n \leqq N} \left\{ 1 + P_{n-1}\, T\left[\left(\frac{p_{n-k}}{P_{n-1}}\right), n-1\right] + (1 - P_{n-1})\, T\left[\left(\frac{p_{n+k}}{1 - P_n}\right), N - n\right] \right\}. \tag{5}$$

Equation (5) is in the formalism of *dynamic programming*, Bellman (1957), yielding as solutions the objective $T[(p_k), N]$ and the optimal policy $n^*[(p_k), N]$. As initial conditions we set $P_0 = 0$, $T(., 0) = 0$, and $T(., 1) = 0$. (Note that this last condition implies that if there is only one cell no comparison is necessary. This is a consequence of (a)).

Bellman, R.: Dynamic Programming, Princeton, N.J., 1957.
Dobbie, J.M.: 'A Survey of Search Theory', Operations Research 16, 1968, 525–537.
de Groot, M.H.: Optimal Statistical Decisions, New York, 1970, (Chap. 14).
Pollock, S.M.: 'Search detection and subsequent action: some problems on the interfaces', Operations Research 19, 1971, 559–586.
Simon, H.A.: 'Theories of Bounded Rationality', Chap. 8 in Decision and Organization, R. Radner and C.B. McGuire eds., Amsterdam 1972.

Modern Textbooks on Statistical Analysis.

Box, G.E.P. and G.C. Tiao: Bayesian Inference in Statistical Analysis, Reading, Mass. 1973.
Dixon, W.J. and F.J. Massey: Introduction to Statistical Analysis, New York, 1969.
Hadley, G.: Elementary Statistics, San Francisco 1969.
Larson, H.J.: Introduction to Probability Theory and Statistical Inference, New York 1969.
Mosteller, F. et al.: Probability with Statistical Applications, 2nd ed., Reading, Mass. 1970.
Silvey, S.D.: Statistical Inference, New York 1970.
Wonnacott, Th.H. and R.J. Wonnacott: Introductory Statistics, New York 1969.

1. Introductory Books emphasizing Applications

Aitchison, J.: Choice against Chance: An Introduction to Statistical Decision Theory, Reading, Mass., 1970.
Biermann, Harold Jr., Bonini, Charles P., Fouraker, Lawrence E. and Robert K. Jaedicke: Quantitative Analysis for Business Decisions. Rev. Ed., Homewood, Ill., 1965.
Bross, I.: Design for Decision, New York, 1953.
Farrar, D.W.: The Investment Decision under Uncertainty, Englewood Cliffs, N.J., 1962.

Fellner, W.: Probability and Profit: A Study of Economic Behavior anlong Bayesian Lines, Homewood, Ill., 1965.
Forester, J.: Statistical Selection of Business Strategies, Homewood, Ill., 1968.
Frank, R. E., and P. E. Green: Quantitative Methods in Marketing, Englewood Cliffs, N.J., 1967.
Grayson, C.J., Jr.: Decisions under Uncertainty: Drilling Decisions by Oil and Gas Operators, Boston: Division of Research, Harvard Business School, 1960.
Hadley, G.: Introduction to Probability and Statistical Decision Theory, San Francisco, 1967.
Hays, W. L., and R. L. Winkler: Statistics: Probability, Inference, and Decisions, 2 Vols., New York, 1970.
Horowitz, I.: An Introduction to Quantitative Business Analysis, 2nd Ed., New York, 1972.
King, William R.: Probability for Management Decisions, New York, 1968.
Lindley, D.V.: Making Decisions, New York, 1971.
Lusted, L.B.: Introduction to Medical Decision Making, Springfield, I.., 1968.
Markowitz, Harry M.: Portofolio Selection, New York, 1959.
Massy, W.F., Montgomery, D.G., and D.G., Morrison: Stochastic Models of Buying Behavior, Cambridge, 1970.
Morris, W.: The Analysis of Management Decisions, Homewood, Ill., 1964.
Morris, W.T.: Management Science: A Bayesian Introduction, Englewood Cliffs, N.J., 1968.
Peters, W.S., and G.W. Summers: Statistical Analysis for Business Decisions, Englewood Cliffs, N.J., 1968.
Pratt, J.W., Raiffa, H., and R. Schlaifer: Introduction to Statistical Decision Theory, preliminary ed., New York, 1965.
Raiffa, Howard: Decision Analysis: Introductory Lectures on Choices under Uncertainty, Reading, Mass., 1968.
Schlaifer, R.: Probability and Statistics for Business Decisions, New York, 1959. (This book is probably the single most important factor leading to the popularization of subjective probability and decision theory. It is written for the economist at a very simple expository level.)
Schlaifer, R.: Analysis of Decisions under Uncertainty, New York, 1969.
Schlaifer, R.: Introduction to Statistics for Business Decisions, New York, 1961.
Starr, Martin K.: Product Design and Decision Theory, Englewood Cliffs, New York, 1963.

2. Theoretical Books

Blackwell, D., and M.A. Girshick: Theory of Games and Statistical Decisions, New York, 1954.
Chernoff, H., and L.E. Moses: Elementary Decision Theory, New York, 1959.
Edwards, Ward and Amos Tversky (eds.): Decision Making: Selected Readings, Harmondsworth, Middlesex., 1967. (15 articles dealing with the theory of decision making, utility and subjective probability, riskless choice models.)
Ferguson, T.S.: Mathematical Statistics: A Decision-Theoretic Approach, New York, 1967.
Fishburn, P.C.: Decision and Value Theory, New York, 1964. (Includes a chapter dealing with differing interpretations of probability.)
Fishburn, P.C.: Utility Theory for Decision-Making, New York, 1970.

Good, I.J.: The Estimation of Probabilities: An Essay on Modern Bayesian Methods, Cambridge, 1965.
Hays, W.L., and R.L. Winkler: Statistics: Probability, Inference and Decision, 2 Vols., New York, 1970.
Horowitz, I.: Decision Making and the Theory of the Firm, New York, 1970.
Jaynes, E.T.: Probability Theory in Science and Engineering, New York, 1961.
LaValle, I.H.: An Introduction to Probability: Decision and Inference, New York, 1970. (This book contains an excellent bibliography.)
Lindley, D.V.: Introduction to Probability and Statistics from a Bayesian Viewpoint, Part 1, "Probability" (259 pages), Part 2 "Inference" (291 pages), New York 1965. (These two volumes represent a college-level text, at approximately the level of Mood's "Introduction to the Theory of Statistics", which presents the basic concepts of probability and statistical inference from a Bayesian point of view.)
Luce, R.D., and H. Raiffa: Games and Decision: Introduction and Critical Survey, New-York, 1957.
Machol, R.E. (ed.): Information and Decision Processes, New York, 1960.
Martin, J.J.: Bayesian Decision Problems and Markov Chains, New York, 1967.
Pratt, John, Raiffa, Howard, and Robert Schlaifer: Introduction to Statistical Decision Theory, New York, 1965.
Page, A.N.: Utility Theory: A Book of Readings, New York, 1968.
Raiffa, Howard, and Robert Schlaifer: Applied Statistical Decision Theory, Boston, 1961.
Savage, L.J.: The Foundations of Statistics, New York, 1954. (A theoretically oriented treatment of Bayesian methods.)
Savage, L.J., and others: The Foundation of Statistical Inference – A Discussion, New York, 1962, 112 pages. (This monograph is based on papers and discussion at a Statistics Seminar held at Birkbeck College in England in Juli 1959. The main speaker was Professor L.J. Savage with other prepared contributions by M.S. Bartlett, G.A. Barnard, D.R. Cox, E.S. Pearson and C.A.B. Smith, and further discussion including H. Ruben, I.J. Good, D.V. Lindley, P. Armitage, C.B. Winsten, R. Syski, E.D. Van Rest, and G.M. Jenkins, The comments of these eminent statisticians with widely diverging views on the subject of Bayesian probability, though at times somewhat technical, makes still interesting reading.)
Sawaragi, Y., Sunahara, Y., and T. Nakamizo: Statistical Decision Theory in Adaptive Control Systems, New York, 1967.
Seal, H.L.: Stochastic Theory of a Risk Business, New York, 1969.
Shelly, M.W., and G.L. Bryan (eds.): Human Judgments and Optimality, New York, 1964.
Tisdell, C.A.: The Theory of Price Uncertainty, Production, and Profit, Princeton, 1968.
Tribus, M.: Rational Descriptions, Decisions, and Designs, New York, 1969.
von Neumann, J., and O. Morgenstern: Theory of Games and Economic Behavior, 2nd ed., Princeton, 1947.
Wald, A.: Sequential Analysis, New York, 1947.
Wald, A.: Statistical Decision Functions, New York, 1950.
Wetherill, G.B.: Sequential Methods in Statistics, New York, 1966.
Winkler, R.L.: An Introduction to Bayesian Inference and Decision, New York, 1972.

3. Works of Historical or Philosophical Interest

Bayes, Thomas: An Essay toward Solving a Problem in the Doctrine of Chances, 1763, reprinted in Biometrika, Vol. 46, 1958.
Bernoulli, Jacob: Ars Conjectandi, Basel, 1713.
Borel, E.: Apropos of a Treatise on Probability, reproduced in: Kyburg, H.E., and H.E.

Smokler: Studies in Subjective Probability, New York, 1963.
Carnap, R.: Logical Foundations or Probability, Chicago, 1950.
Cox, R. T.: The Algebra of Probable Inference, John Hopkins, 1948.
de Finetti, B.: Foresight: Its Logical Laws, Its Subjective Sources, 1937, reproduced in: Kyburg, H. E. and H. E. Smokler: Studies in Subjective Probability, New York, 1963.
De Morgan, Augustus: Formal Logic, London, 1847.
Fisher, R. A.: Statistical Methods for Research Workers, 13th Ed., Edinburgh, 1958.
Fisher, R. A.: Statistical Methods and Scientific Inference, 2nd Ed., Edinburg, 1959.
Hacking, I.: Logic of Statistical Inference, Cambridge, 1965.
Jeffrey, R. C.: The Logic of Decision, New York, 1965.
Jeffreys, Harold: Theory of Probability, 3rd Ed., London, 1961.
Koopman, B. O.: The Bases of Probability, 1940, reproduced in: Kyburg, H. E. and H. E. Smokler: Studies in Subjective Probability, New York, 1963.
Kyburg, H. E., and H. E. Smokler: Studies in Subjective Probability, New York, 1963.
de Laplace, Pierre Simon: Essai philosophique sur les probabilites, 5th Ed., Paris, 1825.
Ramsey, Frank, P.: The Foundations of Mathematics and other Logical Essays (Ed. Braithwaite), New York, 1950.
Ramsey, Frank P.: Truth and Probability, 1926, reproduced in: Kyburg, H. E. and H. E. Smokler: Studies in Subjective Probability, New York, 1963.
Suppes, P.: Studies in the Methodology and Foundations of Science, Dordrecht, Holland 1969.
Stegmüller, W.: Probleme und Resultate der Wissenschaftstheorie und Analytischen Philosophie, Band IV (altogether five issues), Berlin, Heidelberg, New York, 1973. (This fundamental work represents probably the most comprehensive treatment of philosophical aspects of probabilistic reasoning to date.)
Thrall, R. M., Coombs, C. H., and R. L. Davis (eds.): Decision Processes, New York, 1954.
Savage, L. J.: The Foundations of Statistics, New York 1954, 1972.
Todhunter, I.: A History of the Mathematical Theory of Probability, Cambridge 1865.
David, F. N.: Games, God and Gambling, New York 1962.
Epstein, R. E.: Theory of Gambling and Statistical Logic, New York 1967.
Neyman, J. and L. M. LeCam: Bernoulli, Bayes, Laplace, Berlin, New York 1965.
Roberts, V.: Bayesian Statistical Inference and Decision Theory, Chicago 1964.

Subject Index